£2 - 50.
Reduced

The Classification of European
BUTTERFLIES

The Classification of
European
BUTTERFLIES

Lionel G. Higgins

COLLINS
ST JAMES'S PLACE, LONDON

William Collins Sons & Co Ltd
London · Glasgow · Sydney · Auckland
Toronto · Johannesburg

First published 1975
© L. G. Higgins 1975

ISBN 0 00 219624 7

Made and Printed in Great Britain by
William Collins Sons & Co Ltd Glasgow

Contents

Preface

It is the purpose of this book to present in a single volume the recent developments in identification and classification of butterflies, so far as these relate to the fauna of western Europe. This region is taken to extend eastwards to the frontiers of the USSR, the Dardanelles and including Crete. The island of Rhodes and other eastern Aegean islands are more closely related to western Asia and these are not considered. Also included are the Canary Islands, Madeira, the Azores and the African countries of Morocco, Algeria and Tunisia, from the Atlas Mts. northwards to the Mediterranean Sea. All these are part, faunistically, of the western Palearctic Region, and with Europe they support a fauna of great interest and, considering the relatively small area of the region, with a large number of indigenous species.

During the last 45 years great changes have been introduced in the classification of butterflies, with the object of reaching greater precision in specific identification and generic definition. There have been monographic revisions of large groups, entailing great labour, of which the *Monograph of the tribe Hesperiidi* (i.e. *Pyrgus*) by Warren (1926) and the *Monograph of the genus Erebia* (1936) by the same author, are outstanding examples, with many later papers on similar lines by various authors. Still more recently, the extensive investigations into the chromosome numbers of butterflies by Lorković and de Lesse have led to discovery of new species and to the definition of new genera. At present, records of all this work are available only to serious students with access to a good library where the original books and papers can be consulted. Apart from the observations on chromosomes, the new facts and subsequent systematic arrangements are almost all concerned with the anatomy of the male genitalia, which provide taxonomic characters of the highest importance. With the exception of one species not available for dissection, these are now illustrated in the text with line drawings of all species recorded from the region. Space is not available for inclusion of wing venation diagrams for all genera, but those considered most important are shown with figures of legs, palpi, antennae and androconial scales, when taxonomically important, included with the main text.

The genitalia figures make it possible to give short descriptions of the various categories of family, subfamily, tribe and genus, with keys for each rank, based principally upon male characters. A high proportion of European butterflies are sexually dimorphic; often both sexes cannot be covered in a single key. In many cases the classification is based upon male genitalia and in all such cases these characters must be used in composing the relative keys, frequently at generic levels and often most conveniently at higher levels.

7

In a single volume it is not possible to give more than short notes on some of the difficulties and disputed points on the systematic status of European butterflies, and special care has been taken to provide a good bibliography and references to original articles with further information. References to original descriptions of generic names published before the end of 1963 will be found in Hemming (1967). References to specific and subspecific names up to 1930 are included in Seitz vol. 1 and Supplement, also in Bang-Haas 1926–30 (5 parts). References to original descriptions of more recent taxa have been included in the bibliography. Generic and specific synonyms are not included in the main text. They are recorded in the Index with references to the valid names employed in this book. Explanations of certain technical terms will be found in the Glossary.

All figures of genitalia, wing-scales etc. are drawn with the camera lucida from preparations made by the author. The preparations of genitalia almost always are mounted in shallow cells to avoid distortion. The figures are reproduced as nearly as possible in uniform sizes, a difficult task owing to the wide variation in size of the actual structures. It follows that the sizes of the figures are not related to the actual sizes of the parts shown. The short specific descriptions refer almost entirely to anatomical characters. Descriptions of wing-markings etc., with emphasis on identification, will be found in the *Field Guide to the Butterflies of Britain and Europe*, Collins, 2nd Ed. 1973. References to the appropriate page and plate numbers in the guide are given in this book in the heading to each species.

I have to record my grateful thanks to friends who have given help during the preparation of this book. In this connection I must mention especially Mr Norman Riley who has never failed to answer my frequent questions on matters of nomenclature. Mr K. M. Guichard has been more than kind in collecting butterflies from various localities and Mr R. F. Bretherton has given me specimens of great interest, while Mr Riley, Mr Graham Howarth and Professor John Dacie have all read early drafts of the text and have made many helpful suggestions. Finally I have to thank the Trustees of the British Museum (N.H.) for their permission to study the Museum collections.

L. G. Higgins
Focklesbrook Farm
Chobham
Woking
Surrey

Introduction

The principles involved in classification of animals and plants are termed Taxonomy; their application is termed Systematics. The object of classification is to indicate the relationships of species and groups of species to one another, so that the multitude of forms can be arranged in an orderly systematic series, having regard especially to phylogeny. Accurate identification at all levels is clearly of the first importance, since otherwise supposed affinities will be misleading and the system will break down. The taxonomic units (taxa) employed today by taxonomists are grouped into categories in descending order of importance. These are Phylum; Class; Order; Family; Subfamily; Tribe; Genus; Species and Subspecies. Each taxon in each category has its unique name by which it can be recognised and distinguished from all other taxa. Butterflies belong to the Phylum Arthropoda; Class Insecta; Order Lepidoptera. They are separable from all other Lepidoptera by their clubbed antennae, so that they are placed by many authors in a separate sub-order Rhopalocera. Species and all high categories must be described and named in order to allow recognition. They are defined by characters of appearance and especially those of structure, by the presence or absence of which the species can be divided into larger or smaller groups (families etc.), considered to show distant or closer relationship to one another. For example, in a large group of species the ova are more than twice as tall as wide, and the imagines have bifid claws. In classification all species with these characters are assembled in an important group as a Family, to which the name Pieridae is applied. The species composing the Family are divided again by other characters into smaller groups of Subfamily, Tribe and Genus, each having characters in common, which at once unite them and separate them from all other taxa in the same category. This system of classification rests upon the comparative study of individual specimens, and it is obvious that the basic unit is the species. Characters vary in importance, those present in ova, larvae, in wing-venation and genitalia are especially valuable. In general, wing-markings and shapes are less reliable except as specific and subspecific characters, but anatomical indications are usually supported in varying degrees by markings, habitat, food plants, distribution etc. It is realised today that all characters are worthy of study, and a small, apparently insignificant character may give important information concerning relationship. Anatomical characters of imagines are very numerous, and the most important of these are shortly described on p. 19 and following pages.

Species

The concept of a species has varied during the years, and today the word means different things to different people. In Victorian times a species was a well-defined entity, identified by *prima facie* methods of examination and a 'type' specimen, often with a variable number of varieties all identified by a restricted set of taxonomic characters. With increasing study of whole populations, and especially with growing knowledge of genetics, it is generally recognised today that the fully developed species represents a special biological unit which requires a biological definition:

Species are groups of interbreeding natural populations that are reproductively isolated from other such groups (Mayr 1953).

It is rarely necessary to prove the fact of reproductive isolation since almost always, in practice, this can be assumed on circumstantial evidence, but difficulty arises from incomplete speciation, resulting in the appearance of phenotypes with intermediate characters. Such populations in which certain characters point to specific rank and other characters do not, are in an intermediate evolutionary state, sometimes referred to as 'semispecies', a term which implies an advanced degree of subspeciation. Clearly the species concept can be considered from another angle since evolution is a continuous process. We must suppose that living creatures will provide examples of subspeciation and of speciation of every grade, with every grade of reproductive isolation, and the degree of divergence at which a population is considered to achieve specific rank will depend upon the opinions of individual systematists who will sometimes disagree. In other words the category of species is a concept, essential to the systematist but incapable of precise definition, to be interpreted and applied with common sense in a taxonomic formula which denotes, as clearly as possible, the relationships to one another of the various populations under consideration. Hogben (1940) has remarked very truly: 'The concept of the species as a breeding unit has scant relevance to museum practice.' For the museum taxonomist the species becomes:

A group of animals recognisable as a distinct unit which preserves its identity for reasons which are not analysed.

It will be noticed that this definition does not distinguish between subspecies and species. In practice the distinction must be made by the museum taxonomist.

Reference. Wilmot 1942.

Subspecies

It is important to understand the nature of subspecies since they form a most interesting feature of the European butterfly fauna. The concept of a subspecies goes back to the time of Esper (1781), but it was not until much later, at the end of the last century, that the principle was fully accepted and the present formula with trinominal terminology was established

(Rothschild & Jordan 1906, p. 429). It is well known that a mechanism to provide constant variation is present in all living things. This is controlled by genes, invisible particles in chromosomes, with their essential property that the character they control can be inherited. Occasionally a gene will determine an unusual character, i.e. will effect a mutation, which may be of value to the species. In this case the character is likely to persist and will extend through the population. This particulate heredity, as it is called, is the basis for successful evolution or adaptation to changes in environment. Within the territory of a species, individuals will maintain an average phenotype as long as they can breed freely together, i.e. so long as free 'gene flow' is not interrupted. If for some reason free gene flow becomes impossible, e.g. if part of the territory becomes an island or is otherwise isolated, the natural variation of the isolated colony may develop in a direction different from that of the parent colony, and a different phenotype will be produced, a geographical race or subspecies. This term is defined as follows:

Subspecies are geographically limited populations which differ taxonomically from other such subdivisions of the species (Mayr 1970 modified).

Theoretically a subspecies remains fertile with neighbouring subspecies, and it follows that two different subspecies cannot exist together on the same ground, since in that case gene flow would not be interrupted. Among the Lepidoptera, isolation of populations is considered the essential factor in the origin of subspecies. It will explain almost all situations if the wide range of possible isolating mechanisms is kept in mind. All subspecies are graded equal under the Code (p. 289), but that first described is referred to as the nominate subspecies. The term should indicate a population with definite distinctive characters, and with a definite distribution area. There is no acceptable criterion to decide when divergent phenotypes are sufficiently distinct to need subspecific names, nor whether to grade a divergent phenotype as a species or as a subspecies (but see Mayr 1970, p. 193). In such cases the decision will depend upon the observer's attitude, on the one hand to emphasise points of difference, on the other hand to insist more strongly upon points of resemblance. In distant, or formerly distant, populations phenotypical differences may be marked and accompanied by changes in the male genitalia, although on general grounds the forms appear to be specifically related. This situation was first recorded by Jordan (1903) and by Rothschild & Jordan (1906) as an interesting observation following their critical examination of American Papilionidae. It occurs rather commonly in European butterflies, first noticed in *Pyrgus malvae* by Elwes & Edwards (1898). In addition it is now known that dissimilar genitalia distinguish the eastern and western subspecies of *Mellicta athalia*; *Melitaea trivia*; *Maniola jurtina*; *Hipparchia alcyone*; *Pseudophilotes baton*; *Scolitantides bavius*; *Zizeeria knysna* and *Palaeochrysophanus hippothoe*. The geographical subspecies, so clearly expressed in the genitalia, are almost or quite indistinguishable by external examination. The frontiers vary, the two subspecies of *M. athalia* and those

11

of *M. jurtina* interbreed freely at their frontier areas with development of intermediate genitalia forms; *P. baton* may do this but has not been sufficiently well investigated to be proved; the others are too isolated for interbreeding to be possible; all are strictly allopatric. Discussing such situations the late W. H. Evans wrote (1949): '. . . as wide a view as possible has been taken of a species. Whenever a form in one area can be considered as replacing a form in another area, the two are presumed to be conspecific, even though differences in facies, structure and genitalia are considerable'. The writer endorses this point of view which introduces a factor of geographical distribution, i.e. of vicariants (Bernardi 1964), which appears to him highly important and useful in difficult cases. In grading all such forms as subspecies there is the great advantage of trinominal nomenclature, expressing as shortly as possible the two important facts of close relationship and allopatry (Mayr 1970).

During the last 60 years a very large number of phenotypes of European butterflies have been described as subspecies. These wrongly include seasonal forms and clinal phases which are controlled in most cases by polygenes, and which are not strictly of subspecific rank. The term should be restricted to real subspecies, i.e. those with well-defined geographical ranges and well-marked distinctive characters, which alone fit the definition.

Reference. Evans 1949.

Clines

The term indicates a gradual change in any taxonomic character between two extremes, as it occurs in a series of populations, i.e. a character gradient (Huxley 1942). Clines are very common among butterflies, appearing in some degree in the external characters of nearly all species able to adapt to more than one of the various climates and biotopes available in western Europe. It follows that well-marked clines are most common in species with extensive distributions and in mountain species, where a difference in attitude of a few hundred metres leads to a marked change in physical conditions, and changes in humidity, temperature, quality of food-plants etc. appear to be common factors in the production of clinal gradients. Considered from another angle the cline becomes a graduated series of subspecies, but a standard nomenclature is difficult to apply and no satisfactory method has been devised. Extreme forms on a cline are sometimes treated as subspecies, and intermediate phenotypes can be referred to as transitional to one or other of the named taxa.

Nomenclature

This is based upon the binominal system introduced by Linnaeus in 1758, by which every species is given a scientific name based upon Latin or Greek, consisting of two words, firstly the name of a genus (noun), secondly that of a species in the genus (noun in apposition, genitive or adjective). Synonyms were created when different names were given to the same insect. It became recognised in very early times that when this happened the first name given should be the valid name and all later synonyms should cease to be used. Less often, an author would give the same name to different insects creating homonyms. Eventually (1895) the International Commission for Zoological Nomenclature (I.C.Z.N.) was formed, which established a Code of Rules to decide, in cases of doubt, the correct name to be used. The present Code (1964) also governs the construction of certain names; all family names must have the termination -idae; subfamily names must end in -inae; names of tribes in -ini. Names of genera and species do not follow such rules, but should be of Greek or Latin origin or at least 'Latinised'. A subgeneric name, if introduced, is to be enclosed in parentheses, e.g. *Argynnis (Fabriciana) adippe* (the category of sub-genus is not used by all systematists). The specific name, if adjectival, must agree in gender with the generic name. Introduction of the subspecies, the lowest category recognised by the Code, has made it necessary to employ a trinominal nomenclature, e.g. *Fabriciana adippe chlorodippe*, usually shortened to *F.a. chlorodippe*. In Art. 51d of the Code it is directed that, if a species first described in genus X is later transferred to genus Y, the name of the original author of the specific name, if quoted, shall be enclosed in parentheses, e.g. *Fabriciana adippe* (D. & S.). In practice the parentheses are often omitted in all cases, as in this book.

Names of seasonal forms are usually recorded after the prefix 'gen.' = generation; names of sexual forms should be preceded by one or other of the sex-signs ♂ or ♀; polymorphic and mimetic forms, common in tropical countries, are recorded simply as form 'X' or form 'Y'. The Code does not legislate for these names which should not be written as trinominals.

Recent Developments

Much has happened during the present century, and one very striking feature has been the dramatic rise in the number of subspecies of butterflies recognised. No doubt this was a natural sequel to exploration and extension of taxonomic interest to include examination of distant colonies of widely distributed species. The Swiss entomologist H. Fruhstorfer, alone, described over 700 alleged 'subspecies' of butterflies between 1898 and 1918; R. Verity probably at least twice as many, and the total including all Lepidoptera must be many thousands. Unfortunately there was less eagerness to make worth-while comparisons with existing material, and often a new 'subspecies' meant only a new locality, and was sometimes based upon meagre material, much of which it is impossible to trace today.

Another happening has been the development of genetics. Breeding experiments have demonstrated many Mendelian characters in wing markings of moths, but few in butterflies (Ford 1945). An interesting example is that of the fritillary *Argynnis paphia* and its dark ♀-form

13

valesina, shown to be a sex-controlled dominant. Genetics have also provided an explanation of the polymorphic females in *Colias* (Lorković & Herman 1961); knowledge of genetic principles has had a profound effect on all aspects of systematics.

This has been closely associated with interest in chromosomal structure, which has given new specific characters of taxonomic importance in many varying karyotypes found in different butterflies thought previously to be specifically related. Investigation of chromosome numbers, especially by Z. Lorković, H. de Lesse and others, has helped greatly to clarify some of the most puzzling groups of European butterflies, including *Erebia tyndarus* and its close relatives, and the Lycaenid species of the genus *Agrodiaetus*.

Finally, during the last 25 years, the taxonomic importance of specific distribution has been better understood and distribution maps have begun to appear in the literature. Maps are especially important today when so many species are disappearing from their old localities. It is good to know that the British Biological Records Centre is collecting records for a complete European Invertebrate Survey. Provisional maps for the British Butterflies have appeared already. Similar maps for Fennoscandia were published by F. Nordström and others in 1955.

History of Classification

The classification of insects as we understand it today has been developed slowly through the ages in a progressive synthesis that goes back to very early times. The ancient Greek philosophers were interested in animals in their metaphysical researches into the marvels of Nature, seeking the true meaning, or basic plan, ('System') of the Universe. In particular it is known that Aristotle studied animals which were graded by him into classes upon anatomical and other characters, e.g. with blood or bloodless; with two legs or with four legs etc. Animals were then graded into a scale expressing the conception of higher and lower forms of life. This early form of classification was rediscovered with the revival of classical learning during the Renaissance, and was accepted by naturalists until the time of Linnaeus. In fact, the basic idea of a scale of living creatures progressing from primitive to highly developed types must be apparent to every naturalist. During the seventeenth and eighteenth centuries travellers were returning to Europe with unknown animals of every kind, and it became fashionable to collect shells, minerals and other objects in a 'cabinet of curiosities'. Fine illustrated books were published by such authors as Merian (1705); Seba (1734); Sloane (1707) and others, the figures beautifully painted by the miniaturists who were active at this time. Various classes of animals were recognised; usually referred to by the appropriate vernacular Latin word, dating back perhaps for 2,000 years. So, in Rösel's non-binominal books (1746) we find such names as *Vespa*, *Papilio, Locusta* etc., used as group names for various classes of animals,

14

but at this time specific distinctions were indefinite, and the importance of the category scarcely recognised.

When the naturalist Linnaeus began his career, he had at his disposal a considerable reference library and extensive collections of specimens. The information and material were there, but entirely confused and scattered. In 1735, at the age of 28, Linnaeus published the first edition of his famous book, *Systema Naturae*, dealing with the classes of rocks, plants and animals, named and arranged in their 'Natural Order'. As with his contemporaries, the System, explaining the grand plan of the universe, was all important. Species, as such, were not seriously considered until the tenth edition of the *Systema Naturae* in 1758. This book, in which the binominal system of nomenclature is clearly introduced and explained, has been accepted as the work upon which modern nomenclature and classification are based. In it Linnaeus corrected the existing confusion by separating all objects into four groups, viz. Class, Order, Genus and Species; each member of the higher groups was distinguished by some character common to itself and to all other members of the group, and definite names '*nomina propria non confundenda*' were given to each group and to each species, identified by individual characters. A fifth inferior category 'Varietas' is included by Linnaeus in the introduction to his method, but this is very rarely used in Lepidoptera. The definitions for the highest categories are usually good, founded upon constant anatomical characters, e.g. Class 5 Insecta: jaws working sideways, wings present, blood cold; Order 3 Lepidoptera: wings with scales, tongue spiral, body hairy; Genus 203 (i.e. of Insecta) Papilio: antennae clubbed. With enormous labour, Linnaeus devised similar characters and individual names for each category of the entire vegetable and animal kingdoms. By modern standards Linnaeus's generic characters are often crude, especially for his grade of Phalanx, corresponding perhaps to the present grade of sub-genus. His genera are often enormous, including e.g. 192 species in *Papilio* (1758). Nevertheless his method was eagerly accepted everywhere and the convenience and precision of his binominal nomenclature had a tremendously stimulating and lasting impact upon scientific thought. Today we feel that the inclusion of rocks and minerals with the classes of living organisms is surprising, but it must be remembered that Linnaeus lived in a created world. His background was firmly based upon the ancient philosophy of Aristotle; his animals were as they always had been and always would be, as constant in their characters as a piece of granite and therefore susceptible to analysis on similar lines. In his writings there is no hint that he recognised the possibility of a true (cousinly) relationship between them; that knowledge was to come later. The work of describing and naming the vast number of unknown insects was continued energetically for many years by Linnaeus's pupil Fabricius, by Schiffermüller, Goeze and many others without any systematic changes of importance, but at the end of the century it became obvious that the enormous Linnaean genera must be sub-divided. Loyalty to the Linnaean memory was possibly the reason why this process was so long delayed, but the genus *Hesperia* was introduced by Fabricius in 1798, and with the turn of the century came *Pieris*, *Maniola* and *Cupido* by Schrank (1801); *Nymphalis*, *Danaus* and *Heliconius* by Kluk (1802) and in 1804 *Parnassius* and *Polyommatus* by Latreille. In 1807 Fabricius proposed no fewer than 41 new genera in the (unpublished) *Systema Glossatorum* (Illiger Mag.). To explain this great activity it is necessary to return to the last years of the eighteenth century, when several most eminent zoologists were working in Paris, among whom Lamarck, Buffon, and Cuvier were probably the most illustrious, with Latreille a distinguished entomologist. Cuvier was a comparative anatomist and reports of his investigations published in 1798 and 1799–1805 were especially important.

Latreille was greatly influenced by his contact with Cuvier, whom he mentions repeatedly in his publications, referring to Cuvier's first book (1798) as 'ouvrage qui fait époque'. In 1810 Latreille published his work, *Considérations Générales . . . sur l'Ordre Naturelle des Animaux*, in which he presents the old system in a new way, combined with many new genera lately published by various authors in a more precise taxonomic arrangement. The heterogeneous Linnaean genus is replaced by a category termed 'Family' by Latreille, followed by smaller, more homogeneous genera, all defined by anatomical characters, especially those of larva, pupa, legs, palpi and antennae, and finally with a complete Table of all genera and an indication of the typical species in every case, an enormous systematic advance. In the introductory text there are several interesting passages, e.g. at the foot of page 13 he remarks that 'he hopes to show his reasons for establishing the principal groups and also to *explain their reciprocal affinities*' [my italics]. Again on p. 19 he refers to the (anatomical) revolution following Cuvier's researches which made it possible for him to fix the sequence (échelle) of animals 'in accordance with the laws of nature'. Linnaeus could never make such comments and I feel that Latreille in his *Considérations Générales . . .* gives an indication of a break away from the old conception of a static universe, with more than a hint of a common origin for groups of species. From every point of view Latreille was an exceptional and original man, and with this work the general plan for the arrangement of Lepidoptera was firmly established. With relatively small additions and modifications the same order and method are followed today.

Latreille's books were soon followed by the *Verzeichniss der Schmetterlinge* of Hübner (1818–23), surely one of the most remarkable books ever written about Lepidoptera, dealing with the entire World fauna as known at that time, with a large number of new genera based almost entirely upon wing-shape and markings, many of which have proved to be valid. The book shows an exceptional grasp of the whole subject, with real recognition of generic relationships, an astonishing achievement without the help of anatomical characters. The renowned entomologist Boisduval emphasised the importance of the ovum, larva and pupa in defining the higher categories, accepting these along with other conventional characters in his great work, *Species Général des Lépidoptères* (1836 etc.), complaining at the same time that satisfactory taxonomic characters were difficult to find in Lepidoptera. In fact, as more and more new species were discovered, the need for new and more refined taxonomic methods for generic and specific distinction became more urgent. This need was partly met in 1844-45 when Herrich-Schäffer came forward with an entirely new method of classification down to generic level, based largely upon wing-venation. This has proved to be of the greatest importance, usually giving easily identifiable characters for the higher categories. In conjunction with other well-known characters it is in almost universal use today.

A more important and fundamental event occurred in 1858 when Charles Darwin and Alfred Russell Wallace announced publicly their theory of the evolution of species by natural selection, and the following year Darwin published his famous book with the title *The Origin of Species*, enunciating the gradual evolution of new forms of life in response to ecological and other pressures. No other book published during the century produced such religious and scientific excitement. With its superbly simple explanation for the character of life as it exists today, the theory of continuous evolution covered previous difficulties in explaining the close relationship so often present between fossil animals and their living representatives. In the event, the effect on insect classification was not great. The new theory gave strong support to the methods introduced by Latreille 50 years earlier and established firmly the principle of phylogenetic classification, appearing rather as an intellectual stimulus which did not require an immediate response in butterfly taxonomy.

Following the publication of Herrich-Schäffer's book there was some further division of large butterfly genera, but the methods of classification were now static: there is no essential difference between the catalogue of European Lepidoptera published by Heydenreich in 1851 and the last catalogue of Staudinger published in 1901. About this time systematists realised the existence, in the male and female genitalia, of a hitherto undiscovered character, present in all insects and available for use at all taxonomic levels. The importance of this discovery, especially for specific definition, was soon realised and a short account of the development of this new method will be interesting.

The first serious study of male butterfly genitalia for taxonomic purposes was made by Rambur in 1839, when these organs provided critical specific characters for his review of the difficult genus *Pyrgus*. His figures in the last part of the *Faune Entomologique de l'Andalusie* were drawn from genitalia carefully prepared to show the detailed structure of the valves, a most original feature at that time. His book has remained a rare entomological classic since its publication, so rare indeed that the contents of the last part were known to few people. Little further interest appeared for many years, until papers were published in England by Gosse (1881) and in America by Smith and others, with proposals to establish a nomenclature for the various parts of the organs. In 1889 Samuel Scudder, a real pioneer who clearly appreciated the importance of the genitalia in a systematic work, published figures of the male genitalia of all the species of butterflies occurring in the eastern States of U.S.A. Unfortunately Scudder's figures do not show details of structure well enough to be of much value today. By the beginning of the present century the full taxonomic importance of these organs had become widely recognised and important papers appeared by Zander (1903), Rothschild & Jordan (1903) and by McDunnough (1911), while the new principles of generic and specific identification were applied in numerous papers by such authors as T. A. Chapman, F. D. Godman, G. T. Bethune Baker and many others. In 1909 and following years F. N. Pierce compiled his well-known volumes, with genitalia figures of all the species of Lepidoptera (except the Nepticulidae) then known to inhabit Britain, and thereby he was able to clarify the status of several species previously unrecognised as such. From that time until the present day careful examination and illustration of genitalia has been a basic requirement in all important systematic studies of Lepidoptera, including for Europe the publications of Warren (1926, 1936, 1944); Stempffer; Beuret (1953 etc.) and many others.

The genitalia often show good characters at family and subfamily levels which almost always confirm the existing classification based upon other more familiar data. They are certainly of great value at generic level where wing-venation may be constant through large groups (e.g. Polyommatinae) and of outstanding importance in specific diagnosis, often of greater value than any other character (Mayr 1970). Today examination and illustration of the genitalia would be considered essential by lepidopterists for adequate description of any genus or species.

Anatomical Characters

In classification of butterflies, the various categories are determined principally by anatomical characters, which alone are reliable in mimetic species. Characters present in ova, larvae, and pupae are referred to in the text when appropriate. The anatomical characters present in imagines are very numerous but often less apparent. The most important of these are shortly described below, but it is not claimed that the list is exhaustive.

Antennae. Very variable, sometimes of importance in defining higher categories. The terminal club may be poorly defined or well marked, gradual or abrupt, the apex rounded or tapering to a point, sometimes curved into a hook (Hesperiinae, p. 58), when the pointed extremity is known as the *apiculus*. In the Hesperiinae, an area free from scales below the apex, called the *nudum*, has been used as a taxonomic character by Evans (1949).

Palpi. Most variable, sometimes projecting horizontally forwards (porrect), or curving upwards following the curve of the face (ascending). They are rarely of critical importance. A small unscaled (sensory?) area on the inner aspect of basal segment (*basal fleck*) has been used as a taxonomic character.

Head. This may be wide (Hesperiidae) or narrow (others) in relation to the width of the thorax; the eyes smooth or closely set with minute bristles between the facets (hairy). The characters are sometimes of importance, especially in lower categories.

Thorax. This is enclosed in strong chitin, divided by sutures into numerous small plates. Although their arrangement is of taxonomic importance, the specimen must be sacrificed if their structure is examined, and this is not within the scope of this book.

Legs and feet. These are of great importance especially in the classification of family groups and higher categories. Tibiae and tarsi are usually spined, the tibiae with or without the paired appendages known as spurs. When present these arise behind the distal end of the tibia. Their chitin is delicate, covered with minute hairs, clearly with some special function. Spurs rarely appear on forelegs, but a single pair is present in both sexes on hind- and mid-tibiae in all families except the Hesperiidae in which there are two pairs on the hind-tibiae. Spurs are not to be confused with the large spines which are present on the tibiae and tarsi of the legs in all families, excepting the vestigial forelegs of Nymphalids. An elongate chitinised flap (*epiphysis*) is present on the fore-tibiae of the Papilionidae and a similar flap appears on the fore-tibiae of many Hesperiidae. The

19

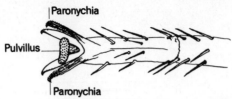

1. Claw and last tarsal segment showing paronychia and pulvillus. (*Argynnis paphia* L.).

2. Tibio-tarsal articulation of middle leg with single pair of spurs and many spines. (*Archon apollinus* Herbst.)

fore-legs of one or both sexes may be degenerate (Nymphalids) or otherwise modified to give basic family-group characters referred to later in the descriptive text. Claws are usually provided with a central pad (*pulvillus*) and paired narrow lobes (*paronychia*) which look like minute feathers when magnified. These appendages may be absent (Papilionidae, Danaidae, *Colias*) or only the pulvillus may be present (*Gonepteryx*).

Wings. The general shape of the wings, and espccially the arrangement of the wing-veins is of great importance, and several systems for naming these have been proposed. In that introduced by Herrich-Schäffer in 1844 the veins are numbered very simply from behind forwards from 1–12 + costa in the fore-wing and from 1–8 in the hind-wing. This numeration is well adapted for butterflies and is adopted in this book. The area of membrane between each vein is termed a *space*; spaces take the number of the vein immediately below them. In the diagram of the basic arrangement of wing-veins in butterflies the nomenclature of the veins is explained, and their conventional abbreviations are indicated.

Wing veins. The FORE-WING usually has 12 veins, enumerated as follows from behind forwards:

v1   runs free from wing-base to outer margin; at its extreme base a small *internal vein* (iv) may run back to inner margin, forming a small cell.

v2, v3, and v4 are branches springing from the large *median vein* (or *cubital vein* c1–c3). This arrangement is constant in all butterflies.

v7–11 are branches springing from the *subcostal* (or *radial*) *vein* (r1–r5 in the numeration of Comstock & Needham). One or more of these branches may be absent in Pieridae, Lycaenidae and Papilionidae.
The *subcostal* and *median veins* are usually connected by three *cross-veins*, referred to as upper- (dc1), middle- (dc2) and lower- (dc3) *discocellular veins*. One or more of these may be absent.

20

The space enclosed by the *subcostal* and *median veins* and *discocellular veins* is the *discoidal cell,* often simply 'the cell'.

v6 extends from the junction of upper and middle *discocellular* veins to the outer margin; when dc1 is absent, absorbed in the subcostal, v6 springs from the stalk of v7–9.

v5 extends from the junction of middle and lower *discocellular* veins to the outer margin.

v12 the *costal vein,* is always strong, never branched; (the vein to be distinguished from the wing costa).

Hind-wing has eight veins + *precostal vein* in many genera.

v1a and v1b are the *anal veins* that run from wing-base to inner margin or anal angle. v1a is absent in Papilionidae.

v2, v3, and v4 spring from the large *median vein* and run to outer margin.

v6 and v7 branch from the *subcostal (radial) vein* and run to outer margin.

v8 *costal vein* has common origin with the subcostal, then runs to costal margin usually with small basal branch, *precostal vein* (pc).
The *subcostal* and *median veins* are often united by upper and lower *discocellular veins* (dc1, dc2). The lower *discocellular vein* is absent in many European butterflies.

v5 extends from the junction of the dc veins and runs to the outer margin. It is absent in some Hesperiidae.

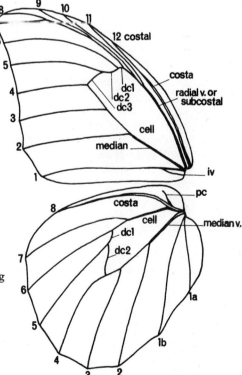

3. Diagrammatic figure of wing venation, veins named and numbered with the terminology used in this book.

Wing scales. The most distinctive features of a butterfly's wing are its scales. These modified hairs appear as minute plates, each with a short pedicle by which it is fixed into a socket in the wing-membrane. Scales are of two basic types. Those covering the wing (cloaking scales), and forming the markings, consist of two delicate lamellae, united by numerous trabeculae, with air spaces between. The shapes vary greatly from simple hairs to flat, oval, or rounded platelets, overlapping (imbricated), and fixed in regular rows across the wing. In many species the scales are strongly ribbed and the brilliant gleaming blue and purple colours, which appear, e.g. in *Apatura iris*, are due to diffraction of light by the ribs acting as prisms.

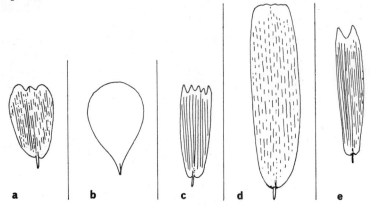

a   b   c   d   e

4. Cloaking scales from uppersides of forewings: **a,** *Iphiclides podalirius* L. **b,** *Parnassius mnemosyne* L. **c,** *Maculinea nausithous* Bergstr. **d,** *Vanessa atalanta* L.. **e,** *Ochlodes venatus* Bremer & Grey.

The second type of scale, termed the androconial scale, is found only in males, and is absent from many species and genera. The shapes of these scales are very different, e.g. in Nymphalids elongate and tapering to a terminal bunch of fibrils, which are supposed to disseminate a perfume which excites the female during mating.

Unlike the cloaking scales, which often vary greatly in form in different areas of the same wing, the form of an androconial scale, within narrow limits, is constant for a species and sometimes for a genus or tribe. In the common Pierid butterflies, the androconial scales have attached to their bases small glands (*Artogeia, Pontia* etc.) and have a scale pattern which differs in each group. In Lycaenidae androconial scales are very common, and in the large subfamily Polyommatinae they are almost always round or oval, and without fibrils. Androconial scales are usually relatively small, either grouped into a sex-brand or scattered across part of the upf mixed with cloaking scales. In some genera they appear capriciously, present in some species but absent from others, e.g. *Coenonympha* (Satyridae).

On certain male sex-brands the scales are quite unlike the common

22

pattern, e.g. those on the brands of *Callophrys*, *Strymonidia*, *Catopsilia* and *Colias* are plain oval, without fibrils, but yet differ from the general cloaking scales that cover the wing. The contrast between these and the plumed androconia occurring in other Pieridae and in Nymphalidae is very marked. The moniliform scales of most Hesperiidae are especially remarkable.

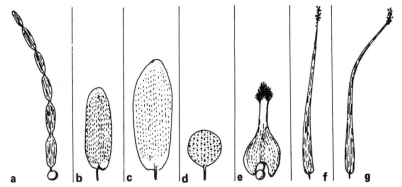

5. Various androconial scales: **a,** *Syrichtus proto* Esper. **b,** *Callophrys rubi* L. **c,** *Colias crocea* Geoffroy. **d,** *Maculinea arion* L. **e,** *Artogeia rapae* L. **f,** *Fabriciana adippe* D. & S. **g,** *Maniola jurtina* L.

The Male Genitalia

These represent the highly modified sclerites of the 9th and 10th body segments. They are of exceptional importance, sometimes for specific identification, and especially for showing relationships of species and groups, giving helpful information on many problems of classification. Basically the parts consist of a rigid chitinous ring which supports the moveable penis. Their structure is rather complicated and the nomenclature of their parts is explained below. The anatomy can be checked by reference to the key figures with examples of every family represented in the region; the names of the different parts are indicated by letters on p. 24-26 and 96.

Tegumen (T). A hooded cap or roof folded down and narrowing on each side to form slender pedicles (*peduncles* PD) joining with the narrow *vinculum* (VI). In some families, e.g. Satyridae, a narrow process is present behind the posterior aspect of the peduncle, called the *apex angularis* (AA), with which the upper anterior angle of the valve articulates. Posteriorly the tegumen is firmly connected with the uncus and the union may be membranous and visible.

Uncus (U). The terminal dorsal structure, usually tapering to a pointed apex, based upon the tegumen and often appearing continuous with it.

23

Key figures to show basic structure of the male genitalia, the principal parts lettered to correspond with the following description.

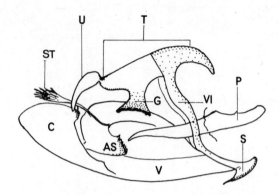

6. HESPERIIDAE. *Pyrgus andromedae* Wallengren.

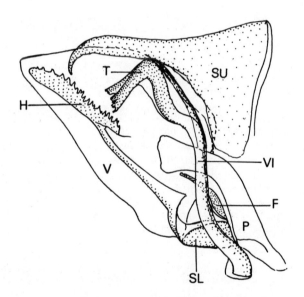

7. PAPILIONIDAE. *Papilio machaon* L.

8. PIERIDAE. *Anthocharis cardamines* L.

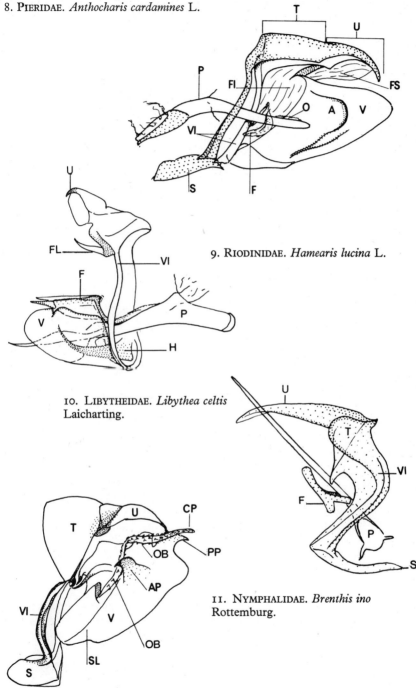

9. RIODINIDAE. *Hamearis lucina* L.

10. LIBYTHEIDAE. *Libythea celtis* Laicharting.

11. NYMPHALIDAE. *Brenthis ino* Rottemburg.

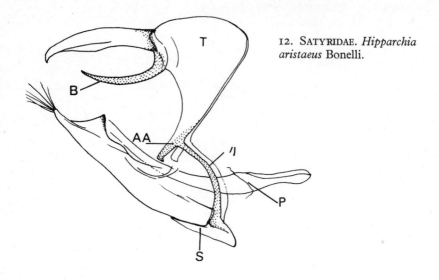

12. Satyridae. *Hipparchia aristaeus* Bonelli.

13. Danaidae. *Danaus plexippus* L.

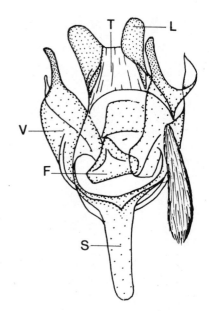

For figures of Lycaenidae see p. 96.

The uncus usually curves gently downwards, the apex sometimes notched; occasionally it is absent as in Melitaeini and Papilioninae. In the latter sub-family, when the reduced uncus fails to give adequate support, its place is taken by the tergite of segment 8, modified to form a *supra-uncus* (SU). The tegumen may be crowned with a process directed posteriorly, known as *uncus anticus*.

Brachia (B). Paired processes arising from the uncus or tegumen on each side, curving backwards. They are present in many Hesperiinae, Nymphalinae and in all European species of Satyridae.

Falx pl. falces (FL). Slender curved appendages arising on each side of the uncus in *Hamearis*, and from the labides in Lycaenidae.

Diaphragm. The membranous sheet that closes the abdominal cavity posteriorly. It is attached all round to the chitinous genital ring, and two distinct parts are recognised in the Nymphalidae and Satyridae. The upper section, called the *fultura superior* (FS), descends from below the uncus to the region of the transtilla or apices angulares, is perforated by the anal gut and closes the anal compartment. The lower section or *fultura inferior* (FI) descends from the region of the transtilla to the base of the vinculum and is perforated by the penis. At the site of the perforation the penis is supported by the diaphragm, termed the *manica* or *anellus* at this point, and further supported by the *furca* (see below), thought to be developed by chitinisation of the fultura inferior.

Gnathos (G). Small but often elaborate structures consisting of paired processes descending from the uncus and approximated, but in butterflies not fusing, to form the floor of the anal compartment. The gnathos arises from chitinisation in the fultura superior, and its development is well shown in *S. s. therapne* (see fig., p. 43). The gnathos is well developed in some Limenitinae and especially in the Pyrginae. The variable shape is often a useful distinctive specific character. The gnathos has been considered homologous with the brachia; the two structures do not occur together in the same species. Chitinised areas are sometimes developed in the diaphragm below the uncus; such areas are referred to as *scaphial* elements. In the isolated Nymphalid species *Issoria lathonia* L. the entire diaphragm in this area is solidified with chitinous plaques.

Transtilla (TR). In some Nymphalidae chitinous plates, formed possibly from the peduncles, are present, which cross the genital ring at the lower limit of the tegumen. Such plates, defining the floor of the anal compartment, form the transtilla, which consists of a single bar in some butterflies. These plates are large in some species of Argynnini, and have been named *vanni* by dos Passos and Grey (1945).

Vinculum (VI). Narrow chitinous rods united below to form a U-shaped frame, which articulates above on each side with the tegumen, or with its peduncles when these are present, completing the genital ring. In some groups it is easy to see the points at which the upper extremities of the vinculum join the tegumen, sometimes with membranous connections. In the Lycaenidae the rami of the vinculum are expanded dorsally and meet centrally giving additional support to the tegumen, represented in this family by a narrow bar between the labides. In the European Papilionidae the genital ring appears to be formed completely by the vinculum, with the tegumen minute and degenerate.

Saccus (S). A median process of variable length which arises from the floor or lower margin of the vinculum, extending forwards into the abdominal cavity. Among European butterflies it is greatly developed in the Apaturinae, Charaxinae and in the Hesperine genus *Thymelicus*. The length of the saccus appears to bear a close relation to the length of the penis.

Furca (F). A chitinous prop beneath the penis, of varying shape, formed in the membrane of the fultura inferior. It is usually bifid and attached on each side to the vinculum, but in Lycaenidae it is a forked structure based upon the valves at their junction. Rarely the chitinisation surrounds the penis entirely, forming a complete collar (*anellus*) as e.g. in *Laeosopis*, p. 108.

Penis (P). The intromittent male organ is a tubular structure firmly chitinised which varies greatly in size and in other features. It is connected anteriorly by its proximal orifice (PO) with the ejaculatory duct, which brings the sperms (more correctly the spermatophore) for storage in a tube or small pouch (*vesica*) which is enclosed within the stiff outer wall (*aedeagus*). During copulation the vesica is extruded through the ostium penis (O) to deposit the spermatophore in the bursa copulatrix of the female. The wall of the vesica may be armed with chitinous structures varying in size from minute spicules to large dense spines (*cornuti* see fig. 38). The vesica may be partly extruded by pressure during preparation of a specimen, and this may distort the arrangement of the cornuti. The characters of the penis are often of taxonomic value, the basic features remaining similar through whole genera or tribes. The point at which it is supported by the manica is termed the *zone*, sometimes indicated by a chitinised collar as in *Aricia* (Lycaenidae). A minute chitinised structure, sometimes present at the ostium penis in Lycaeninae, is called the *cuneus*.

Valve, valva or clasper (V). Paired lateral appendages, usually flat and wide in side view, in fact collapsed hollow organs with internal and external walls, each usually articulated anteriorly with the vinculum in the region of the saccus, and above with the tegumen or apex angularis. The valves are mobile, and open freely during copulation, in order to expose the penis. In many species, and especially in the Argynninae valves bear elaborate processes and spines arising from the inner wall, which show important characters.

Certain areas of the valve are recognised as follows:
Costal Margin or **Costa** (CM). The superior border. This border is often folded or thickened to form a band which may terminate posteriorly in complicated structures (Pyrginae), or it may be continued as a free costal process (CP) extending above the cuillier.

Cuillier or **Cucullus** (C). The broad expanded posterior region of the valve, greatly developed in the species of *Pyrgus*.

28

Sacculus (SL). The anterior (lower) basal angle of the valve where the inferior border is usually rolled into a shallow gutter. In some groups an important process (harpe) appears to arise in this area.

Harpe (H). In this book the term is applied to a prominent densely chitinised and often toothed process arising from the inner aspect of the valve, and fully developed near the central area, often appearing as a continuation from the sacculus. A harpe of this type is common in the Nymphalidae, e.g. *Mellicta athalia*, p. 201.

Ampulla (A). The central area of the inner aspect of the valve. An *ampullary process* (AP) may arise at this point which does not appear to be connected with the sacculus, as in *Limenitis populi* fig. 263a and in some Pieridae.

Nymphalid valves, often elaborately modified, may show special characters. These include a *costal process* (CP), the *oblique dentate crest* (OB) in the Argynnini and a *posterior process* (PP) which forms the valve apex in many species.

Hesperid valves. In many species of Pyrginae the costal border terminates posteriorly in an irregular spiny area, the *stylifer* (SF). A slender process arising from the stylifer and curving upwards is the *style* (ST), a shorter inferior extension of the stylifer, present in some species, is the *antistyle* (AS).

Lycaenidae. In their genitalia, described on pp. 95-6, most species differ greatly from all other butterflies.

The anatomical characters are shown in Key Figures lettered as follows:

A.	Ampulla	O.	Ostium penis
AA.	Apex angularis	OB.	Oblique dentate crest
AE.	Aedeagus		(Argynnini)
AP.	Ampullary process	P.	Penis
AO.	Opening for anal gut	PD.	Peduncle
	(Argynnini)	PO.	Anterior orifice of penis
AS.	Antistyle	PP.	Posterior process of valve
B.	Brachium	S.	Saccus
C.	Cuillier or cucullus	SL.	Sacculus
CM.	Costal margin of valve	SF.	Stylifer
CP.	Costal process of valve	ST.	Style
F.	Furca (fultura penis)	SU.	Supra-uncus
FI.	Fultura inferior (diaphragm)	T.	Tegumen
FL.	Falx (Lycaenidae) (pl. falces)	TR.	Transtilla
FS.	Fultura superior	U.	Uncus
G.	Gnathos	V.	Valve
H.	Harpe	VI.	Vinculum
L.	Labides (Lycaenidae)		

Reference. Tuxen 1970

Abbreviations

♂	= male	CN	= chromosome number
♀	= female		(haploid)
dcv	= discoidal or disco-cellular vein	FG	= references to text page and/ or plate number in *A Field Guide to the Butter-flies of Britain & Europe*
pd	= postdiscal area (of wings)		
gc	= ground-colour		
fw	= fore-wing	TS	= Type species (of genera)
hw	= hind-wing	D. & S.	= Denis & Schiffermüller, authors of the *Wiener Verzeichniss* 1775
ups	= upper-surface (of wings)		
uns	= under-surface (of wings)		
upf	= upper-surface of fore-wing	F.	= Fabricius J. C.
unf	= under-surface of fore-wing	L.	= Linnaeus (Carl von Linné)
uph	= upper-surface of hind-wing	N	= north
unh	= under-surface of hind-wing	S	= south
ups	= upper-surface	E	= east
v	= vein (of wings)	W	= west
A-P	= antero-posterior	C	= central

N Africa. When used without qualification = Morocco, Algeria & Tunisia together, from the Atlas Mountains northwards.

In the illustrations of genitalia the names and provenances of specimens recorded for the first figure apply also to all subsequent figures unless the contrary is indicated.

The region = the area of W Europe and of N Africa defined in the Preface.

Systematics

Order LEPIDOPTERA Linnaeus 1758

Mouth parts suctorial. Four wings with scales. The Lepidoptera form a very large Order with sections showing extreme variety of physical characters, and their classification is proportionally difficult. Fossil remains of such fragile insects are rare, until recently none had been discovered of earlier date than Tertiary (about 30 million years ago), and these have been referable to existing families in all cases, but a fossil insect described from the Trias in Australia (Bourgogne in Grassé 1951: 365) is thought probably to be a Lepidopteron, and much more ancient. On general grounds, the large insect group considered most closely related is that of the Trichoptera (Caddis Flies), but beyond this association the evolutionary stages of the Lepidoptera are lost in the mists of antiquity. Today the main butterfly groups are so well defined and species with intermediate characters are so rare, that it is possible to speculate upon an ancestry that goes back far beyond Tertiary times. Since the phylogeny cannot be traced precisely, classification has to be based upon existing species, and it is convenient to recognise the major group Rhopalocera, with clear-cut and easily identified characters, as distinct from the remaining Lepidoptera Hetcrocera, with characters extremely diverse.

Sub-Order RHOPALOCERA Boisduval 1840

Antenna simple, apex more or less expanded, forming a terminal club; fore- and hind-wings overlap without frenulum.

Four Superfamilies are recognised. They are distinguished by the characters used in the following Key, with indication of the families to be associated with each.

1 Six legs all fully functional for walking **2**
  Fore-legs not fully functional as walking legs . . **3**

2 Fore-wings with 12 veins all running unbranched from wing
  base or cell to costa or outer margin . . . . . Hesperioidea
  Represented in Europe by a single family Hesperiidae.
  Fore-wings with 10-12 veins, one or more branching between
  cell and costa or outer margin . . . . . . Papilionoidea
  Includes Papilionidae. and Pieridae.

3 ♂ forelegs modified, single tarsal segment with or without single
  terminal claw; ♀ unmodified, 5 tarsal segments, simple claws,
  paronychia and pulvilli . . . . Lycaenoidea
  Includes Riodinidae and Lycaenidae.
  Fore-legs modified in both sexes; ♂ very small, 1-3 tarsal
  segments without claws; ♀ larger, 5 tarsal segments usually
  without claws . . . . Nymphaloidea
  Includes Libytheidae. Nymphalidae, Satyridae and Danaidae.

Note 1. In Libytheidae ♀ fore-leg tarsal segments imperfectly defined but claws present with paronychia and pulvilli of Nymphalid type.
Note 2. The wide head and other distinctive characters of the Hesperioidea are considered especially important by many authors, who rank the group as an independent Sub-Order GRYPOCERA Karsch 1893.

Key to families of Papilionoidea, Lycaenoidea and Nymphaloidea

1 Six legs all normal, fore-legs not modified **2**
  Fore-legs modified in one or both sexes **3**

2 On all feet claws simple . . . . . . Papilionidae
  On all feet claws bifid . . . . Pieridae

3 Palpi 4 times as long as head . . . . . Libytheidae
  Palpi not very long. **4**

4 Fore-legs modified in ♂ only **5**
  Fore-legs modified in both sexes **6**

5 ♂ fore-tarsus with single segment and claw . . . Lycaenidae
  ♂ fore-tarsus degenerate, lacking claw . . . . Riodinidae

6 Claws acutely angled, lacking pulvilli and paronychia . . Danaidae
  Claws normal with pulvilli and paronychia . . . **7**

7 One or more veins dilated at fw base . . . . Satyridae*
  Veins at fw base not dilated . . . . . Nymphalidae†
*Character not well developed in Oeneini.
† Character not well developed in Araschniinae.

Family **HESPERIIDAE** Latreille 1809

Small butterflies, wing margins entire, fw pointed, males upf often with sex-brand. *Androconial scales* usually moniliform. *Head* wider than thorax, face horizontal rather than vertical, frons wide, thorax usually robust. *Eyes* smooth. *Antennae* short, bases widely separated, 'eyelash' present. *Palpi* characteristic; short, basal segment large, 'basal fleck' extensive, middle segment more or less inflated, terminal segment very short, depressed. *Legs* fully functional for walking, claws simple, usually with paronychia and pulvilli, fore-tibia almost always with epiphysis, lacking spurs, mid-tibia with single pair of spurs, hind-tibia with two pairs of spurs. *Venation.* Each wing cell closed by vestigial veins, sometimes obsolescent; fw upper discoidal vein often present; a short internal vein present anastomosing with v1 to form a small cell; hw precostal vein absent.

Genitalia. All typical anatomical features present.

Early stages. Ovum variable. Larval head wide, first thoracic segment (neck) narrow, body slightly fusiform, pubescent, often with pigmented prothoracic dorsal collar (shield), living concealed in shelter spun with leaves or grass. Pupa concealed in larval shelter, slender, fixed by cremastral or nasal hooks, often with silken girdle.

The group is extremely well differentiated, distinctive features appearing with relatively little variation in almost all species, structure of palpi clothed with long bushy hair-scales especially striking. The stout abdomens of most species, wing venation, larval and pupal habits are among the characters showing affinity with Heterocera. Distinctive characters of legs are least well developed in the small subfamily Heteropterinae, in which the abdomen is long and slender.

References. Reuter 1897. Tutt 1905. Lindsey, Bell & Williams 1931. Evans 1949.

Key to subfamilies of Hesperiidae

1 Fw v5 curved proximally to approach v4 . . . Hesperiinae

  Fw v5 straight **2**

2 Fw v5 slightly nearer to v4 than to v6, genitalia brachia present but without gnathos . . . . . . Heteropterinae
  Fw v5 central between v4 and v6, or nearer the latter, genitalia usually with gnathos, never with brachia . . . . Pyrginae

Subfamily PYRGINAE Burmeister 1878

Ups gc usually dark grey, marked with small white spots in both sexes. Males upf often with costal fold covering androconial scales. *Eyes* smooth. *Palpi* middle segment densely hairy, erect, terminal segment depressed, scaled but not hairy. *Antennae* short, club abrupt, blunt, slightly arcuate. *Venation.* Fw cell elongate, v5 often weak, arising centrally between v4 and v6.

Genitalia. Basic anatomy with uncus, tegumen, valve, furca and penis all perfectly developed. Special features of gnathos, cucullus and stylifer are described on pages 27–29.

Early stages. Ovum spherical with flat base, ribbed and reticulate. Larva pilose, slender, living within a leaf shelter. Pupa slender, tapering, attached by cremastral hooks to a silken pad within the shelter (puparium). Pupal dorsum covered with long, fine pubescence. Larval food plants Dicotyledons, commonly *Potentilla, Rubus* etc.

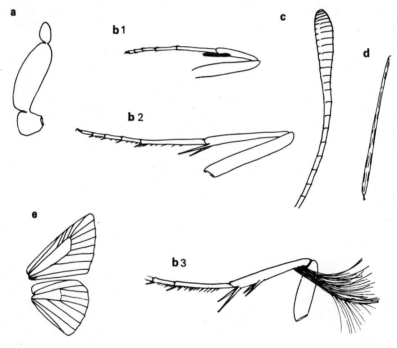

14. PYRGINAE, key characters. **a,** palpus; **b1** fore-leg; **b2** middle-leg; **b3** hind -leg (hair pencil only in *Pyrgus*); **c,** antenna; **d,** androconial scale; **e,** wing venation. See also fig. 6, p. 24.

Key to genera of Pyrginae

1 Gnathos absent . . . . *Carcharodus*
  Gnathos present 2

2 Valves asymmetrical . . . . *Erynnis*
  Valves symmetrical 3

3 Upf male costal fold absent . . . . . . *Spialia*
  Upf male costal fold present 4

4 Upf white spots present in s4 & s5 . . . . . *Pyrgus*
  Upf spots in s4 & s5 absent . . . . . . *Syrichtus*

Genus **PYRGUS** Hübner 1819   TS: *Papilio malvae* L.

On upf white pd spots in s4 and s5 displaced distally; ♂ upf with sex-brand in costal fold. *Legs* hair-pencil present on hind-tibia, absent in related genera. *Androconial scales* very slender, not moniliform. *Venation.* Hw v5 always well developed.
Genitalia. Valve with clearly defined style and antistyle; penis small, almost straight, without marked characters.
Note. The species of *Pyrgus* form a difficult group without well-marked external specific characters, but usually identifiable by their genitalia. Important characters are present in the shape of the gnathos, style, anti-style and cuillier of the valve. The precise taxonomic status of *P. scandi-navicus* Strand and of *P. alticolus* Rebel (*warrenensis* Verity) are uncertain. It has been suggested that both are distinct species (Warren 1953).

References. Warren 1926. Reverdin 1911. Picard 1948. Guillaumin 1964.

PYRGUS MALVAE L. CN 31 Federley; 33 Bigger   FG p. 312; Pl. 58
A complex species represented in Europe by 3 subspecies each with distinctive genitalia. Additional subspecies occur in W Asia and in N America.

P. m. malvae L. 1758.
Genitalia. Uncus straight, bifid; gnathos bifid, dorsal limb sickle-shaped, dentate upper margin closely applied to tegumen; valve rather wide, style very wide, antistyle absent.
Range. All European mainland except boreal and SW regions, extending across C Asia and Siberia to the Amur.

P. m. malvoides Elwes & Edwards 1898.
Genitalia. Uncus curved, not bifid; gnathos small, descending, not applied to tegumen, tapering to pointed process; valve narrower, style longer, antistyle present but small.
Range. SW Europe including Spain, Portugal, S France, Italy and Sicily.

35

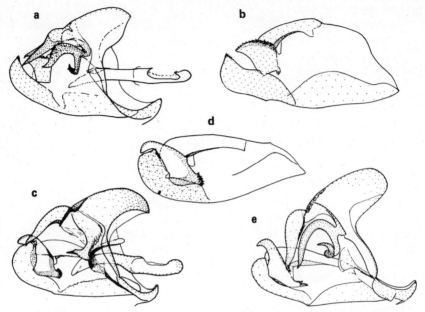

15. *Pyrgus malvae malvae*, England: **a,** genitalia; **b,** valve. *P. m. malvoides,* Italy; **c,** genitalia; **d,** valve. *P. m. melotis,* Lebanon: **e,** genitalia, penis removed.

P. m. melotis Duponchel 1832.

Unh pale, markings almost obsolete.

Genitalia. Like *P. m. malvoides* but gnathos highly developed as a large hook-shaped process.

Range. Syria, Lebanon, Israel. Reported from the Grecian Cyclades, on the island of Milos? Not seen from Turkey, distribution imperfectly understood.

References. Reverdin 1911. Kauffmann 1955. Guillaumin 1962.

Note. In the main the subspecies *malvae* and *malvoides* are allopatric, but mixed races with some individuals showing anomalous genitalia or intermediate characters occur near Innsbrück, in S Switzerland and especially in C France near Clermont-Ferrand in the Puy de Dôme. The two forms are graded subspecies by Evans 1949 and by other authors, in a compact group to which the Asiatic *P. m. ponticus* and the American *P. ruralis* also belong.

PYRGUS ALVEUS Hübner CN 24 FG p. 313; Pl. 58

A widely distributed butterfly occurring in several closely related forms variously ranked by different authors as species or subspecies.

Range extends across temperate Europe and Asia to Mongolia and W China.

P. a. alveus Hübner 1803.

Genitalia. In side view uncus slender, gnathos triangular; style short, slender; antistyle wide; cuillier broad, posterior margin regularly curved, more than a semicircle, proximal margin vertical or inclined slightly backwards.

Range. C Europe, commonly in mountains.

P. a. centralhispaniae Verity 1925.

Genitalia like *P. a. alveus* but curve of cuillier often less regular, somewhat inconstant, proximal margin inclining forwards. More extensive external markings distinctive.

Range. Spain, Pyrenees, S Alps and Apennines, blending further north with *P. a. alveus.*

Reference. Agenjo 1963(C).

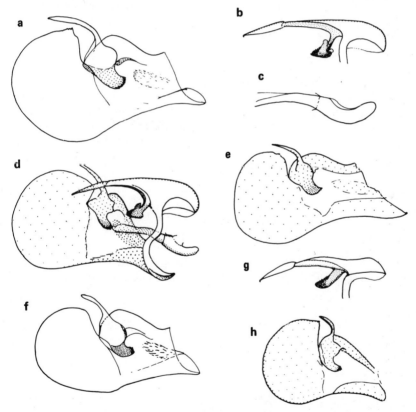

16. *Pyrgus alveus alveus,* Engadin, Switzerland: **a,** valve; **b,** dorsal structures; **c,** penis. *P. a. centralhispaniae,* C Spain: **d,** genitalia. *P. a. alticolus,* Gross-Glockner, Austria: **e,** valve. *P. a. scandinavicus,* Jotenheim, Norway: **f,** valve. Dovre, Norway: **g,** dorsal structures. *P. a. numidus,* Middle Atlas, Morocco: **h,** valve.

P. a. alticolus Rebel 1910. Small, ♂ fw 10–11mm.
Genitalia like *L. a. alveus*, cuillier inclined backwards, apex often rounded (character inconstant ?).
Range. Austria, at high altitudes near Brenner Pass, Stelvio, Gross-Glockner etc. France, Hautes Alpes, perhaps not identical. Switzerland, Grisons ?

P. a. scandinavicus Strand 1903. ♂ fw 11–12mm., occurs at moderate altitudes.
Genitalia. Gnathos not triangular, cuillier slightly flattened posteriorly, inclined backwards.
Range. Fennoscandia to 63°N, commonly in mountains.
Reference. Warren 1953.

P. a. numidus Oberthur 1910. ♂ fw 15mm.
Genitalia like *P. a. alveus* but cuillier narrow and vertical height increased to extend above costal border of valve.
Range. Confined to Morocco and Algeria.
Reference. Warren 1953.

PYRGUS ARMORICANUS Oberthur   CN unknown FG p. 315; Pl. 58
Distribution extends from Morocco across S and C Europe and W Asia to N Iran, perhaps further east. Two subspecies with similar genitalia.

17. *Pyrgus armoricanus*, Brittany, N France: valve.

P. a. armoricanus Oberthur 1910.
Genitalia. Like *L. alveus*; style more slender, antistyle slightly longer, narrower, apex hooked forwards; cuillier narrower, distal border less than a semicircle, inclined obliquely backwards with increased space behind style.
Range. S and C Europe, northwards to S Germany, absent from Britain.

P. a. maroccanus Picard 1950. Slightly larger, white markings ups larger.
Range. Morocco. Algeria.

PYRGUS FOULQUIERI Oberthur 1910   CN 27   FG p. 316; Pl. 58
Genitalia. Like *P. alveus*; antistyle longer, narrower, apex hooked forwards, cuillier longer than wide.
Range. N Spain (Catalonia). SE France in Bouches du Rhône, Aveyron, Lozère and from Var through the Basses and Hautes Alpes. C Italy, very local in Sibillini Mts., Sabine Mts., Sorrento.

18. *Pyrgus foulquieri*, Basses Alpes: valve.

PYRGUS SERRATULAE Rambur   CN 30   FG p. 316; Pl. 58
Distributed from W Europe across C Asia to Transbaicalia, Lebanon and
Asia Minor. Two subspecies with similar genitalia.

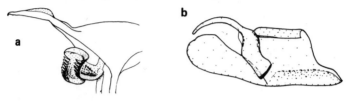

19. *Pyrgus serratulae*, Valais, Switzerland: **a,** dorsal structures and gnathos;
b, valve.

P. s. serratulae Rambur 1839. Small, ♂ fw 11–12mm.
Genitalia. Uncus short, gnathos prominent, posteriorly strongly dentate;
valve narrow, style long, cuillier narrow, inclined backwards, apex
rounded; penis short.
Range. Usually in mountains, from C Spain, Pyrenees and Alps northwards to Germany.

P. s. major Staudinger 1879. Large, ♂ fw 14–15mm.
Genitalia. Indistinguishable.
Range. Constant in Greece; also occurs in SW France flying at low alti-
tudes, a local form.

PYRGUS CARLINAE Rambur 1839   CN 30 FG p. 317; Pl. 58
Genitalia. Gnathos small, angled, with four or five teeth along upper margin of horizontal arm; valve like *P. serratulae*, cuillier narrow, inclined

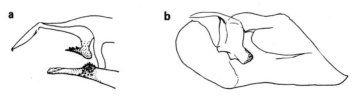

20. *Pyrgus carlinae*, Valais, Switzerland: **a,** dorsal structures including penis
apex; **b,** valve.

39

backwards; penis on upper margin before apex has bulbous swelling armed with small teeth.
Range. At high altitudes from Maritime Alps to Savoie and through S Alps to Carinthia and Trentino.

PYRGUS CIRSII Rambur 1839   CN 30   FG p. 317; Pl. 58
Genitalia. Like *P. carlinae,* gnathos slightly longer with 7–8 teeth along upper margin of horizontal arm; style longer, curved, with small apical teeth; penis apex armed with teeth along lower border and sides.
Range. Local in SW Europe including Spain, Portugal, S France, Switzerland (Vaud) and W Germany (near Nürnberg).

21. *Pyrgus cirsii,* C Spain: **a,** dorsal structures including penis apex; **b,** valve.

PYRGUS ONOPORDI Rambur 1839   CN 30 FG p. 318; Pl. 58
Genitalia. Like *P. serratulae;* gnathos has prominent spiculate knob on stem, extremity long, slender, with small teeth; style short; antistyle large; penis short, slightly curved, without teeth on shaft.
Range. SW Europe including Spain, Portugal, SE France and northwards to Rhône valley in Valais, Switzerland. Morocco. Algeria.

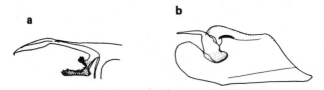

22. *Pyrgus onopordi,* C Italy: **a,** dorsal structures; **b,** valve.

PYRGUS CINARAE Rambur 1839   CN unknown FG p. 318; Pl. 59
Genitalia. Like *P. alveus;* uncus longer, slender and almost straight;

23. *Pyrgus cinarae,* Yugoslav Macedonia: valve.

gnathos triangular; valve elongate, style very long, straight, with fine terminal teeth, cuillier narrow, oblique, apex truncate.
Range. C Spain (Cuenca), Albania, Greece, S Russia and Asia Minor.

PYRGUS FRITILLARIUS Poda 1761   CN 29 FG p. 322; Pl. 58
Genitalia. Tegumen domed, uncus short, curved, gnathos forming a complete sling, lower border strongly chitinised and lined with fine teeth which extend over the more fragile lateral walls; valve elongate, style robust, extremely short with fine terminal spines, cuillier narrow; penis stout, almost straight.
Range. S and C Europe northwards to Poland, S Russia and eastwards to C Asia. Absent from NW Europe.

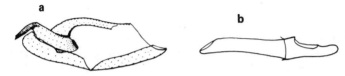

24. *Pyrgus fritillarius*, S Spain: **a,** valve; **b,** penis.

PYRGUS SIDAE Esper   CN unknown   FG p. 319; Pl. 58
Distributed locally in S Europe and more commonly eastwards through Asia Minor, Lebanon and Iran. Two subspecies with similar genitalia.

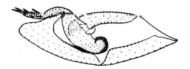

25. *Pyrgus sidae occiduus*, S France: valve.

P. s. sidae Esper 1784. Large fw ♂ 15–17mm.
Genitalia. Like *P. fritillarius*; style more slender with apical brush of long spines, antistyle toothed, cuillier with posterior dorsal lobe; penis slightly sinuous.
Range. Balkans including Yugoslav Macedonia, Albania and Greece.

P. s. occiduus Verity 1925. Smaller, fw ♂ 13–14mm.
Genitalia. Indistinguishable.
Range. S France in Maritime and Basses Alpes, and eastwards in Italy locally in Tuscany, Emilia and Lazio.

PYRGUS ANDROMEDAE Wallengren 1853   CN unknown
                                              FG p. 322; Pl. 58
Genitalia. Like *P. fritillarius*; uncus short, domed, curved; style slender with six terminal spines, antistyle wider, apex of cuillier with small anterior lobe; penis as in *P. fritillarius*.

Range. Confined to Europe; Scandinavia in the far north. Pyrenees, Alps and Balkans, probably widely distributed on the highest mountains at high altitudes.

26. *Pyrgus andromedae*, Valais, Switzerland: genitalia.

PYRGUS CACALIAE Rambur 1839   CN 30   FG p. 323; Pl. 58
Genitalia. Like *P. andromedae*, valve elongate, style short, horizontal, with many spines along upper border, cuillier expanded posteriorly; penis as in *P. fritillarius*.
Range. Alps at high altitudes, Rumania, Bulgaria (Rilo Mts.), Pyrenees.

Reference. Picard 1946.

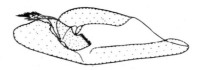

27. *Pyrgus cacaliae*, Albula Pass, Engadin: valve.

PYRGUS CENTAUREAE Rambur 1839   CN unknown
FG p. 323; Pl. 58
Genitalia. Like *P. andromedae*; gnathos less wide; valve less elongate, style short with many short stiff hairs near apex, cuillier very narrow, expanding gradually to blunt apex.
Range. In Europe confined to Fennoscandia. In Asia range probably extensive in northern regions, known also from Altai and Sajan Mts. Widely distributed in northern Canada.

28. *Pyrgus centaureae*, Dovre, Norway: valve.

Genus **SPIALIA**   Swinhoe 1913   TS: *Hesperia galba* F.

Like *Pyrgus* but upf ♂ lacks costal fold (sex-brand); hind tibia without hair-pencil; upf white spots in s4 and s5, if present, not displaced distally, pale discal spots in s1b usually placed distal to spot in s2.

Genitalia. Gnathos prominent, situated below costal margin of valve (fig. **h**, *S. s. ali*); valve oval, broad, with bowed costal margin which terminates in a spiny stylifer as it meets the narrow cuillier, style and antistyle absent; diaphragm (futura superior) lightly chitinised.

Reference. Picard 1948(1950).

SPIALIA SERTORIUS Hoffmannsegg   CN 31 FG p. 324; Pl. 59

Range. N Africa, S Europe and widely distributed eastwards across S Russia and W Asia to Chitral, Altai Mts. and Tibet. A complex species represented in the region by four subspecies, each with distinctive markings but differences in genitalia small. The subspecies are described separately.

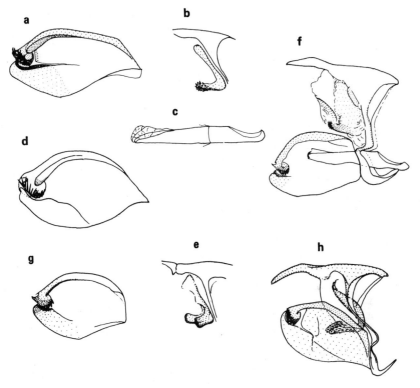

29. *Spialia sertorius sertorius*, C Spain: **a,** valve; **b,** gnathos; **c,** penis. *S. s. orbifer*, Macedonia: **d,** valve; **e,** gnathos. *S. s. therapne*, Corsica: **f,** genitalia; **g,** valve. *S. s. ali*, Morocco: **h,** genitalia, penis removed.

S. s. sertorius Hoffmannsegg 1804.
Genitalia. Uncus long, gnathos L-shaped, slender, hooked; valve costal fold narrow, stylifer small, flattened posteriorly, cuillier elongate; penis short, almost straight.
Range. SW and C Europe to 52°N, eastwards to Czechoslovakia, Hungary and Trieste, occasionally reported from Corsica.

S. s. orbifer Hübner 1823. CN 30–31.
Genitalia. Like *S. s. sertorius*; terminal hook of gnathos shorter and wider; valve slightly wider, costal fold and stylifer slightly larger.
Range. Europe, east of the Adriatic, northwards to Vienna, and east to S Russia, Lebanon and W Asia to Iran.

S. s. therapne Rambur 1832.
Genitalia. Small, like *S. s. sertorius*; gnathos short, stout, intimately connected with the lightly chitinised and finely spiculate diaphragm; cuillier short, wide.
Range. Corsica and Sardinia.
Reference. Kauffmann 1955.

S. s. ali Oberthur 1881   FG p. 325; Pl. 59
Genitalia. Like *S. s. sertorius* but gnathos more massive, terminating in a larger hook and more heavily spined; cuillier tapering abruptly to upturned point; penis as in *S. s. sertorius*.
Range. Confined to Morocco, Algeria and Tunisia.

SPIALIA PHLOMIDIS Herrich-Schäffer 1845
   CN 31   FG p. 325; Pl. 59
Genitalia. Uncus short, gnathos semicircular with long terminal curve; valve wide, costal fold expanding posteriorly, apex truncate with short apical teeth, apex of cuillier sharply upturned with apical teeth; penis long, expanded apex downturned, preceded by small dorsal tooth.
Range. S Balkans and eastwards across Asia Minor to Caucasus and Iran.

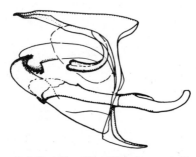

30. *Spialia phlomidis*, Albania: genitalia.

44

Genus **SYRICHTUS** Boisduval 1834   TS: *Papilio proto* Ochsenheimer.
Like *Spialia* but upf costal fold present, pale discal spot in s1b slightly
proximal to or below spot in s2.
Genitalia. Gnathos large; apex of cuillier toothed and with strong dorsal
process before apex. The apparent shape of the process varies with any
change in inclination of the valve; apex of penis usually spiny.

Note. The generic name *Muschampia* Tutt 1906, often used for this genus,
is a junior synonym of *Syrichtus* Boisduval (See Hemming 1967).

SYRICHTUS PROTO Ochsenheimer 1808   CN 30 FG p. 327; Pl. 59
Androconial scale, fig. 5, p. 23.
Genitalia. Gnathos horizontal, spiny, tapering at each end; valve with
wide costal fold not expanded posteriorly, cuillier tapering to upturned
apex, dorsal process small, almost rectangular, upper margin evenly
toothed; penis almost straight.
Range. N Africa and S Europe and eastwards to Greece and W Asia.

31. *Syrichtus proto*, S Spain: **a**, valve; **b**, penis.

Note. The species was named and described by Ochsenheimer 1808, with
reference to Esper, Schmett. Europ. 1(2): 210, Pl. 123, figs. 5, 6; also
published again by Ochsenheimer in the same year.

SYRICHTUS MOHAMMED   Oberthur 1887   CN unknown
FG p. 327; Pl. 59
Genitalia. Like *S. proto*; valve costal fold expanded posteriorly; gnathos
wider.
Range. Restricted to Morocco and Algeria.

32. *Syrichtus mohammed*, Morocco: valve.

45

SYRICHTUS TESSELLUM Hübner 1803   CN 30 FG p. 326; Pl. 59
Genitalia. Gnathos elongate oval; valve wide, cuillier small, erect, apex sharply toothed, with strong proximal dorsal spine; penis rather long, slender and sinuous. The genitalia show considerable local variation.
Range. SE Europe in Greece, Macedonia and Albania, W Asia and eastwards to Mongolia in several subspecies.

33. *Syrichtus tessellum nomas*, Iraq: genitalia, penis removed. European specimen not available.

SYRICHTUS CRIBRELLUM   Eversmann 1841   CN unknown
FG p. 326; Pl. 59
Genitalia. Gnathos slender, elongate, valve narrower than that of *S. tessellum*, costal border less bowed, cuillier apex rounded, proximal process very prominent, densely chitinised and toothed, not erect; penis with numerous large cornuti.
Range. Hungary and S Russia and eastwards to Mongolia and the Amur.

Note. Warren 1926 has introduced the generic name *Tuttia* for this species. It does not appear to the writer that generic distinction is required.

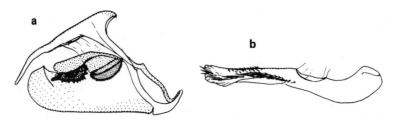

34. *Syrichtus cribrellum*, S Russia: **a,** genitalia, penis removed; **b,** penis.

SYRICHTUS LEUZEAE Oberthur 1881
CN unknown FG p. 328; Pl. 59
Genitalia. Gnathos tapering to a sharp point with few teeth on dorsal and ventral borders; valve very wide, almost quadrilateral, cuillier long,

narrow, upturned, costal border terminates in a rounded knob; penis slender with small lateral teeth.
Range. Restricted to Algeria.

35. *Syrichtus leuzeae*, Algeria: genitalia, penis removed.

Genus **CARCHARODUS** Hübner 1820   TS: *Papilio alceae* Esper
Small brown or grey butterflies, ups with small dark markings, fw with small hyaline areas and costal fold (sex-brand); a conspicuous hair-tuft unf in males of some species; hw margin slightly sinuous, fringes long, scalloped and ups chequered to form dentate margins.
Genitalia. Uncus long, slender; gnathos absent but diaphragm lightly chitinised to form a floor to the anal compartment; valves variable, costal fold terminated posteriorly in densely chitinised spinose expansions; penis usually large.
Early stages. Larval food plants Labiatae, rarely Malvaceae.

References. Reverdin 1913. de Lesse 1960. (A).

CARCHARODUS ALCEAE Esper 1780   CN 31   FG p. 328; Pl. 59
♂ unf without hair-tuft. *Antennal club* obtuse, straight.
Genitalia. Folds of diaphragm extensive but feebly chitinised; valve triangular, short, apex of costal fold greatly expanded, style represented by a densely spiny process, antistyle long, curved, tapering to a point, cuillier ascending, narrow, apex pointed and embracing the style; penis large with long caecum, rounded apex dilated and spinous.
Range. S Europe to France and N Germany (rare). W Asia.

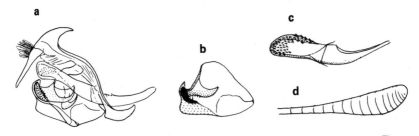

36. *Carcharodus alceae*, Yugoslav Macedonia: **a,** genitalia; **b,** valve; **c,** penis; **d,** apex of antenna.

CARCHARODUS LAVATHERAE Esper 1780

CN 30   FG p. 328; Pl. 59

♂ unf lacking hair-tuft. *Antennal club* slightly arcuate. *Androconial scales* very slender.

Genitalia. Diaphragm below uncus extensively chitinised; valve triangular, spinous area of costal fold not expanded posteriorly; cuillier narrow, apex rounded and capped with spines; furca prominent, encircling penis, dorsal plate conspicuous; penis rather slender.

Range. Morocco, Algeria, Tunisia, S Europe northwards to S Switzerland and S Germany (rare). Asia Minor.

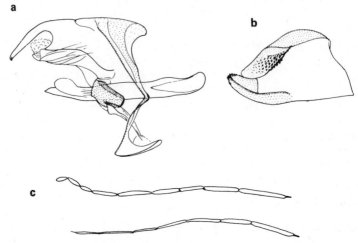

37. *Carcharodus lavatherae*, C Pyrenees: **a,** genitalia, valves removed; **b,** valve; **c,** androconial scales (two).

Note. Verity (1940) proposed a new genus *Lavatheria* for this species, but it does not appear to the writer that generic distinction is required.

The chromosome karyotype in the following species, *C. boeticus* and *C. flocciferus*, is often confused by the presence of a variable number of small supernumerary chromosomes. When these are ignored, the value is probably n=30 or very near. In the subspecies *C. b. stauderi* the value appears constantly to be n=30, and again in *C. f. orientalis* also n=30 in Lebanon, but variable in other localities.

CARCHARODUS BOETICUS Rambur

CN 38–47   FG p. 329; Pl. 59

♂ unf with hair-pencil, usually dark, from inner margin. *Antennal club* slightly arcuate. Eastern and western forms, here treated as subspecies, are considered specifically distinct by many authors.

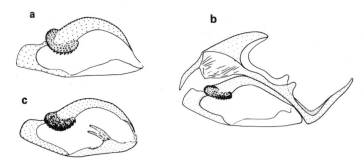

38. *Carcharodus boeticus boeticus,* C Spain: **a,** valve. *C. b. stauderi,* Morocco: **b,** genitalia, penis removed; **c,** valve.

C. b. boeticus Rambur 1839.
Genitalia. Like *C. lavatherae,* stylifer larger, almost semicircular, densely chitinised and spiny, cuillier narrow, almost rectangular in side view; penis slender, a few small spines near apex.
Range. Widely distributed in Spain and Portugal, very local in SW Alps and C Italy.

C. b. stauderi Reverdin 1913. CN 30.
Genitalia. Stylifer less symmetrical, usually slightly compressed but variable.
Range. N Africa including Cyrenaica. Asia Minor, Lebanon, Iran.

CARCHARODUS FLOCCIFERUS Zeller
CN 36–48 FG p. 330; Pl. 59
♂ unf with dark hair-pencil from inner margin. *Antennal club* slightly arcuate and tapering. Eastern and western forms, treated here as subspecies, are considered specifically distinct by many authors.

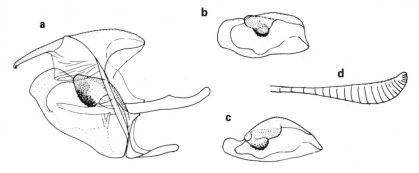

39. *Carcharodus flocciferus flocciferus,* C Pyrenees: **a,** genitalia; **b,** valve. *C. f. orientalis,* N Turkey: **c,** valve; **d,** antennal apex.

C. f. flocciferus Zeller 1847.

Genitalia. Like *C. boeticus*; chitinous gutter below uncus well defined; valve rather wide, apex of cuillier broad, stylifer large with dense spines along lower border; penis slender with small cornuti and very small apical spines.

Range. SW Europe including Italy, eastwards to Dalmatia (Ostarija). Records from Sicily need confirmation.

C. f. orientalis Reverdin 1913. CN 30–37.

Genitalia. As above but apex of valve narrow.

Range. S Yugoslavia, Bulgaria, Greece and eastwards across W Asia to Kashmir and Afghanistan.

Note 1. In prepared specimens the shape of the stylifer is seen best in a detached valve. It appears quite different with a valve *in situ.* In external characters seasonal variation may be marked, especially in *C. f. orientalis*, in which first-brood specimens may be dark, resembling the western *C. f. flocciferus.* The situation of the frontier between *orientalis* and *flocciferus* is not known.

Note 2. Ragusa 1919 proposed a new genus *Reverdinus* for this species. It does not appear to the author that generic distinction is necessary.

Genus **ERYNNIS** Schrank 1801   TS: *Papilio tages* L.

Small brown butterflies, markings generally obscure; *antennal club* slender, arcuate; male ups with costal fold; outer margins of wings entire; epiphysis on fore-tibia large, claws lack paronychia.

Genitalia. Tegumen domed, uncus short, strongly curved, connected with tegumen by narrow chitinised band and with small chitinised plate below; gnathos conspicuous, strongly curved; valves asymmetrical; penis short, without marked features.

Early stages. Larva with 'trumpet' hairs (cf. pupal Lycaeninae).

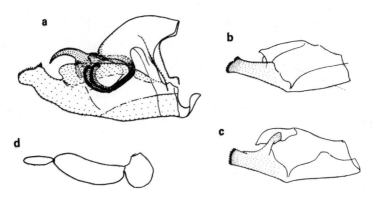

40. *Erynnis tages,* N Yugoslavia: **a,** genitalia, penis removed; **b,** left valve; **c,** right valve; **d,** palpus.

ERYNNIS TAGES L. 1758   CN 31   FG p. 331; Pl. 59
Genitalia. Uncus sickle-shaped; costal margin of left valve short, cuillier narrow, apex oblique; costal margin of right valve longer, cuillier with short chitinised dorsal process, apex rectangular.
Range. Europe, except boreal regions, thence across Asia to China.

ERYNNIS MARLOYI Boisduval 1834   CN 31 FG p. 331; Pl. 59
Genitalia. Small bilobed dorsal process at base of uncus, gnathos more elongate than in *E. tages*; costal margin of left valve extends to triangular cuillier, in which dorsal margin is regularly dentate; cuillier of right valve more elongate.
Range. Balkans, across W Asia to Himalaya Mts.

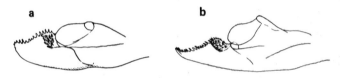

41. *Erynnis marloyi,* Iraq: **a,** left valve; **b,** right valve. European specimen not available.

Subfamily HETEROPTERINAE Aurivillius 1925

Description. Abdomen slender, longer than inner margin of hw; ♂ without sex-brand. *Palpi* long, porrect, middle segment very hairy. *Antennae* short, club arcuate, lacking apiculus. *Legs* epiphysis absent from fore-tibia; spurs on middle and hind legs variable, but distal spurs always present on hind tibia. *Venation.* Wings broad, cells long and narrow; in fw v5 straight, lying slightly nearer to v4 than to v6, lower dc vein curved; hw ample, costa longer than inner margin.
Genitalia. Fragile, elongate, tegumen domed, uncus almost straight, brachia parallel with and close to uncus; dorsal structures very small in relation to size of valve and long slender saccus; penis very long and slender.
Early stages. Ovum spherical with flat base, shell with faint vertical grooves.

Genus **HETEROPTERUS** Dumeril 1806   TS: *Papilio morpheus* Pallas
The characters are those of *H. morpheus* Pallas.

HETEROPTERUS MORPHEUS Pallas 1771   CN unknown
FG p. 332; Pl. 60

Genitalia. Valve more than twice as long as uncus+tegumen, costal margin terminating abruptly in right-angle point, cuillier narrow, upturned and finely spined.

Range. From N Spain across temperate Europe and Asia to Amurland, occurring in scattered colonies.

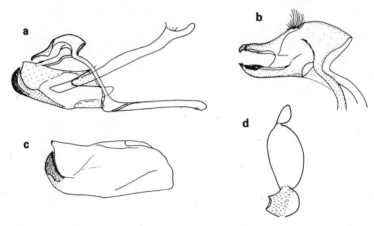

42. *Heteropterus morpheus*, Rome: **a,** genitalia; **b,** dorsal structures enlarged; **c,** valve; **d,** palpus.

Genus **CARTEROCEPHALUS** Lederer 1852 TS: *Papilio palaemon* Pallas. Like *Heteropterus*, ups yellow markings more extensive.

CARTEROCEPHALUS PALAEMON Pallas 1771   CN unknown
FG p. 332; Pl. 60

Genitalia. Like *H. morpheus*; uncus bears elaborate bristles; costal margin of valve sinuous, rounded posteriorly, cuillier more pointed, shorter and less heavily spined; penis very long and slender.

Range. Across temperate and N Europe, Asia and N America.

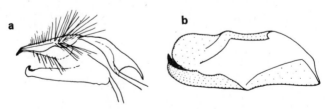

43. *Carterocephalus palaemon*, Switzerland: **a,** dorsal structures; **b,** valve.

CARTEROCEPHALUS SILVICOLUS   Meigen 1829
CN unknown   FG p. 333; Pl. 60

Genitalia. Like *C. palaemon.*

Range: N Europe and eastwards across N Asia to Kamschatka and Japan.

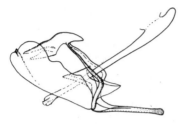

44. *Carterocephalus silvicolus,* Lithuania: genitalia.

Subfamily HESPERIINAE Latreille 1809

Description. In this extensive subfamily characters vary greatly. Males upf often with black sex-brand across discal area but never with costal fold. *Eyes* smooth. *Palpi* variable. *Antennae* short, club slender, often with apiculus. *Legs* and feet with usual family characters. *Venation.* Fw apex pointed, v5 proximally curved to approach v4; hw usually with anal lobe, v5 weak or absent; cell in fw elongate, in hw short. *Genitalia.* Brachia usually present; gnathos absent in all European species; furca usually well developed.

Early stages. Ovum without strong ribs, sometimes faintly grooved, reticulate or pitted, shape variable. Larva slender with neck well defined, smooth or finely pubescent. Pupa very slender, in *T. acteon* without cremaster but with 'nose horn' or beak provided with hooks, fixed in puparium by the beak hooked into a silken pad and with silken girdle. Larval food plants Monocotyledons (grasses). Larvae often pass entire larval stage in a tunnel formed of grass stems spun together. All European species single brooded.

Key to genera of Hesperiinae

1 Antennal club blunt, without apiculus   .   .   .   .   *Thymelicus*
  Antennal club with apiculus **2**

2 Antennal apiculus short, upf ♂ sex-brand present   .   .   **3**
  Antennal apiculus long, upf ♂ sex-brand absent .   .   .   **4**

3 Penis stout, straight   .   .   .   .   *Hesperia*
  Penis with irregular apical processes   .   .   .   .   *Ochlodes*

4 Mid-tibia heavily spined   .   .   .   .   .   .   *Gegenes*
  Mid-tibia with scanty feeble spines .   .   .   .   .   *Borbo*

Genus **THYMELICUS** Hübner 1819   TS: *Papilio acteon* Rottemburg
Description. Small species, ups gc yellow or tawny; hw anal lobe poorly developed; upf with black linear sex-brand. *Androconial scales* moniliform, usually broken into separate particles by removal for examination. *Palpi* terminal segment slender, almost as long as middle segment. *Antennae* short, club slender, slightly arcuate, without apiculus. *Venation*. Hw v5 absent.
Genitalia. Uncus and brachia slender; valve simple, elongate, cuillier upturned, pointed; saccus very slender, as long as valve; penis about twice as long as valve.
Early stages. Ovum oval, flattened, shell smooth or faintly reticulated. Larva and pupa with usual subfamily characters.

THYMELICUS ACTEON Rottemburg
CN unknown   FG p. 333; Pl. 60
Distribution very extensive through Mediterranean sub-region. Two poorly defined subspecies with similar genitalia.

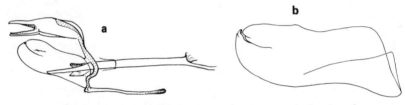

45. *Thymelicus acteon*, Piedmont, N Italy: **a**, genitalia; **b**, valve.

T. a. acteon Rottemburg 1775.
Genitalia. Uncus and brachia of equal length, valve apex rounded, cuillier terminating in two small teeth closely applied to costal margin.
Range. N Africa, S and C Europe including S England, and eastwards across Asia Minor to Lebanon, Iraq and N Iran.

T. a. christi Rebel 1894.
Distinguished by brightly marked ups.
Genitalia. Indistinguishable.
Range. Confined to Canary Islands

THYMELICUS HAMZA Oberthur 1876
CN unknown   FG p. 334; Pl. 60
Genitalia. Like *T. acteon*; cuillier longer, apex rising above costal margin, lacking teeth.

46. *Thymelicus hamza*, Middle Atlas, Morocco: valve.

Range. N Africa, including Cyrenaica; W Asia extending to Pamirs. Not recorded from Europe.

THYMELICUS LINEOLUS Ochsenheimer 1808
CN 27-29 FG p. 335; Pl. 60

Genitalia. Like *T. acteon*; brachia longer, cuillier wider, apex with small teeth.

Range. N Africa, S and C Europe including S England, and across W Asia to N Iran and Amurland and Ussuri.

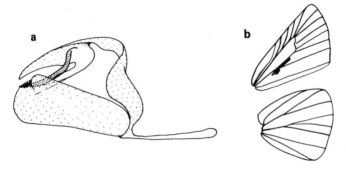

47. *Thymelicus lineolus,* Austria: **a,** genitalia, penis removed; **b,** wing venation.

THYMELICUS FLAVUS Brünnich 1763   CN 27   FG p. 335; Pl. 60
Androconical scales long, slender.

Genitalia. Uncus horizontal, brachia widely divergent; apex of cuillier rounded.

Range. N Africa, S and C Europe and eastwards to Lebanon, Iraq and Iran.

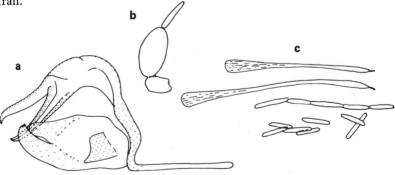

48. *Thymelicus flavus,* Austria: **a,** genitalia, penis removed; **b,** palpus; **c,** androconial scales.

Genus **HESPERIA** F. 1793   TS: *Papilio comma* L.
Hw cell short, anal lobe defined, v5 absent. *Palpi* apical segment shorter than middle segment. *Antennal club* with short apiculus.
Genitalia. Uncus very short, bifid in dorsal view, brachia short, robust; valve in side view slender, cuillier upturned, pointed apex erect and parallel with slender costal process; penis straight.
Early Stages. Ovum slightly compressed dome, shell minutely pitted.

HESPERIA COMMA   L.   CN unknown   FG p. 336; Pl. 60
Distribution Holarctic with numerous ill-defined subspecies, of which two occur in the region. It seems restricted to areas where rocks are calcareous.

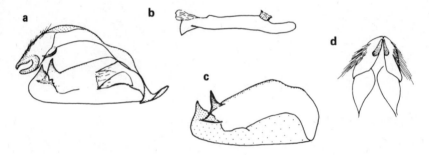

49. *Hesperia comma,* Austria: **a,** genitalia, penis removed; **b,** penis; **c,** valve; **d,** uncus and tegumen, dorsal view.

H. c. comma L. 1758.
Genitalia. Described above.
Range. Widely distributed in Europe to 70°N and across N and C Asia to Amurland, in N America in the western mountains.

H. c. benuncas Oberthur 1912.
Genitalia. Valve differs in slightly smaller dorsal processes.
Range. Morocco, Algeria.

Genus **OCHLODES** Scudder 1872   TS: *Hesperia nemorum* Boisduval
A small genus with Holarctic distribution. Like *Hesperia*, hw anal lobe less well defined. *Antennal club* with small apiculus.
Genitalia. Like *H. comma*; uncus longer, in dorsal view bifid with slender limbs, brachia slender, about twice as long as uncus; apex of valve rounded; penis with complicated apical structure.

OCHLODES VENATUS   Bremer & Grey 1853
                                        CN 29 FG p. 336; Pl. 60
Range. Very extensive, from W Europe eastwards across temperate Asia.
The nominate subspecies *O. v. venatus* Bremer described from N China.

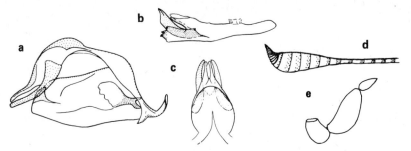

50. *Ochlodes venatus faunus,* S England: **a,** genitalia, penis removed; **b,** penis; **c,** uncus and tegumen, dorsal view; **d,** antennal apex; **e,** palpus.

O. v. faunus Turati 1905.
Genitalia. Described above.
Range. Widely distributed in S and C Europe including Spain and Portugal extending eastwards to Asia Minor, Lebanon and C Asia (Turkestan).

Gegenes Group
Small or rather small species, ups brown, fw often with hyaline spots, males with or without sex-brand upf. Early stages of European species not recorded.

Genus **GEGENES**   Hübner 1819   TS: *Papilio pumilio* Hoffmannsegg
Description. Male upf without sex-brand. *Antennae* short, apiculus well developed. *Palpi* small, middle segment oval, swollen, terminal segment very short, pointed. *Legs* mid-tibiae strongly spined. *Venation.* Fw cell narrow, upper angle acute; hw v5 absent, anal lobe well developed.

GEGENES PUMILIO Hoffmannsegg 1804   CN 24   FG p. 337; Pl. 60
Genitalia. Cuillier short, scarcely reaching costa of valve, upper margin with two pairs of prominent teeth; saccus rather short.
Range. Mediterranean region and eastwards to Himalaya Mts. and Iran.

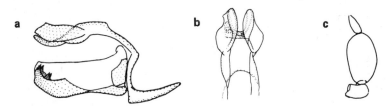

51. *Gegenes pumilio,* Lebanon: **a,** genitalia, penis removed; **b,** uncus and tegumen, dorsal view; **c,** palpus.

57

GEGENES NOSTRODAMUS Fabricius 1793   CN unknown
FG p. 337; Pl. 60

Genitalia. Like *G. pumilio*; cuillier longer, upper margin evenly serrate; saccus almost as long as tegumen+uncus.

Range. Ethiopian Africa. Coastal regions of Mediterranean and eastwards to Himalaya Mts.

52. *Gegenes nostrodamus,* Algeria; **a,** genitalia, penis removed; **b,** uncus and tegumen, dorsal view.

Genus **BORBO** Evans 1949   TS: *Hesperia borbonica* Boisduval
Like *Gegenes,* but differs in the longer antennal apiculus and hw anal lobe better defined. *Legs.* Tibial spines inconspicuous.

Genitalia. Uncus rather slender, bifid in dorsal view; a strongly chitinised gutter forms a floor to the anal compartment; furca elaborate, forming a complete anellus; penis slender, apex upturned.

BORBO BORBONICA Boisduval 1833   CN unknown
FG p. 338; Pl. 60

Genitalia. Described above; valve elongate, cuillier upturned and recurved, longer than that of *G. nostrodamus,* dorsal border toothed.

Range. Africa, with Seychelles Islands and Réunion, widely distributed as *B. b. borbonica* Boisduval. Syria, Egypt, Algeria and Morocco, occurs as the subspecies *B. b. zelleri* Lederer 1855 especially in Mediterranean coastal regions.

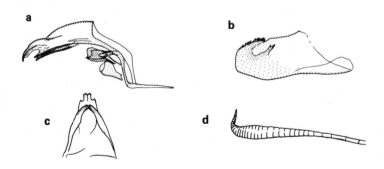

53. *Borbo borbonica,* Algeria: **a,** genitalia, valves and penis removed; **b,** valve; **c,** uncus and tegumen, dorsal view; **d,** antennal apex.

Family **PAPILIONIDAE** Latreille 1809

Large, conspicuous butterflies with most varied characters, but subfamily groups well defined. *Eyes* smooth. *Palpi* variable. *Antennae* short, club variable. *Legs and feet* all species with six fully functional legs of almost equal size, fore-tibia with epiphysis, each foot with a single pair of claws, lacking pulvilli and paronychia. True androconial scales lacking in all European species. *Venation.* Variable, fw with 11 or 12 veins and internal vein; cell closed in both wings; hw with single anal vein, inner margin concave.

Genitalia. Variable, without any constant family character.

Early stages. Ovum hemispherical, surface granular, domed. Larva with osmaterium. Pupa variable, see under subfamilies.

Note. This large family includes several rather isolated ('relict') forms, e.g. *Zerynthia, Hypermnestra* etc. and a very large assembly of true Swallowtails with over 500 species presenting enormous variation. Many of these are extremely rare. The European species *P. machaon* and *I. podalirius* are not closely related.

References. Ford 1944. Munroe 1961.

Key to subfamilies of Papilionidae

1 Fw with 11 veins . . . . Parnassiinae
  Fw with 12 veins . , ... **2**

2 Tegumen vestigial, uncus absent . . . . . Papilioninae
  Tegumen and uncus developed . . . . . Zerynthiinae

Subfamily PAPILIONINAE Latreille 1809

Description. Most species with tail on hw at v4. The subfamily is greatly developed in tropical countries but only four species occur in Europe. *Palpi* very short, ascending. *Antennae* short, less than half the length of fw, club rather gradual, usually slightly arcuate (upturned). *Feet* claws on each foot of equal length. *Venation.* Fw with 12 veins, upper dcv absent; median and submedian veins united near base by a strong transverse vein; a short internal vein present; hw with precostal cell.

Genitalia. Tegumen vestigial, depressed, degenerate, very small; vinculum forming the genital ring; valve wide, largely exposed, articulating with tegumen by a membranous strand, sacculus sometimes a partly independent structure, extending along valve to terminate in the harpe; furca not large; saccus variable; penis rather short, stout, curved or angled.

Early stages. Pupa slender, fixed upright or nearly so by cremastral hooks and silken girdle.

Note. This description is based upon European species only.

References. Rothschild 1895. Rothschild & Jordan 1906.

54. PAPILIONINAE, key characters. *Papilio machaon*: **a,** wing venation; **b,** genitalia, including supra-uncus. *Iphiclides podalirius*: **c,** ♂ fore-leg; **d,** middle-leg; **e,** hind-leg; **f,** mid-tarsal claw.

Genus **PAPILIO** L. TS: *Papilio machaon* L.

Hw tail on v4 often spatulate if present, body groove folded; sexes similar.
Genitalia. Uncus absent, scaphium surmounted by supra-uncus in all European species; valve wide, harpe well chitinised, margin usually finely toothed; saccus absent.
Early stages. Larva cylindrical, plump, thoracic segments slightly tapered, skin smooth. Pupa with bifid cephalic processes and a row of small tubercles on each side of the dorsum. Hibernates as pupa.

References. Rothschild & Jordan 1906. Stichel 1907(B).

PAPILIO MACHAON L. 1758 CN 30-32 FG p. 35; Pl. 1

Genitalia. Supra-uncus well formed with slender pointed apex; scaphium vestigial, depressed, with vestiges of tegumen, both covered by supra-uncus; valve broad, harpe densely chitinised, elongate, with many dorsal teeth; penis bowed, short and massive.
Range. N Africa, Europe and temperate Asia eastwards to Japan, with closely related species or subspecies in N America.

Reference. Eller 1936.

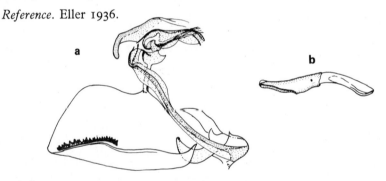

55. *Papilio machaon,* Switzerland: **a,** genitalia, spread, showing vestigial scaphium and tegumen; **b,** penis.

PAPILIO HOSPITON Géné 1839 CN unknown

FG p. 35; Pl. 1

Genitalia. Like *P. machaon* but supra-uncus smaller, apex short; valve wide, posterior margin almost straight, harpe short with four or five small teeth; penis bowed.
Range. Confined to Corsica and Sardinia.

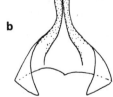

56. *Papilio hospiton,* Corsica: **a,** valve; **b,** supra-uncus, dorsal view.

PAPILIO ALEXANOR   Esper 1799   CN 30 FG p. 36; Pl. 1
Antennal club straight.
Genitalia. Supra-uncus blunt, downturned; valve small, harpe expanded
into a wide curve and serrated all round; penis short, curved to a right-
angle; furca short and wide.
Range. Local in S Europe from SE France to Greece and eastwards to
Lebanon, Iran and Turkestan.

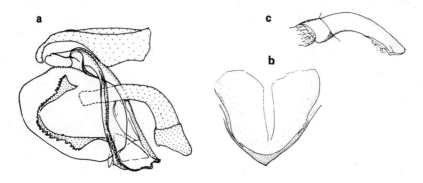

57. *Papilio alexanor,* Basses Alpes: **a,** genitalia; **b,** furca enlarged; **c,** penis.

Genus **IPHICLIDES** Hübner 1820   TS: *Papilio podalirius* L.
Ups usually white or pale yellow, thinly scaled, marked by black transverse bars; hw tail when present, slender, tapering, body groove not
folded, anal region often slightly extended in ♂; sexes similar; male
abdomen with prominent lateral grooves enclosing yellow hair scales,
abundant in fresh specimens.
Genitalia. See *I. podalirius* L.
Range. The genus is well represented in N America and in SE Asia.
Early stages. Larva fusiform, thorax humped. Pupa as in *Papilio.*

IPHICLIDES PODALIRIUS L.   CN 30   FG p. 36; Pl. 1
The species has an extensive distribution from N Africa through temperate Europe and Asia to China. Two subspecies with similar genitalia.

I. p. podalirius L. 1758.
Genitalia. Tegumen vestigial, supra-uncus not present but organs closely
embraced by eighth sclerite; valve large, pyriform, sacculus as in *Papilio,*
harpe not toothed, small, densely chitinised; saccus short but massive;
penis curved, stout, rather long.
Range. Temperate S and C Europe and eastwards to C Asia, including
Lebanon and N Iran.

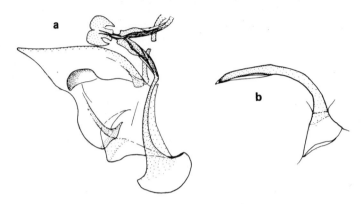

58. *Iphiclides podalirius*, Romania: **a,** genitalia spread, showing left valve and dorsal structures; **b,** penis.

I. p. feisthamelii Duponchel 1832.   CN 30
Slightly larger than *I. p. podalirius*.
Range. N Africa, extending far into the Sahara oases, Spain, Portugal and S France. The two subspecies appear to be allopatric, but the situation at the frontiers in S France has not been investigated.

Subfamily ZERYNTHIINAE Grote 1900

Description. A small heterogeneous subfamily, including relict forms which show transition from Papilioninae to Parnassiinae. Four species occur in the Mediterranean region and a small number of rather isolated but related forms are known from temperate eastern Asia. *Palpi* variable. *Antennae* short, club cylindrical, slightly arcuate, upturned. *Claws* unequal, medial claw small or vestigial. *Venation.* Fw with 12 veins, upper dc vein absent, transverse vein absent, internal vein present; hw precostal vein directed inwards, precostal cell small. Sphragial escutcheon present in ♀.
Genitalia. Uncus present, apex cleft.
Early stages. See generic descriptions. Larval food plants *Aristolochia* species.

References. Le Cerf 1913. Stichel 1907(B).

Genus **ZERYNTHIA** Ochsenheimer 1816   TS: *Papilio polyxena* D. & S.
Outer margin of hw deeply scalloped.
Genitalia. Uncus very small; valve large, wide; saccus vestigial; penis small, straight, base bilobed.
Early stages. Ovum domed, surface granular. Larva cylindrical with dorsal and three lateral rows of small fleshy processes. Pupa slender, on the ground in a light cocoon, secured by silken thoracic girdle and silken threads to a small cephalic prominence.

ZERYNTHIA POLYXENA D. & S.   CN 30-31   FG p. 37; Pl. 2

Two poorly defined subspecies with similar genitalia.

Z. p. polyxena D. & S. 1775.

Genitalia. Valve wide, almost three times as long as small uncus and tegumen, posterior margin irregular, dentate near apex, harpe narrow, pointed, arising from inferior margin; penis straight, narrow, tapering to pointed apex, base bilobed.

Range. SE Europe, northwards to Vienna, extending to W Turkey. Sicily.

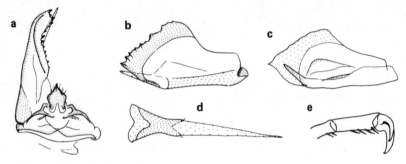

59. *Zerynthia polyxena polyxena,* Montenegro: **a,** genitalia, penis and right valve removed, dorsal view; **b,** valve. *Z. p. cassandra,* S France: **c,** valve; **d,** penis; **e,** mid-tarsal claw.

Z. p. cassandra Hübner-Geyer 1828.

Wing markings differ slightly.
Genitalia. Valve margin less irregular.
Range. S France, Italy (characters often intermediate).

ZERYNTHIA RUMINA L. 1758.   CN unknown

FG p. 38; Pl. 2

Genitalia. Like *Z. polyxena* but tegumen narrower; valve shorter, costal border irregular, apex pointed, harpe shorter, arising near apex; penis as in *Z. polyxena.*

Range. N Africa, Spain, Portugal and SE France, in local colonies. Size variable, large in N Africa, but genitalia indistinguishable.

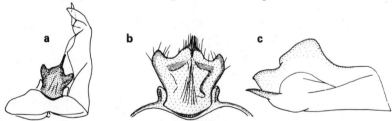

60. *Zerynthia rumina,* S France: **a,** genitalia, penis and left valve removed; **b,** uncus and tegumen enlarged; **c,** valve.

Genus **ALLANCASTRIA** Bryk 1934   TS: *Thais cerisyi* Godart
Description. Outer margin of hw deeply scalloped, in some races forming
a short tail on v4. *Palpi* terminal segment long. *Antennae* as in *Zerynthia*.
Venation. Hw precostal cell very small, precostal vein curved inwards.
Genitalia. See below *A. cerisyi*.

ALLANCASTRIA CERISYI   Godart·   CN unknown

FG p. 39; Pl. 2

A. c. cerisyi Godart 1822.
Genitalia. Uncus long, narrow, apex cleft; tegumen substantial; valve
broad, pointed, harpe absent; penis slender, shorter than valve, base
bilobed; furca prominent.
Range. SE Europe, usually near Black Sea coast, in Albania, N Greece,
Bulgaria and Rumania. W Asia, widely distributed to Lebanon and Iran.
Also in Crete, *A. c. cretica* Rebel 1902, small, margin of hw not scalloped,
genitalia similar. Colonies flying at high levels in W Asia are specifically
distinct. (T. Larsen *in litt.*).

Reference. Bernardi 1971.

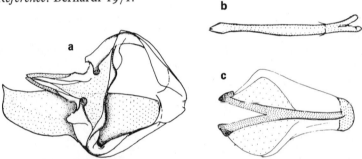

61. *Allancastria cerisyi,* Bulgaria: **a,** genitalia, penis and right valve removed,
dorsal view; **b,** penis; **c,** furca enlarged.

Genus **ARCHON** Hübner 1822   TS: *Papilio apollinus* Herbst
Description. The single species is of moderate size, wings broad, unf with
bristles, membrane wrinkled, largely hyaline, margins entire; ♂ abdomen
with terminal hair-tuft; ♀ lacks sphragial pouch (see *Parnassius*). *Antennae*
as in *Zerynthia. Palpi* very small, porrect. *Legs and feet* modified, front tibia
short with two anterior curved spines, epiphysis large, tarsus very long;
middle and hind-tibiae with spurs and smaller spines; on each foot external claw well developed, inner claw thin and small, vestigial on fore-
foot. *Venation.* As in *Zerynthia,* fw with 12 veins.
Genitalia. Uncus slender, apex cleft; tegumen broad, extending into
massive peduncles which fuse with vinculum and continue into long
saccus; valve very small, attached to expanded vinculum; penis substantial, long and straight.

Early stages. Larva stout, hairy, resembling *Parnassius*. Pupa rigid, short and wide, on the ground in a light cocoon. Hibernation as pupa.

ARCHON APOLLINUS Herbst 1798   CN unknown

FG p. 39; Pl. 2

Genitalia. Described above.

Range. Widely distributed in W Asia eastwards to Iran; reported from N Greece and Turkey.

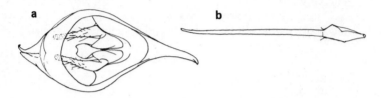

62. *Archon apollinus,* Lebanon: **a,** genitalia, penis removed, dorsal view; **b,** penis.

Note. By venation and genitalia characters *A. apollinus* is related to *Zerynthia,* by larval and pupal characters and by markings it is closer to *Parnassius.* It represents an archaic relict form with intermediate taxonomic characters.

Subfamily PARNASSIINAE Swainson 1840

The characters of the subfamily are those of the genus *Parnassius*.

Genus **PARNASSIUS** Latreille 1804   TS: *Papilio apollo* L.

Description. Butterflies of medium or large size, head small and hairy, wings often thinly scaled or partly hyaline with bristles beneath, margins entire. Most species are white, fw with large black spots in cell and at cell-end, hw usually with red spots or ocelli in spaces five and seven. A sphragis is formed around the ostium bursae of the ♀ during copulation. *Palpi* small, porrect. *Antennae* short, club straight, fusiform. *Legs* ♂ foreleg hair-tufts often present at tarsal sutures, sometimes prominent (*P. apollo*); claws unequal, internal claw short. *Venation.* Fw with 11 veins, v9 absent; in hw precostal cell absent, precostal vein strong, directed basally.

Genitalia. Large, horny; uncus vestigial or absent; tegumen broad, hooded, with brachia on each side curving downwards; valve variable, saccus present only in *P. mnemosyne* among European species; penis straight, robust, as long as or longer than tegumen+vinculum, base bifid.

Early stages. Ovum domed or compressed. Larva usually black, plump, with small hairy warts on each segment. Pupa short, rigid, thorax very wide, lying upon the ground in a light cocoon. Hibernation as ovum.

References. Bryk 1915, 1930–39, 1962. Eisner 1954–56. Stichel 1907(A). Bollow 1929.

PARNASSIUS APOLLO L.   CN 30   FG p. 39; Pl. 3

Widely distributed in Fennoscandia and occurring on all important mountain ranges in Europe, in well marked local races usually ranked as subspecies. In all those examined including *P. a. siciliae* Oberthur, *P. a. pumilus* Stichel, *P. a. nevadensis* Oberthur, genitalia indistinguishable.

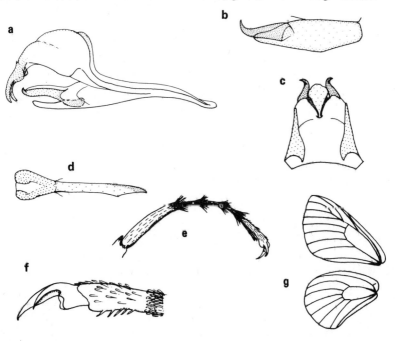

63. *Parnassius apollo,* Valais, Switzerland: **a,** genitalia, penis removed; **b,** valve; **c,** tegumen and uncus, ventral view; **d,** penis; **e,** ♂ fore-leg; **f,** fore-tarsal claw; **g,** wing venation.

P. a. apollo L. 1758.

Genitalia. Uncus vestigial; valve horizontal, elongate, narrow, harpe massive; penis straight, substantial, base bilobed.
Range. Widely distributed in mountainous districts of Europe and eastwards to the Ural Mts., Caucasus and C Asia.

PARNASSIUS PHOEBUS F. 1793 CN 30 FG p. 40; Pl. 3

Occurs at high altitudes in the Alps, Urals and in C and E Asia. Also in N America (Alaska).

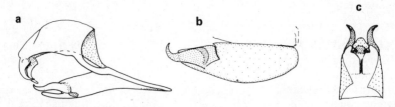

64. *Parnassius phoebus,* Cottian Alps, NW Italy: **a,** genitalia, penis removed; **b,** valve; **c,** tegumen and uncus, ventral view.

P. p. sacerdos Stichel 1906.

Genitalia. Like *P. apollo* but smaller; uncus narrow, brachia more slender; valve shorter, tapering to rounded apex, harpe massive.

Range. High alpine peaks from Alpes Maritimes and Savoie to Gross Glockner. Absent from Spain, Pyrenees, Apennines, Carpathians and Balkan Mts.

References. Oberthur 1891, 1913. Bryk 1915. Eisner 1966.

PARNASSIUS MNEMOSYNE. L. 1758 CN 29–30

FG p. 41; Pl. 3

Genitalia. Uncus absent; tegumen with deep posterior notch and lateral arms terminating in sharp points, a slender process arising from ventral surface on each side; valve vertical, wide, lacking harpe; saccus pyriform; penis as in *P. apollo* but more slender, straight, base bilobed in dorsal view.

Range. Widely distributed at sub-alpine levels in mountainous areas of Europe and W Asia, but often at valley levels in northern range. Absent from Spain and Portugal.

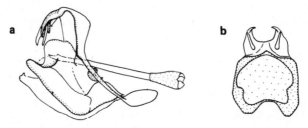

65. *Parnassius mnemosyne,* Switzerland: **a,** genitalia, side view; **b,** tegumen and uncus, ventral view showing brachia.

Family **PIERIDAE** Duponchel 1832

Description. All species in the region are of medium size or little more, with white or orange wings easily recognisable; the sexes usually differ. Subfamily and generic characters are well marked in the genitalia, but specific characters often less well defined. *Androconial scales* usually present upf. Fresh specimens may exhale a faint perfume. *Eyes* smooth. *Palpi* longer than the head, porrect or slightly ascending. *Antennae* variable, usually of medium length, very slender with small, rather gradual pyriform club, but in *Leptidea* short, club more abrupt. *Legs* all functional, feet with bifid claw, with or without pulvilli and paronychia. *Venation*. Fw with 10, 11 or 12 veins; cell closed in both wings.

Genitalia. Uncus well developed; tegumen connected with vinculum without defined peduncle; valve flat, flexible, partially exposed, attached below in the region of the saccus, and above by a membranous band to the tegumen; penis often sharply curved, with caecum and trochanter (but see note below).

Early stages. Ovum between two and three times as tall as wide. Larva pubescent, usually green simply marked with longitudinal stripes. Pupa fixed upright by cremaster and silken thoracic girdle.

References. Klots 1931–32. Niculescu 1963. Verity 1905, 1947.

Key to subfamilies of Pieridae

1 Hw precostal vein absent **2**
  Hw precostal vein present **3**

2 Fw subcostal vein with 4 branches after cell-end . Dismorphiinae
  Fw subcostal vein with 2 branches after cell-end . . Coliadinae

3 Fw with 10–11 veins . . . . Pierinae
  Fw with 12 veins . . . . Anthocharinae

The shape of the penis is unusual in most Pierinae, in Coliadinae and in Catopsiliini, and no doubt in other tribes not represented in Europe. The aedeagus is bent and the ejaculatory duct enters dorsally behind a small closed section which is termed the *caecum penis*, i.e. the blind end. On the inferior surface just beyond the caecum, there is a striking process referred to in this book as the *trochanter penis*. This is well developed in *Artogeia* and in most species of Pierinae, but is unaccountably absent in Anthocharinae. The structure has not received much attention from systematists. It is referred to by Niculescu as the apophysis, but this term has been used already in genitalia nomenclature in a different sense. Since the process is obviously an important centre for muscular attachments, the name *trochanter penis* appears suitable.

Subfamily PIERINAE Swainson 1840

Description. Wings broad, margins entire, sexes dissimilar. Many species have two or three annual broods with marked seasonal polymorphism. Antennae one third to half the length of fw, club pyriform or cylindrical. Feet with paronychia and pulvilli. *Androconial scales* present upf carry a gland cell at their bases. *Venation.* Slightly variable, fw with 10 or 11 veins; hw precostal vein present.
Early stages. Pupa slender, usually with cephalic and dorsal prominences.

Key to tribes of Pierinae

1 Fw apex sharply pointed, slightly falcate . . . . Callidryini
  Fw apex rounded **2**

2 Fw upper angle of cell obtuse . . . . . Pierini
  Fw upper angle of cell acute . . . . . . Teracolini

Key to genera of Pierini

1 Wing-markings similar on both surfaces . . . . *Aporia*
  Wing-markings differ on the two surfaces **2**

2 Unh with conspicuous mottled greenish markings . . *Pontia*
  Unh almost unmarked or dusted with grey along veins . **3**

3 Androconial scale 6 times as long as greatest width . . *Pieris*
  Androconial scale short, pyriform . . . . . *Artogeia*

Tribe PIERINI Godman & Salvin 1889

Description. Ups gc milk-white with scanty black or grey markings; frons not tufted. *Palpi* middle and apical segments of almost equal length. *Venation.* Fw upper angle of cell obtuse.
Genitalia. Penis usually with caecum and trochanter well developed.

Genus **APORIA** Hübner 1820   TS: *Papilio crataegi* L.
The characters are those of *A. crataegi*, the single European species.

APORIA CRATAEGI L. 1758   CN 25-26   FG p. 42; Pl. 13
Androconial scales present like those of *Pontia*, scale about twice as long as wide, tapering to a blunt point.
Genitalia. Uncus strong, curving sharply downwards; tegumen bilobed at junction with uncus; valve broad, tapering rapidly to a pointed apex, with rudimentary harpe; furca vestigial; penis gently curved, trochanter small.
Range. From N Africa and W Europe across temperate Asia to Japan.
Early stages. Pupa with protruding head, dorsum humped, lacking sharp prominences.

70

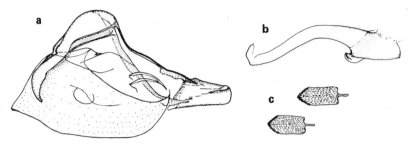

66. *Aporia crataegi*, C Spain: **a**, genitalia, penis removed; **b**, penis; **c**, androconial scales.

Genus **PIERIS** Schrank 1801   TS: *Papilio brassicae* L.
Androconial scales abundant, long and slender.
Genitalia. Uncus short, slender; tegumen about twice as long as uncus; valve with deep incision or short process near inferior posterior angle; penis robust, almost straight, longer than valve, caecum short, trochanter well developed, shaft with slight dorsal hump.

PIERIS BRASSICAE L.   CN 15   FG p. 42; Pl. 4
Range. Extends widely across temperate Asia to Siberia, Himalaya Mts. and Tibet. Absent from NE Siberia. Two subspecies occur in the region.

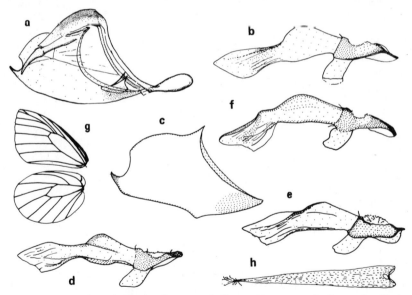

67. *Pieris brassicae*, S England: **a**, genitalia, penis removed; **b**, penis. *P. b. cheiranthi*, La Palma, Canary Islands: **c**, valve; **d**, penis. Azores: **e**, penis. Madeira: **f**, penis; **g**, wing venation; **h**, androconial scale.

71

P. b. brassicae L. 1758.
Genitalia. Described above.
Range. All Europe excepting boreal regions.

P. b. cheiranthi Hübner 1808.
Genitalia. Like *P. b. brassicae* but valve slightly shorter, wider, posterior notch emphasised; penis dorsal hump larger. These characters most marked in specimens from Madeira, least obvious in a specimen from Azores, scarcely distinct from continental *P. b. brassicae*.
Range. Canary Islands, Madeira and Azores.

The five species following, placed here in the genus *Artogeia* Verity, are usually included in *Pieris* by many authors. Their genitalia, androconial scales and chromosome numbers differ from those of *P. brassicae* and it is not satisfactory to include them in the same genus.

Genus **ARTOGEIA** Verity 1947   TS: *Papilio napi* L.
Androconial scales small, pyriform.
Genitalia. Valve margins entire; penis curved, trochanter large; specific characters not well developed.

ARTOGEIA NAPI   L.   CN 25-32   FG p. 45; Pl. 6
Genitalia. In dorsal view uncus articulating with bilobed apex of tegumen; valve posterior margin bluntly angled; penis slightly sinuous.
Range. Extensive, from N Africa and Europe across temperate Asia to W North America. Three subspecies based upon phenotypic characters, all with similar genitalia.

A. n. napi L. 1758.
Size small to moderate, ♀ gc white (rarely yellowish), two or more annual broods.
Range. Europe including England and Scandinavia. In S Europe second brood larger, wings broader, sometimes graded as subspecies *A. n. meridionalis* Heyne 1895.

A. n. bryoniae Hübner 1804.
In SE Europe CN variable. Size moderate; ups ♂ veins lined black, ♀ ups dusky, gc often yellowish. *Androconial scale* wide.
Range. Alps and Carpathians at high altitudes, Austria and N Yugoslavia, often at relatively low altitudes.

A. n. segonzaci le Cerf 1923.   CN unknown.
Large, heavily marked, ♀ gc white, usually with bryo-streak (Bowden).
Range. Confined to High Atlas in Morocco, a mountain form flying at almost 3,000m. In Middle Atlas, flying at about 1750m, *A. n. atlantis* Oberthur 1925, lightly marked in both sexes, perhaps low level summer form of *P. n. segonzaci*.

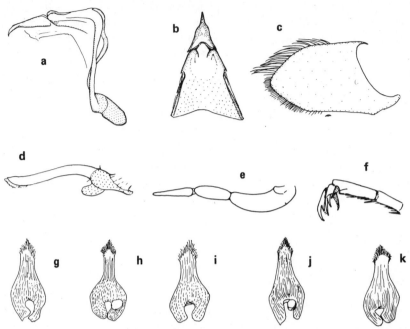

68. *Artogeia napi napi*, S England: **a,** genitalia, valves and penis removed; **b,** uncus and tegumen, dorsal view; **c,** valve; **d,** penis; **e,** palpus; **f,** mid-tarsal claw. ANDROCONIAL SCALES: **g,** Sicily; **h,** S England; **i,** Switzerland, *A. n. bryoniae*; **j,** Norway, *A. n. adalwinda*; **k,** High Atlas, Morocco, *A. n. segonzaci*.

Artogeia napi – A. bryoniae

The relationship between *Artogeia napi* and *Artogeia bryoniae* has been the subject of active study for many years. The situation has a genetic basis which is seen to be extremely complicated. In captivity the forms interbreed without great difficulty, and very many families have been reared and studied by Peterson (1955), Lorković (1962) and Bowden (1954–55). The dark *bryoniae* proves to be dominant over the white *napi*, the colour controlled by a single autosomal gene with alleles BB or Bb, i.e. *bryoniae* may consist of homozygous or of heterozygous individuals, but all *napi* must be homozygous bb. In many districts, and especially in the Karawanken and Julian Alps, it is found that what appear to be pure *bryoniae* females may be heterozygotes from which *napi* can be segregated. In nature both forms normally retain their individuality although intermediates may appear. These are very rare in the western and northern Alps, but they become more common in the east and south-east, where there seems to be a gradual passage from one to another, judging by such characters as dark markings and ground-colour (Peterson 1954, 1955). In some districts, e.g. Mödling near Vienna and in Slovenia, *bryoniae* and *napi*

73

may be found flying together, but blending is not total, and both forms have appeared with clearly defined phenotypical characters in families bred from single *bryoniae*-females taken in the latter district (Lorković 1962, p. 111). In view of these findings it seems clear that *napi* and *bryoniae* are properly united as subspecies of a single taxon. Lorković has reported that the hybrid chromosome cytology remains normal, i.e. there is not any disturbance of chromosome pairing during mitosis. In some areas the undersides of the hind-wing of male *bryoniae* may be white instead of the usual yellow. This rather striking form *subtalba* Schima is absent or very rare in the western and northern Alps, but in the southeast, in Austria and Slovenia, it is common and predominates in some areas. It is most obvious in males and may be present in females or replaced by pale buff, form *subtochracea* Kautz. This variant is completely dominant over the normal yellow colour and is also controlled genetically. The dusky Scandinavian form *adalwinda* Fruhstorfer is more closely related to nominate *A. n. napi*.

References. Müller & Kautz 1938. Bowden 1956. Petersen 1955. Lorković 1962. Ford 1964. Warren 1961, 1963. Robinson, R. 1971 Lepidoptera Genetics. Pergamon Press. Schima 1909.

ARTOGEIA ERGANE   Geyer 1828   CN 26   FG p. 44; Pl. 5

Androconial scale like *A. napi*.
Genitalia. Like *A. napi*; uncus long, slender, articulation with tegumen less well defined; posterior margin of valve bluntly angled; penis trochanter smaller.
Range. From SE France through S Europe to Asia Minor and Iran.

Reference. Lorković 1968(B).

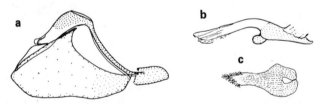

69. *Artogeia ergane,* Dalmatia: **a,** genitalia, penis removed; **b,** penis; **c,** androconial scale.

ARTOGEIA RAPAE   L. 1758   CN 25   FG p. 43; Pl. 5
Androconial scale like *A. napi*, but shaft more slender.
Genitalia. Like *A. napi* but uncus more slender, articulation with tegumen not prominent; posterior margin of valve evenly rounded; shaft of penis straight.
Range. Canary Islands, Azores and N Africa across Europe and Asia to Japan. Introduced into N America.

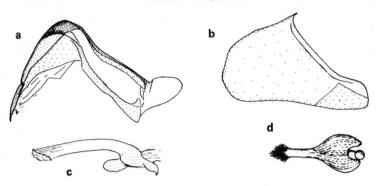

70. *Artogeia rapae*, S England: **a,** genitalia, valves and penis removed; **b,** valve; **c,** penis; **d,** androconial scale.

ARTOGEIA MANNII   Mayer 1851   CN 25   FG p. 44; Pl. 5
Androconial scales like *A. rapae.*
Genitalia. Like *A. rapae*; uncus more slender, shorter; posterior margin of valve less evenly rounded; penis as in *A. rapae.*
Range. Morocco (rare and local), S Europe from NE Spain and S France across S Europe to Asia Minor and Syria.

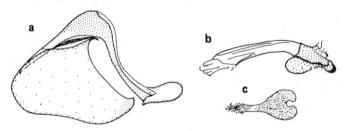

71. *Artogeia mannii*, S France: **a,** genitalia, penis removed; **b,** penis; **c,** androconial scale.

ARTOGEIA KRUEPERI   Staudinger 1860   CN 24
FG p. 46; Pl. 5
Androconial scale like *A. rapae* but more slender, apex elongate.
Genitalia. Like *A. rapae*; uncus slightly more robust; posterior margin of

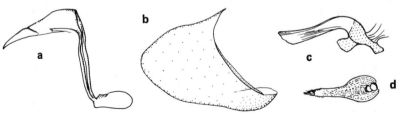

72. *Artogeia krueperi*, Bulgaria: **a,** genitalia, valves and penis removed; **b,** valve; **c,** penis; **d,** androconial scale.

valve evenly curved, central point rather prominent; penis curved, trochanter prominent.
Range. S Balkans and eastwards to Iran and Baluchistan, flying in rocky places.

Genus **PONTIA** F. 1807   TS: *Papilio daplidice* L.
Description. Ups like *Pieris* but upf with black discoidal spot; unh extensive green or yellowish markings. *Androconial scales* when present, not pyriform. *Venation.* Fw 10 or 11 veins.
Genitalia. Uncus stout, gently curved, junction with tegumen well defined; penis strongly curved, trochanter present.

PONTIA DAPLIDICE   L. 1758   CN 26   FG p. 47; Pl. 7
Androconial scale narrow, tapering slightly to apex. *Venation.* Fw with 10 veins.
Genitalia. Uncus robust, in side view obscured by wide valve; penis curved to right-angle.
Range. Canary Islands, N Africa, S and C Europe and eastwards to India and Japan.

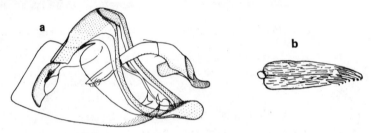

73. *Pontia daplidice,* S France: **a,** genitalia; **b,** androconial scale.

PONTIA CHLORIDICE   Hübner 1808   CN unknown
FG p. 47; Pl. 7
Androconial scale like *P. daplidice* but shorter and narrower. *Venation.* Fw ♂ 11 veins, ♀ often 10 veins.
Genitalia. Like *P. daplidice,* posterior margin of valve more rounded; penis less strongly curved, trochanter large, caecum small.
Range. Mountainous areas from Balkans to Iran and Mongolia, also in N America (*P. beckeri* Edwards, CN 26, Remington 1960).

74. *Pontia chloridice,* Bulgaria: **a,** genitalia; **b,** penis; **c,** androconial scale.

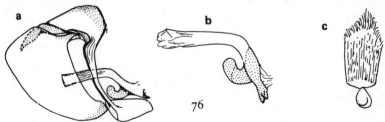

76

PONTIA CALLIDICE Hübner 1800   CN 26   FG p. 50; Pl. 7
Androconial scales absent. *Venation*. Fw with 11 veins.
Genitalia. Like *P. daplidice*, valve less wide, does not obscure uncus in side view; penis less strongly curved.
Range. On high mountains from Pyrenees and Alps to Lebanon, Himalaya Mts., Tibet and Mongolia, also in N America (*P. occidentalis* Reakirt).

75. *Pontia callidice,* Valais, Switzerland: genitalia.

Tribe **Teracolini** Reuter 1897

Description. Butterflies of small to medium size, frons slightly tufted, usually white or yellow, ♂ upf often with brightly coloured apical patch, ♀ fw apex more rounded, coloured patch reduced or absent and ups dark markings more extensive. Seasonal variation often marked. Sexes dissimilar. *Palpi* short, basal segment about half total length, apical segment very short. *Antennae* less than half the length of fw, club abrupt. *Androconial scales* abundant, very small. *Venation*. Fw with 11 veins, upper angle of cell acute.
Genitalia. Similar to *Artogeia*, saccus longer.
Early stages. Ovum and larva like *Artogeia*. Pupa slender, head and tail pointed, wing-cases forming ventral bulge.

Genus **COLOTIS** Hübner 1819   TS: *Papilio amata* F.
Characters are those of *C. evagore* Klug.

COLOTIS EVAGORE   Klug 1829   CN unknown   FG p. 50; Pl. 7
Range. Widely distributed in SW Asia and Africa, a single subspecies flies in the region on barren areas in the Atlas Mts.

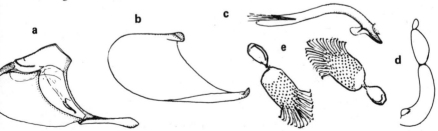

76. *Colotis evagore,* Morocco: **a,** genitalia, penis removed; **b,** valve; **c,** penis; **d,** palpus; **e,** androconial scales.

77

C. e. nouna Lucas 1849.
Genitalia. Like *A. rapae* L., posterior margin of valve evenly rounded; saccus long, slender; penis slightly sinuous, a small brush of fine hair present near apex, trochanter well developed.
Range. N Africa in desert areas.

Tribe CALLIDRYINI Kirby 1896
For present purposes the characters are those of the genus *Catopsilia*.

Genus **CATOPSILIA** Hübner 1820 TS: *Papilio crocale* Cramer
Description. Large butterflies, fw apex pointed, gc greenish-white to yellow, markings scanty but a small dark discoidal spot always present upf; uph sex-brand associated with hair-pencils unf; no frontal tuft. *Antennae* short, gradually expanded to form a slender club apex truncate. *Palpi* stout, clothed with flat scales, terminal segment very short, conical, the whole crested beneath with long shining scales. *Feet* with paronychia and pulvilli. *Androconia* restricted to patch uph; scales little modified, do not carry a gland-cell, attached by peg and socket. *Venation.* Fw with 11 veins; hw precostal vein present (*C. florella*) or absent.
Genitalia. Described below (*C. florella*).
The genus is widely distributed in tropical Asia and Africa.

CATOPSILIA FLORELLA F. 1775 CN 31 FG p. 57; Pl. 13
Genitalia. Uncus slender with narrow uncus anticus, tegumen short; valve triangular, costal process prominent; penis slender, trochanter long.
Range. Within the region, only in Canary Islands; further widely distributed in Africa south of the Sahara and eastwards to India and China.
   Correct taxonomic position of this species is uncertain.

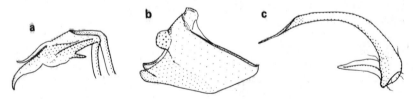

77. *Catopsilia florella,* Canary Islands: **a,** uncus and tegumen, side view; **b,** valve; **c,** penis.

Subfamily ANTHOCHARINAE Tutt 1896

Description. Small or medium-sized butterflies with white or yellow wings; upf with black discoidal spot; distinctive green markings unh; head with large frontal hair-tuft. *Antennae* less than half the length of fw, club oval, abrupt. *Palpi* porrect, slender, hairy, obscured by frontal hair-tuft, middle segment as long as basal segment. *Androconial scales* generally abundant. *Venation.* Fw with 12 veins, hw precostal vein present, curving inwards.

Genitalia. Uncus generally fused with tegumen without visible suture; valve elongate, harpe well developed; penis slender, slightly sinuous, lacking trochanter and caecum except in *Elphinstonia*, genital opening posterior.

Early stages. Ovum and larva as in *Pieris.* Pupa rigid, elongate, dorsi-flexed, tapering to terminate in anterior and posterior pointed extremities, fixed upright by cremaster and a silken girdle.

Reference. Klots 1930.

Key to genera of Anthocharinae

1 Male upf with red apical patch 2
   Male upf without red apical patch 3

2 Pupa slender . . . . *Anthocharis*
   Pupa stout . . . . *Zegris*

3 Unh with greenish marbling . . . . . . *Euchloe*
   Unh greenish with scanty pale striae. . . . . *Elphinstonia*

Genus **EUCHLOE** Hübner 1823   TS: *Euchloe crameri* Butler
Ups gc milk-white, upf apical markings and discoidal spot black; unh confused pattern of green spots resembling *Anthocharis.* Sexes almost similar.

Genitalia. Valve little or not at all longer than uncus+tegumen, often posteriorly truncate.

EUCHLOE AUSONIA Hübner   CN 31   FG p. 51; Pl. 7
Two subspecies with similar genitalia.

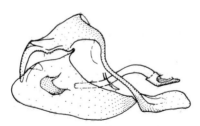

78. *Euchloe ausonia,* Asturias Mts., N Spain: genitalia.

E. a. ausonia Hübner 1804.
Posterior margin of valve slightly oblique, costal angle reflexed, harpe short.

Range. Cantabrian Mts., Pyrenees and SW Alps, eastwards to Valais and Bernese Oberland. Flies in a single brood at sub-alpine levels to 2,000m.

The forms *E. orientalis* Bremer 1864 and *E. ausonides* Boisduval 1852 are probably referable to this subspecies.

E. a. insularis Staudinger 1861.
Genitalia. Small, otherwise indistinguishable from *E. a. ausonia.*
Range. Confined to Corsica and Sardinia.

Note. A larval description has not been found, and it is uncertain whether *insularis* should be associated with *E. ausonia* or with *E. crameri*, or perhaps is specifically distinct.

EUCHLOE CRAMERI Butler 1869   CN 31   FG p. 51; Pl. 7
Specific characters based upon markings of larva and imago. Flies in a single prolonged emergence or perhaps in two annual broods.
Genitalia. Indistinguishable from *E. a. ausonia.*
Range. N Africa, S Europe and W Asia. Local but widely distributed at low or moderate altitudes.

References. Catherine 1920. Verity 1947.

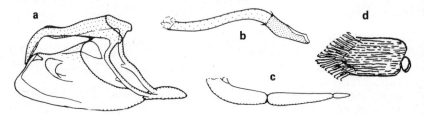

79. *Euchloe crameri,* Turin, N Italy: **a,** genitalia, penis removed; **b,** penis; **c,** palpus; **d,** androconial scale.

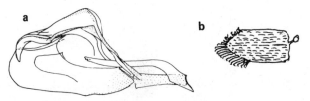

80. *Euchloe tagis,* S Spain: **a,** genitalia; **b,** androconial scale.

EUCHLOE TAGIS Hübner   CN unknown   FG p. 52; Pl. 8
Range. Restricted to Morocco, Portugal, Spain and S France. Two subspecies with similar genitalia. *Androconial scales* like *E. ausonia.*

E. t. tagis Hübner 1804.
Genitalia. Like *E. ausonia*, small, uncus more sharply curved; valve truncate, costal angle not reflexed, harpe longer.
Range. Portugal and S Spain.

E. t. bellezina Boisduval 1828.
Subspecific characters present in wing markings.
Genitalia. Indistinguishable from *E. t. tagis.*
Range. Local in SE France, C Spain. Moroccan specimens very similar.

EUCHLOE FALLOUI Allard 1867   CN unknown   FG p. 53; Pl. 8
Genitalia. Like *E. tagis*, valve short, truncate, base wide.
Range. N Africa on southern slopes of Atlas Mts. from Morocco eastwards
and as a desert insect in Egypt, Sinai and Negev desert.

81. *Euchloe falloui,* Algeria: genitalia.

EUCHLOE BELEMIA Esper 1799   CN unknown   FG p. 53; Pl. 8
Genitalia. Like *E. ausonia*, valve shorter, posterior margin truncate,
costal angle reflexed, harpe short; penis more slender.
Range. Africa north of the Atlas Mts., eastwards across Cyrenaica and
Egypt to Lebanon and Baluchistan. S Spain and S Portugal. Canary
Islands.

a

b

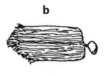

82. *Euchloe belemia,* S Spain: **a,** valve; **b,** androconial scale.

EUCHLOE PECHI Staudinger 1885   CN unknown
FG p. 52; Pl. 8
Genitalia. Like *E. tagis*, small, tegumen short; valve slightly longer,
tapering posteriorly with angle rounded; harpe narrow, almost straight.
Range. Known only from Algeria, in the Djebel Aures.

83. *Euchloe pechi,* Algeria: genitalia, penis removed.

Genus **ELPHINSTONIA** Klots 1931   TS: *Anthocharis charlonia* Donzel
A single species of this small genus occurs in the region. It is usually
placed near *Euchloe*, but the characters of the genitalia suggest close relationship with *Pontia*.

ELPHINSTONIA CHARLONIA   Donzel 1842   CN 30–32
FG p. 54; Pl. 8

Androconial scales absent. Frontal hair-tuft large.
Genitalia. Suture between uncus and tegumen clearly defined; valve
truncate posteriorly, forming a prominent angle with costal margin, harpe
small; penis curved to a rt. angle, trochanter large.
Range. Canary Islands. N Africa south of the Atlas Mts. Yugoslav
Macedonia. W Asia to Iran.

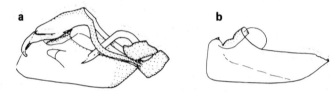

84. *Elphinstonia charlonia*, Canary Islands: **a,** genitalia; **b,** valve.

Genus **ANTHOCHARIS** Boisduval 1835   TS: *Papilio cardamines* L.
Description. Rather small white or yellow butterflies closely related to
Euchloe, all flying in spring in a single annual brood. Sexes dissimilar,
♂ with broad orange-red patch at apex of fw which is absent or vestigial
in ♀. *Androconial scales* rectangular with pointed apices, terminal fibrils
long.
Genitalia. Valve longer than uncus+tegumen, narrow, apex rounded,
harpe large; saccus long; penis slightly angled beyond zone. Specific
characters not well marked in genitalia.

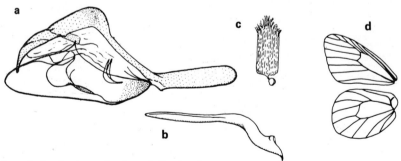

85. *Anthocharis cardamines*, S England: **a,** genitalia, penis removed; **b,** penis;
c, androconial scale; **d,** wing venation.

ANTHOCHARIS CARDAMINES L. 1758   CN 31   FG p. 54; Pl. 8

Genitalia. Described above.
Range. From W Europe across temperate Asia to China.

ANTHOCHARIS BELIA L.   CN unknown   FG p. 55; Pl. 8

Genitalia like *A. cardamines,* valve slightly narrower. Two rather poorly defined subspecies with similar genitalia.

86. *Anthocharis belia,* Middle Atlas, Morocco: valve.

A. b. belia L. 1767.

Genitalia. Like *A. cardamines.*
Range. N Africa on northern slopes of Atlas Mts.

A. b. euphenoides Staudinger 1869.

Subspecific characters present in wing-markings.
Genitalia. Indistinguishable.
Range. Spain, Portugal, Pyrenees, SE France, N and C Italy in the mountains.

ANTHOCHARIS DAMONE Boisduval 1836   CN unknown
FG p. 55, Pl. 8

Genitalia. Like *A. cardamines;* valve slightly narrower, harpe large.
Range. Sicily, S Italy and Greece and eastwards to Syria and Kurdistan.

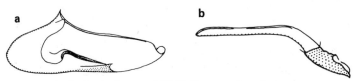

87. *Anthocharis damone,* NE Sicily: **a,** valve; **b,** penis.

ANTHOCHARIS GRUNERI Herrich-Schäffer 1851   CN 24
FG p. 56; Pl. 8

Genitalia. Like *A. cardamines;* valve slightly shorter and wider.
Range. Greece and Asia Minor and eastwards to Syria and Iran.

88. *Anthocharis gruneri,* Greece: valve.

Genus **ZEGRIS** Boisduval 1836   TS: *Papilio eupheme* Esper
Description. Like *Anthocharis* but differs in more robust thorax and
abdomen; fw costa slightly concave, apex more pointed; unh markings as
in *A. belia* L. *Antennae* very short, large club abrupt, oval. *Palpi* porrect.
Androconial scales as in *Anthocharis*.
Genitalia. As in *Anthocharis*, but suture between uncus and tegumen
better defined; saccus short.
Early stages. Pupa distinctive, with marked ventral thoracic bulge, silken
girdle vestigial if present, enclosed in a slight cocoon.

ZEGRIS EUPHEME   Esper 1805   CN unknown
                                        FG p. 56; Pl. 9
Range. Morocco, E Spain, Asia Minor, S Russia and Iran. A single subspecies is described in the region.

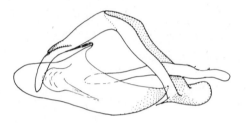

89. *Zegris eupheme,* S Spain: genitalia.

Z. e. meridionalis Lederer 1852.
Genitalia. Described above.
Range. E Spain and Morocco.

Subfamily COLIADINAE Swainson 1827

Description. Medium-sized or rather large butterflies, yellow, orange or
greenish-white. In Europe they are represented by two genera, *Colias*
with wing margins entire, and *Gonepteryx* in which the wings are more or
less angled. The sexes differ in all species. *Sex-brand* present or absent in
males. *Antennae* short, shaft stout, expanded gradually to form a slender
club. *Palpi* porrect, clothed beneath with a crest of hair, terminal segment
very short, basal segment longer than middle segment. *Legs* with strong
tarsal spines. *Venation.* Fw with 11 veins, hw precostal vein absent.
Early stages. Ovum of usual Pierid shape. Larva slender, often green with
longitudinal stripes. Pupa with single anterior process and dilated thorax,
held upright by cremastral hooks and silken girdle.

Key to genera of Coliadinae

1 Apex of fw falcate .   .   .   .   *Gonepteryx*
2 Apex of fw rounded   .   .   .   .   .   .   *Colias*

Genus **COLIAS** Fabricius 1807   TS: *Papilio hyale* L.

Description. Black wing borders ups usually solid in ♂, broken in ♀ by spots of ground-colour. Males of all species except *hecla, palaeno* and *chrysotheme* have a sex-brand uph near costa covered with many long and fewer short, oval scales. These are unlike the cloaking scales covering the wing-surfaces. On unf opposite this brand, there are small, deeply grooved and highly refractive asymmetrical scales of unusual shape. Associated with males of this genus a faint perfume has been noticed by many observers. Paronychia and pulvilli absent.

Genitalia. More than twice as tall as wide, tegumen with small uncus anticus; valve tall, firmly attached above to margin of tegumen; furca prominent, composed of two wide lateral plates; penis strongly curved with large trochanter in all species. Specific characters are poorly defined and the genitalia are of little value in identification.

Note. The complete genitalia of *C. hyale* are figured, but only the valves of other species, since in all other respects the specific characters are so ill defined. When genitalia of this group are examined valves cannot be detached without injury. It is best to divide the tegumen when the parts can be spread flat upon a slide, giving good views of the valves.
Reference. Lorković & Herman 1961.

Group 1: tooth present on posterior margin of valve.

COLIAS HYALE   L. 1758   CN 31   FG p. 62; Pl. 11
Genitalia. In side view head of valve narrow, tooth on posterior margin slender, set at acute angle; in posterior-anterior view of valves *in situ*, dorsal expansion of valve rather small.
Range. S and C Europe, chiefly in eastern regions, S Russia (Kief) and Asia Minor to Caucasus and C Asia. Exact range uncertain owing to difficulty of identification. Occurs with *C. australis* in many areas.

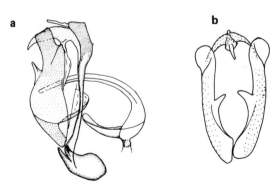

90. *Colias hyale,* Styria, Austria: **a,** genitalia, side view; **b,** genitalia, A-P view, Romania.

COLIAS AUSTRALIS Verity 1911   CN 31   FG p. 62; Pl. 11
Genitalia. Like *C. hyale*; in side view head of valve wider, tooth on posterior margin larger, base wider, more widely separated from posterior border of valve; in posterior-anterior view of valve *in situ*, dorsal expansion of valve larger.
Range. S and C Europe, especially in western regions, Spain, Italy and France, but also in Balkans. Absent from N Africa. Occurs in Asia Minor, perhaps even further east.

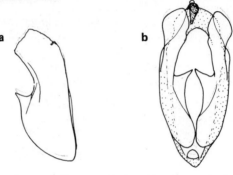

91. *Colias australis*, Switzerland: **a,** valve; **b,** genitalia, A-P view.

Note. It is uncertain whether genitalia characters are sufficiently definite to be helpful. The characters described above, first recorded by Niculescu, appear sufficiently constant to be useful, but perhaps not well marked in all specimens.
References. Berger 1948. Reissinger 1960. Niculescu 1963.

Group 2: without tooth on posterior margin of valve.

COLIAS HECLA Lefèbvre   CN 31   FG p. 61; Pl. 11
Sex-brand uph absent.
Genitalia. Valve small, neck wide, posterior angle prominent, posterior border evenly curved. Two subspecies with similar genitalia.

92. *Colias hecla*, Norway: valve.

C. h. hecla Lefèbvre 1836.
Genitalia. Described above.
Range. Greenland, N America.

C. h. sulitelma Aurivillius 1890.
Range. Boreal Scandinavia, N Siberia. Probably circumpolar.

COLIAS NASTES Boisduval   CN 31   FG p. 57; Pl. 9
Genitalia. Valve small, posterior border bulging strongly below mid-point. Two subspecies with similar genitalia.

93. *Colias nastes,* N Sweden: valve.

C. n. nastes Boisduval 1832.
Genitalia. Described above.
Range. Labrador, Greenland, N Siberia.

C. n. werdandi Zetterstedt 1840.
Range. Arctic Norway, Sweden. Nova Semlya. Probably circumpolar; many subspecies named.

COLIAS PHICOMONE Esper 1780   CN 30   FG p. 57; Pl. 9
Genitalia. Valve slender, head wide, posterior border smoothly curved, not prominent.
Range. Cantabrian Mts., Pyrenees, Alps, Carpathians. Absent from Balkans and Apennines.

94. *Colias phicomone,* Cottian Alps, NW Italy: valve.

COLIAS ERATE Esper 1804   CN 31   FG p. 63; Pl. 11
Genitalia. Valve short, posterior border strongly angled below head.
Range. Europe, near shores of Black Sea in Rumania, Turkey and Greece
(rare). Abyssinia, Somalia and eastwards across Russia and Siberia to
Japan and Formosa.

95. *Colias erate,* Romania: valve.

COLIAS PALAENO L.   CN 31–32   FG p. 58; Pl. 9
Widely distributed across boreal and temperate regions of Europe and
Asia to Japan. Also in N. America (?). Two subspecies with similar
genitalia.

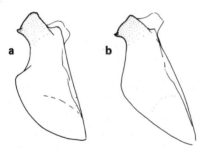

96. *Colias palaeno palaeno,* Arctic
Norway: **a,** valve. *C. p. europomene,* Switzerland: **b,** valve.

C. p. palaeno L. 1761.
Genitalia. Head of valve narrow, upper border slightly domed, posterior
border has abrupt bulge or angle above central point.
Range. Fennoscandia and Baltic countries to Lithuania; extension further
east uncertain.
C. p. europome Esper 1779.
Subspecific characters present in wing-markings.
Genitalia. Valve posterior border often more evenly curved.
Range. On moors and mountains in C Europe, Alps, Bavarian moors,
etc. Flies to 2,000m or over in Alps, specimens often slightly smaller
C. p. europomene Ochsenheimer 1816.

COLIAS CHRYSOTHEME Esper 1781   CN unknown
                                        FG p. 59; Pl. 10
Sex-brand uph absent.
Genitalia. Valve short, posterior margin strongly bowed.

97. *Colias chrysotheme*, Austria: valve.

Range. Danube countries of E Europe, Austria (Burgenland), Hungary, Czechoslovakia, Poland and across Russia to Altai Mts. and Mongolia.

COLIAS LIBANOTICA Lederer 1858   CN 32   FG p. 59; Pl. 10

Widely distributed in W Asia. A single subspecies occurs in Greece.

C. l. heldreichi Staudinger 1862.
Genitalia. Valve large, posterior border bulging in even curve, dorsal border of head undulant, neck short and wide.
Range. Greece, in Peloponessus, Veluchi Mts. and Parnnasus. Lebanon, very similar.

98. *Colias libanotica heldreichi*, Peloponnesus, Greece: valve.

COLIAS MYRMIDONE   Esper 1781   CN 30–31
FG p. 59; Pl. 10
Genitalia. Valve rather narrow, head small, narrow with deep posterior notch making an angle with almost straight posterior border.
Range. In Europe, only in Austria, Hungary, E Germany and Rumania, then across S Russia to W Asia.

99. *Colias myrmidone*, Styria, Austria: valve.

COLIAS BALCANICA Rebel 1903   CN unknown

FG p. 61; Pl. 11

Genitalia. Valve large, wide, with deep notch below wide head forming prominent angle with posterior border.

Range. Confined to mountains of Yugoslavia, Bulgaria and Albania. Not recorded from Greece.

100. *Colias balcanica,* Bulgaria: valve.

COLIAS CROCEA Geoffroy in Fourcroy 1785   CN 31

FG p. 60; Pl. 10

Genitalia. Head of valve wide, posterior border evenly curved without an angle.

Range. N Africa, Canary Islands, S and C Europe and eastwards to W Asia.

Reference. Lorković & Herman 1961.

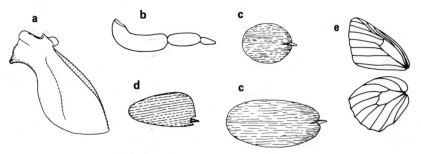

101. *Colias crocea,* N Italy: **a,** valve; **b,** palpus; **c,** androconial scales; **d,** asymmetrical scale from uns base of fore-wing; **e,** wing venation.

Genus **GONEPTERYX** Leach 1815   TS: *Papilio rhamni* L.

Description. Rather large butterflies, fw apex falcate, hw with marginal projection at v3, males ups yellow or orange, females greenish-white, the species very similar. *Palpi* clothed above with smooth scales, long basal segment sharply curved. *Antennae* red, stout and short, thickened gradually to club-shaped apex. *Feet* with paronychia, pulvilli absent. *Androconial scales* absent.

Genitalia. Uncus and tegumen very small; valve pyriform, about two and a half times as long as tegumen+uncus, a narrow process arises from costal margin a little before the sharply pointed apex; furca prominent with wide lateral plates; saccus slender, almost as long as valve; penis very slender, about one and a half times as long as valve, apex downturned. Specific characters are present in uncus and tegumen.

Early stages. Ovum, larva and pupa like *Colias*. In C Europe the imago hibernates (*G. rhamni*), mating occurs in spring and ova are laid, producing a single brood in summer. In S Europe and in N Africa (*G. rhamni* and *G. cleopatra*) two annual broods are recorded following winter hibernation. It is uncertain whether hibernation occurs in the Canary Islands (*G. c. cleobule*).

GONEPTERYX RHAMNI L. 1758   CN 31–32 FG p. 63; Pl. 12

Genitalia. Uncus small, slightly shorter than tegumen; apex of valve short, abrupt; penis as in *G. cleopatra*, long and slender.

Range. N Africa, temperate Europe and Asia to Siberia.

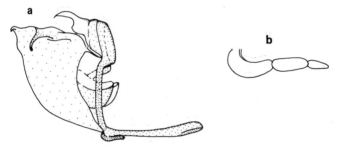

102. *Gonepteryx rhamni,* S England: **a,** genitalia, penis removed; **b,** palpus.

GONEPTERYX CLEOPATRA L.   CN unknown
FG p. 66; Pl. 12

Genitalia. Uncus very small, bifid, about half the length of small tegumen; valve tapering gradually to pointed apex; penis long, slender.

Range. Canary Islands, N Africa, S Europe and W Asia. Two subspecies with similar genitalia.

G. c. cleopatra L. 1767.

Genitalia. Described above.

Range. N Africa, S Europe including most Mediterranean islands and Crete, Asia Minor, Syria and Lebanon.

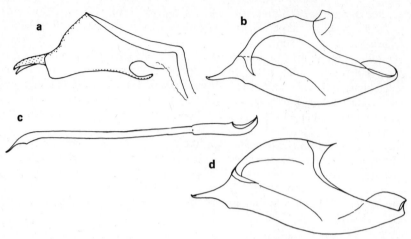

103. *Gonepteryx cleopatra cleopatra*, S France: **a,** uncus and tegumen, side view; **b,** valve; **c,** penis. *G. c. cleobule*, Gomera, Canary Islands: **d,** valve.

G. c. cleobule Hübner 1825.

Range. Canary Islands, with variation in wing markings on different islands. Madeira.

GONEPTERYX FARINOSA Zeller 1847   CN 32
FG p. 70; Pl. 12

Genitalia. Like *G. rhamni*; uncus slightly larger, longer than tegumen; valve longer, tapering more gradually; penis as in *G. cleopatra*.
Range. S Balkans and widely distributed in W Asia.

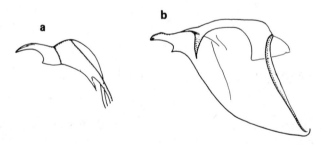

104. *Gonepteryx farinosa*, S Greece: **a,** uncus and tegumen, side view; **b,** valve.

Subfamily DISMORPHIINAE Godman & Salvin 1886

Members of this subfamily are characteristic of Central and South America, where many species occur, some of which are mimetic of the *Heliconiinæ* and other protected butterflies with which they fly. In the Old World the *Dismorphiinae* occur only in the Palearctic Region, represented by the single genus *Leptidea* (Wood Whites). They differ greatly from all other butterflies in their structural characters. They are unique in the Family in having scale pigments, at least in the genera *Enantia* and *Leptidea*, which contain flavones (anthoxanthines), plant pigments not yet detected in other Pierines, whose pigments are pterines (urea derivatives). For present purposes the characters are those of the single Palearctic genus *Leptidea* Billberg.

Genus **LEPTIDEA**   Billberg 1820   TS: *Papilio sinapis* L.
Description. Small fragile butterflies with long fw and simple markings. Apex of fw rounded or slightly falcate; thorax and abdomen slender, the latter longer than hw. *Palpi* porrect, short. *Antennae* one-third the length of fw, club pyriform. *Feet* with paronychia, pulvilli absent, claws strongly abducted. *Androconial scales* absent. *Venation.* Fw with 11 veins, cell short in both wings.
Genitalia. Distinctive, very small, globular; uncus depressed, bifid, terminating in bilateral small rounded heavily chitinised processes; valves immobile, fused to tegumen; saccus well developed, slightly variable; penis slender, slightly curved, apex pointing downwards, supported by small furca.
Early stages. Ovum almost three times as high as wide, ribbed and pitted. Larva of usual Pierid form, slender, green. Pupa rigid, tapering at each end to a point and attached vertically with a silken girdle. Hibernation as pupa.
Reference. Lorković 1949.

LEPTIDEA SINAPIS   L. 1758   CN 28–41   FG p. 70; Pl. 13
Genitalia. Described above, upper posterior process of valve blunt; apex of saccus slightly bulbous; furca (anellus?) prominent in side view.

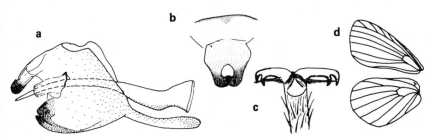

105. *Leptidea sinapis,* Switzerland: **a,** genitalia; **b,** uncus, A-P view; **c,** midtarsal claw; **d,** wing venation.

93

Range. W Europe and eastwards to Asia Minor, Lebanon and Caucasus Mts.

LEPTIDEA DUPONCHELI Staudinger 1871 CN 102–103

FG p. 71; Pl. 13

Genitalia. Like *L. sinapis*, saccus with conspicuous bulbous apex.
Range. Local in SE France, Greece, Yugoslav Macedonia and Bulgaria. More widely distributed in Asia Minor and Lebanon and eastwards to Iran.

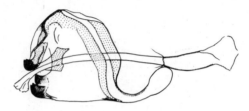

106. *Leptidea duponcheli*, SE France: genitalia.

LEPTIDEA MORSEI Fenton CN unknown

A single subspecies occurs within the region.
Genitalia. Like *P. sinapis*, furca (anellus) more densely chitinised; saccus straight, rather wide and abruptly tapered at apex (not bulbous).

L. m. major Grund 1905. FG p. 71; Pl. 13

Like *L. m. morsei*, but larger average size.
Range. SE Europe, from Mt. Nanos eastwards through N Yugoslavia. Hungary. Rumania. Often associated with *Neptis sappho*, food plant of both species is *Lathyrus niger*.

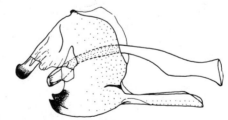

107. *Leptidea morsei*, Croatia, Yugoslavia: genitalia.

Family **LYCAENIDAE** Leach 1815

Description. In this most extensive family there are great variations in structure, including wing venation, legs and genitalia. The following account relates only to species occurring in the region defined on p. 7. Small butterflies, males often brightly coloured, gleaming blue or golden. Specific identification may be difficult with wing markings almost constant through large groups, the specific characters best developed unh in the precise arrangement of small markings, spots or striae, which usually are identical in both sexes. *Eyes* smooth or hairy. *Palpi* variable, in most European species slender, porrect or slightly ascending. *Antennae* distinctly clubbed but variable. *Legs* with single pair of tibial spurs, often absent from fore-tibia, ♂ fore-tarsus unsegmented with single claw; ♀ fore-tarsus with five segments and normal claws, middle and hind-legs normal in both sexes, claws with paronychia and pulvilli. Additional anterior tibial spines present in many species. *Androconial scales* usually present upf. *Venation.* Fw with 10 or 11 veins, v8 or v8+v9 absent; in hw precostal vein absent; cell usually weakly closed in both wings; a short filamentous tail common on hw at v1b and v2. Venation variable throughout the family, genera often based upon details of genitalia. *Genitalia.* Small, compact. The anatomy differs from other major families as follows:

1. A central uncus is not present in European genera except in Everini. Its place is taken by paired lobes, characteristic of almost all Lycaenid genera and referred to in this book as *labides*. Labides are usually regarded as a divided uncus, referred to as *sub-unci* by many authors.

2. From the labides arise slender processes, curved or sickle-shaped, referred to as *falces*. These are most characteristic of the Lycaenidae and may represent the brachia of other groups.

3. The valves do not articulate with the tegumen and scarcely with the vinculum. Except in the Lycaeninae and in some Theclinae, they are attached at their bases to one another and feebly connected with the vinculum at its lowest point. In this way the valves together form a single unit ('lobuli basales' Toxopaeus 1925), relatively immobile and probably without any possibility of abduction, so that their physiological function (as 'claspers'?) may differ from that of valves in other groups.

4. The ascending rami of the vinculum are expanded dorsally to unite and complete the genital ring, reinforcing the tegumen which is reduced to a narrow chitinous central band in this area.

5. The valve formation is usually simple; among European species a harpe is present only in the genus *Tarucus*.

Early stages. Ovum bun-shaped or discoid, shell reticulate and pitted but without ribs. Larva onisciform, usually with a lateral flange on each side.

95

LYCAENIDAE, key characters of male genitalia.

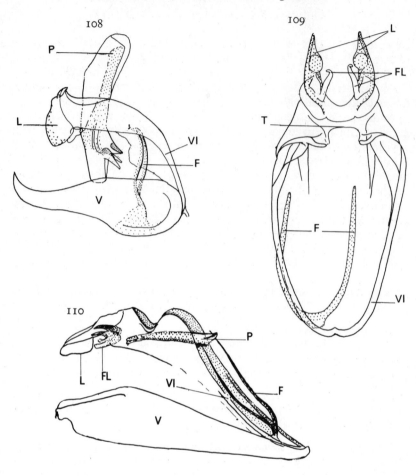

108. *Lampides boeticus*: side view showing labides (L), vinculum (VI), valve (V), furca (F), penis (P).

109. *Plebicula dorylas*: A-P view, valves and penis removed, showing labides (L), falces (FL), tegumen (T), vinculum (VI), furca (F).

110. *Plebicula dorylas*: side view, penis in natural position, parts lettered as above.

dorsum hairy, head small, often retractile. Pupa short, oval, abdominal segments rigid, lying free, or suspended by cremaster, and with a silken girdle. Many larvae have a gland on abdominal segment seven which secretes a liquid ('honey') much sought after by ants. This has led to the evolution of symbiotic associations in many genera.

References. Tutt 1905–14. Bethune Baker 1910, 1914. Beuret 1955–60 and many papers in Mitt. ent. Ges. Basel. Forster 1938.

Key to subfamilies of Lycaenidae by Genitalia

1 Valves not joined basally **2**
  Valves joined basally **3**

2 Dorsal structures slender (unf 2 black spots in cell) . . Lycaeninae
  Dorsal structures more massive (unf without such spots) Theclinae (part)

3 Valve with dorsal expansion embracing penis . . . Aphnaeinae
  Valve without dorsal expansion **4**

4 Dorsal structures massive . . . . . Theclinae (part)
  Dorsal structures not massive **5**

5 Genitalia elongate, lacking furca . . . . . . Strymoninae
  Genitalia not elongate, furca present . . . Polyommatinae

Subfamily LYCAENINAE Leach 1815

Description. ♂ ups often gleaming golden red; ♀ less bright, uph often brown. In both sexes markings consist of small black spots in a pattern which is constant throughout the subfamily, but in ♂ ups markings often reduced or absent; unf always with two black spots in cell. *Androconial scales* absent. *Eyes* smooth. *Palpi* slender, slightly ascending, apical segment about half the length of middle segment. *Antennae* slender, club abrupt, oval. *Legs* with typical family-group characters. *Venation.* Fw with 11 veins; anal angle of hw often produced in ♂, sometimes with projection or filamentous tail at v2.

Genitalia. Characteristic; labides narrow, drooping, falces curved; valves not joined basally, articulated with delicate membranous expansion from vinculum, a small crest or tooth at proximal costal angle indicates point of attachment to vincular membrane; furca usually prominent with basal attachments to each valve; saccus well defined; penis slender, tapering to a fine point, slightly curved and with minute cuneus at base of ostium in most species.

Early stages. Ovum bun-shaped, sculptured with large pits. Larva tapered at head and tail, lateral ridges little developed and with short branched hairs (Bäumchenhaare), dorsal gland absent. Pupa smooth, oval, suspended by cremaster and with silken girdle, surface bearing 'trumpet' hairs (Trichtehaare). Larval food plants *Polygonaceae.*
References. Beuret 1953. Malicky 1969.

Note. In many respects this subfamily differs from other European Lycaenidae. The articulation of the valve with the vinculum, giving lateral instead of ventral mobility, is especially noteworthy. Generic divisions based upon the structure of the genitalia are commonly accepted today. In this connection the furca is important. An A-P view of the furca is not difficult to mount if the saccus and dorsal structures are cut away and the valves spread widely or removed.

Key to genera of Lycaeninae

1 Valve with 1 or 2 posterior processes . . . *Palaeochrysophanus*
 Valve without posterior processes **2**

2 Furca very large extending beyond vinculum . . . *Thersamonia*
 Furca not extending beyond vinculum **3**

3 Valve narrow, apex rounded . . . . . . *Lycaena*
 Valve cusp-shaped, oval or rectangular . . . . *Heodes*

Genus **LYCAENA** F. 1807   TS: *Papilio phlaeas* L.
Genitalia. Valve rather narrow, distal extremity rounded; furca in side view triangular, pedicle curved or sinuous, in A-P view with two elongate or triangular (*L. helle*) lamellae; penis almost straight with minute cuneus at ostium.
Note. The name *Chrysophanus* Hübner by which this group was known for many years, was suppressed by the I.C.Z.N., Opinion No. 541. See also Hemming 1967.

LYCAENA PHLAEAS L. 1761   CN 24   FG p. 242; Pl. 51
Genitalia. Described above; furca rather small, apex of each lamella slightly hooked; dorsal cuneus of penis obscure.
Range. Canary Islands and Madeira, N and C Africa and Europe, very widely distributed extending eastwards across Asia to Japan; also in N America, most common in the eastern States.
Early stages. Larval food plants *Rumex* species.

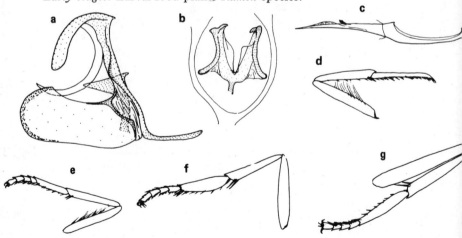

111. *Lycaena phlaeas,* Sicily: **a,** genitalia, penis removed; **b,** furca within vinculum; **c,** penis; **d,** ♂ fore-leg; **e,** ♂ middle-leg; **f,** ♂ hind-leg; **g,** ♀ hind-leg.

LYCAENA HELLE D. & S. 1775.   CN 24   FG p. 239; Pl. 51
Genitalia. Like *L. phlaeas*; valve narrow, slightly constricted before apex; furca small, lobes almost quadrilateral; dorsal cuneus of penis not well defined.
Range. N and C Europe and eastwards across Siberia to Amurland.
Early stages. Larval food-plant *Polygonum bistorta*.

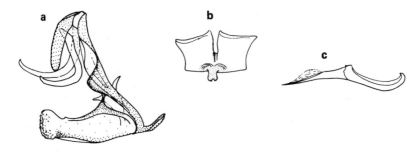

112. *Lycaena helle*, Geneva, Switzerland: **a,** genitalia, penis removed; **b,** furca; **c,** penis.

LYCAENA DISPAR   Haworth 1803   CN unknown
FG p. 243; Pl. 51
Genitalia. Like *L. helle*; valve narrow, slightly constricted before rounded apex which is armed with minute teeth; furca large, lateral lamellae narrow, sharply pointed; penis sinuous, dorsal cuneus present.
Range. Widely distributed across C Europe but very local from France eastwards across Asia to Amurland; absent from SW Europe and Fennoscandia, extinct in England.
Early stages. Larval food plants *Rumex*.

Reference. Le Moult 1945.

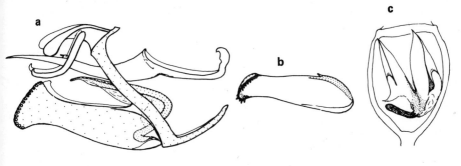

113. *Lycaena dispar*, Bulgaria: **a,** genitalia; **b,** valve; **c,** furca within vinculum.

Genus **HEODES** Dalman 1816   TS: *Papilio virgaureae* L.
Genitalia. Like *Lycaena* but valve shorter, wider and cup-shaped like the cusp of a bivalve shell, with prominent, densely chitinised tooth at costal angle connected by fibrous articulation with vinculum; furca like *Lycaena* with two triangular lamellae; penis as in *Lycaena*.

HEODES VIRGAUREAE   L. 1758   CN 24   FG p. 244; Pl. 51
Genitalia. Valve in side view almost quadrilateral; furca prominent, enclosed within the chitinous genital ring.
Range. N and C Europe and Asia Minor across temperate Asia to Mongolia.

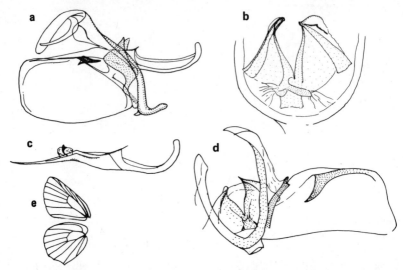

114. *Heodes virgaureae*, Guarda, Engadin: **a,** genitalia, including proximal part of penis; **b,** furca within vinculum; **c,** penis; **d,** genitalia spread, showing mobility of valve and articulation with vinculum; **e,** wing venation.

HEODES TITYRUS   Poda   CN 24   FG p. 245; Pl. 52
Genitalia. Like *H. virgaureae*; valve shorter, oval; furca apices turned slightly outwards. Two subspecies with similar genitalia.

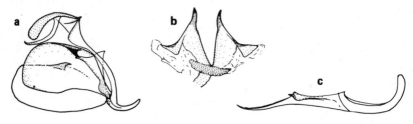

115. *Heodes tityrus*, Glarus, Switzerland: **a,** genitalia, penis removed; **b,** furca; **c,** penis.

H. t. tityrus Poda 1761.
Genitalia. Described above.
Range. S and C Europe, and through Asia Minor, Lebanon to Iran.

H. t. subalpinus Speyer 1851.
Subspecific characters in wing markings. The extreme form of a clinal series, perhaps better graded as an ecological modification.
Range. At high altitudes within the range of *H. t. tityrus*, Cantabrian Mts., Pyrenees, Alps etc.

HEODES OTTOMANUS Lefèbvre 1830   CN unknown
FG p. 245; Pl. 51
Genitalia. Like *H. virgaureae* but slightly smaller, labides and falces longer and more slender; valve narrower; in side view furca less prominent; penis as in *H. virgaureae*.
Range. Restricted to S Balkans, Greece and western Asia Minor.

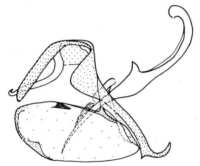

116. *Heodes ottomanus,* W Greece: genitalia.

HEODES ALCIPHRON Rottemburg 1775   CN 24
FG p. 246; Pl. 52
Genitalia. Like *H. virgaureae* but furca larger, lateral lamellae longer almost filling genital ring, stem longer, geniculate in side view; valve more elongate, costal spine prominent; penis cuneus extremely delicate.

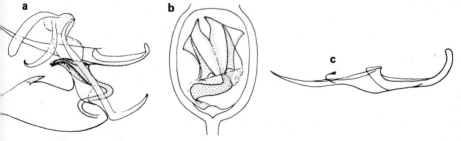

117. *Heodes alciphron,* N Italy: **a,** genitalia, penis *in situ;* **b,** furca within vinculum; **c,** penis.

Range. Morocco, only in High Atlas. S and C Europe and eastwards to Mongolia.

Genus **THERSAMONIA** Verity 1919   TS: *Papilio thersamon* Esper
Genitalia. Valve like *Lycaena*, elongate, slightly constricted before apex, without teeth on costal border; furca very large, geniculate in side view and extending far outside the genital ring, lamellae tapering gradually to slender pointed apices; penis sinuous, raised by the curve of the furca to enter the genital ring near its apex.
Early stages. Larval food plants *Rumex* and *Sarothamnus.*

THERSAMONIA THERSAMON   Esper 1784   CN 24
FG p. 247; Pl. 51
Genitalia. Vinculum very oblique; furca massive.
Range. From Italy and E Europe eastwards to Lebanon and Iran.

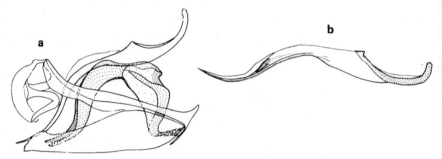

118. *Thersamonia thersamon,* Hungary: **a,** genitalia, penis *in situ*; **b,** penis.

THERSAMONIA PHOEBUS   Blachier 1908   CN unknown
FG p. 248; Pl. 51
Genitalia. Like *T. thersamon*; furca slightly shorter.
Range. Confined to W Morocco.

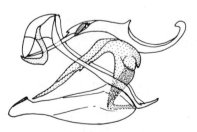

119. *Thersamonia phoebus,* High Atlas, Morocco: genitalia.

THERSAMONIA THETIS   Klug 1834   CN 24

FG p. 248; Pl. 51

Genitalia. Like *T. thersamon*; furca less massive but still very large, labides more slender; apex of valve rounded with apical point recurved; penis as in *T. thersamon*.

Range. S Greece and across W Asia to Lebanon and Iran.

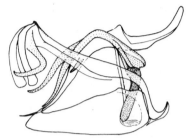

120. *Thersamonia thetis,* Peloponnesus, S Greece: genitalia.

Genus **PALAEOCHRYSOPHANUS** Verity 1943

TS: *Papilio hippothoe* L.

Genitalia. Valve small, oval, robust, with one or two posterior processes; furca small with dense Y-shaped central lamella and lightly chitinised narrow lamellae on each side; base of penis steeply flexed, distal part almost straight.

PALAEOCHRYSOPHANUS HIPPOTHOE   L.   CN 24

FG p. 249; Pl. 51

Range. Very extensive, across N and temperate Europe and Asia to the Amur, with several well marked subspecies of which three occur in Europe.

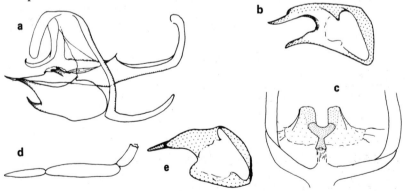

121. *Palaeochrysophanus hippothoe hippothoe,* Czechoslovakia: **a,** genitalia; **b,** valve; **c,** furca within vinculum; **d,** palpus. *P. h. leonhardi,* Yugoslavia: **e,** valve.

P. h. hippothoe L. 1761.
Genitalia. Valve with two posterior processes.
Range. W Europe from N Spain to Scandinavia and eastwards to Slovenia and N Carpathians.

P. h. eurydame Hoffmannsegg 1806.
Subspecific distinctive characters in wing-markings.
Genitalia. Indistinguishable.
Range. Hautes Alpes, Savoie, Switzerland from Valais to Engadin, Brenner, Stelvio, N Italy and in C Apennines, flying always at high altitudes.

P. h. leonhardi Fruhstorfer 1917.
Genitalia. Valve with single posterior process.
Range. Balkans in mountains, northwards to Sarajevo. Greece. Asia Minor ?

Note. P. h. hippothoe and *P. h. leonhardi* are graded distinct species by many authors. Their distribution areas are almost in contact in NW Yugoslavia, but cohabitation has not been reported. Related forms of *P. h. hippothoe* occur eastwards to Iran (*P. h. candens* H.-S.) and further to the Amur, but their genitalia have not been described.

Subfamily APHNAEINAE Swinhoe 1912

Small butterflies related to the Theclinae, unh with oblique stripes or rows of spots. They occur widely in tropical Asia and Africa. For present purposes the characters are those of the genus *Cigaritis*.
Reference. Riley 1925.

Genus **CIGARITIS** Donzel 1847   TS: *Cigaritis zohra* Donzel
Description. Eyes smooth. *Palpi* very slender, long, porrect. *Antennae* slightly thickened in terminal third. *Legs* mid-tibia short in both sexes; first tarsal segment of hind-leg slightly dilated in ♂. *Venation.* Fw with 11 veins.
Genitalia. Dorsal structures somewhat massive, labides large, falces curving horizontally; valve about the same size as labides with costal process meeting its fellow on opposite side, embracing the straight massive penis; furca small, almost square in side view; saccus well defined.
Early stages. In *C. myrmecophila* Dumont, larvae feed at night, passing the day in ants' nests.

CIGARITIS ZOHRA   Donzel 1847   CN unknown
FG p. 232; Pl. 52
Genitalia. Described above.
Range. Restricted to Africa north of the Sahara, in Morocco, Algeria and Tunisia.

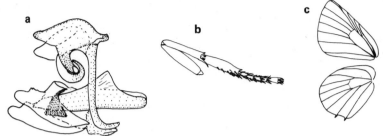

122. *Cigaritis zohra,* Morocco: **a,** genitalia; **b,** ♂ hind-leg; **c,** wing venation.

CIGARITIS ALLARDI Oberthur 1909   CN unknown

FG p. 233; Pl. 52

Genitalia. Like those of *C. zohra.*
Range. Morocco and Algeria.

123. *Cigaritis allardi,* Algeria: genitalia, side view.

CIGARITIS SIPHAX Lucas 1847   CN unknown FG p. 232; Pl. 52

Genitalia. Like those of *C. zohra*
Range. Morocco, Algeria, Tunisia.

124. *Cigaritis siphax,* Tunisia: genitalia.

CIGARITIS MYRMECOPHILA Dumont 1922   CN unknown
FG not described

Genitalia. Like those of *C. zohra.*

Range. Tripolitania, Egypt, SW Iran. Has occurred near Tozeur in S Tunisia. A desert species not inhabiting the Mediterranean region of N Africa.

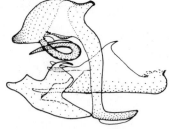

125. *Cigaritis myrmecophila,* SW Iran: genitalia. Algerian specimen not available.

Subfamily THECLINAE Butler 1869

Small, single-brooded butterflies associated with forest trees upon which their larvae feed. On ups most species are marked with brilliant gleaming colours. Sexes dissimilar. *Androconial scales* absent. The species are widely distributed in E Asia and three occur in Europe, each representing a different genus, of which one – *Laeosopis* Rambur – is peculiar to Europe.

Description. Eyes hairy. *Palpi* slender, porrect, longer in ♂. *Antennae* thickened rather gradually to form a slender club. *Legs* robust, with usual Lycaenid characters; feet with large pulvilli. *Venation.* Fw with 11 veins and internal vein; hw often with slender tail or projection at v2.

Genitalia. Tall but short from front to back, very variable, uncus developed in many Oriental species (Shirozu & Yamamato 1956) none of which occurs in Europe; labides usually massive, falces relatively small; valves small, often rounded, bases joined together (*Quercusia*) or well separated (*Laeosopis*); furca most variable, sometimes encircling penis (*Laeosopis*); saccus often present, usually well developed; penis variable.

Early stages. Ovum bun-shaped, deeply pitted. Larva onisciform and pilose, lateral ridges well developed. Pupa short, oval, cremastral hooks absent (Malicky), lying free upon the ground beneath a leaf, integument with so-called 'stellate' hairs.

Key to genera of Theclinae

1 Hw not tailed	*Laeosopis*
Hw tailed	**2**
2 Penis twice total height of genitalia	*Quercusia*
Penis length less than height of genitalia	*Thecla*

Genus **THECLA** F. 1807   TS: *Papilio betulae* L.
Refraction colours absent upf in both sexes. *Venation.* Hw with filamentous tail on v2.
Genitalia. Tegumen very massive; valve small, almost circular; penis slender.

THECLA BETULAE   L. 1758   CN 16   FG p. 233; Pl. 50
Genitalia. Described above.
Range. W Europe including Fennoscandia and across temperate Europe and Asia to Korea; absent generally from boreal regions and Mediterranean countries.

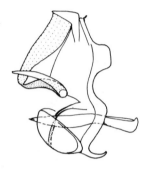

126.   *Thecla betulae,* S England: genitalia.

Genus **QUERCUSIA**   Verity 1943   TS: *Papilio quercus* L.
Refraction colours present in both sexes. *Venation.* Hw with filamentous tail on v2.
Genitalia. Tegumen hood-shaped; valve elongate, small with narrow posterior process, valve bases joined; furca a small oval plate; penis about two and a half times as long as valve, apex massive.

QUERCUSIA QUERCUS   L.   CN 24   FG p. 234; Pl. 50
Widely distributed across temperate Europe and Asia to Korea excluding boreal regions. Two subspecies with similar genitalia.

Q. q. quercus L. 1758.
Genitalia. Described above.
Range. N Spain, France and northwards to S Sweden, eastwards across Europe and Russia; also in Corsica, Sardinia and Sicily, N Turkey.

Q. q. iberica Staudinger 1901.
Subspecific characters in wing markings.
Genitalia. Indistinguishable.
Range. C and S Spain, Portugal, Morocco and Algeria.

107

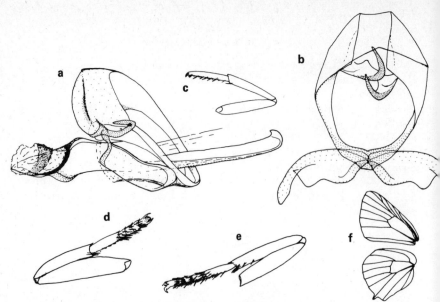

127. *Quercusia quercus,* N Switzerland: **a,** genitalia, penis *in situ*; **b,** genitalia, A-P view, valves spread; **c,** ♂ fore-leg; **d,** ♂ middle-leg; **e,** ♂ hind-leg; **f,** wing venation.

Genus **LAEOSOPIS** Rambur 1858   TS: *Papilio roboris* Esper
Ups with blue refraction colour in both sexes. *Eyes* with scanty hair.
Venation. Fw v12 short; hw lacks tail on v2.
Genitalia. Labides elongate, oblique at about 45° from axis of vinculum; valves small, rounded, bases widely separated; furca an oval ring; saccus large; penis short but massive.

LAEOSOPIS ROBORIS Esper 1793   CN unknown   FG p. 234; Pl. 50
Genitalia. Described above.
Range. Restricted to Portugal, Spain and SE France.
Reference. Agenjo 1963B.

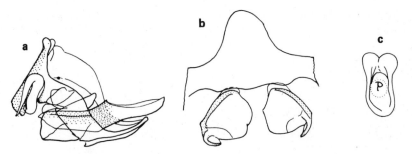

128. *Laeosopis roboris,* C Spain: **a,** genitalia, penis *in situ*; **b,** genitalia, A-P view, valves spread; **c,** furca.

Subfamily STRYMONINAE Tutt 1907

Description. Small single-brooded butterflies, ups wing colours subdued; upf with or without sex-brand near cell-end; hw with or without filamentous tail at v2; sexes similar or nearly so. *Eyes* hairy. *Palpi* small, slender, porrect, slightly longer in ♀. *Antennae* short, shaft slender with rather long narrow club. *Legs* ♂ femora hairy; large anterior tibial spines present in *Tomares*. *Venation.* Fw usually with 10 veins but 11 veins in *Tomares*; hw often with short tail or projection on v2 and small anal lobe.

Genitalia. Compressed and remarkably elongate; valves very small, narrow, horizontal and basally joined together, in ventral view appear to be enclosed within the vinculum; falces very long; furca absent; penis slender, longer than vinculum+labides with dense terminal cornuti which may show specific characters.

Early stages. As for Theclinae; larvae pilose, usually with dorsal gland on abdominal segment seven, dorsal and lateral ridges well developed. Pupa short, generally suspended and with silken girdle. As far as is known the species hibernate as fully formed larvae within the ova. Larval food plants usually trees and bushes, but variable in some species.

Note. The cornuti in the vesica are partly eversible. When comparing preparations of these organs, the condition of the vesica must be recognised or appearances may be misleading.

Key to genera of Strymoninae

1 Legs greatly modified (large tibial spines) . . .	*Tomares*
Legs not greatly modified	**2**
2 Unh green	*Callophrys*
Unh not green	**3**
3 Unh with white discal stripe firmly marked . . .	*Strymonidia*
Unh discal stripe formed of short white striae . . .	*Nordmannia*

Reference. Clench 1961.

Genus **NORDMANNIA** Tutt 1907   TS: *Lycaena myrtale* Klug
Male ups lacking sex-brands; unh grey or brown with slightly irregular pd series of white striae, often incomplete but rarely absent.

NORDMANNIA ILICIS   Esper 1779   CN unknown
FG p. 235; Pl. 50

Genitalia. Very elongate, about two and a half times as long as wide; in ventral view falces vertical, narrow, almost straight; valve narrow, terminal section very slender; penis with two dense cornuti, a third ventral cornutus with rounded apex is less dense.

Range. S and C Europe northwards to S Sweden, eastwards to Asia Minor and Lebanon. Absent from Mediterranean islands except Sicily, and from NW Europe including Britain.

109

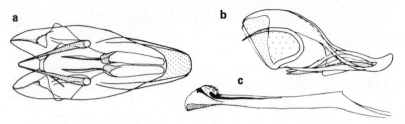

129. *Nordmannia ilicis,* C Pyrenees: **a,** genitalia, dorsal view; **b,** genitalia, side view; **c,** penis.

NORDMANNIA ESCULI Hübner   CN unknown

FG p. 236; Pl. 50

Range. SW Europe and N Africa. Two subspecies with similar genitalia.

N. e. esculi Hübner 1804.
Genitalia. Like *N. ilicis* but shorter; valve slightly wider, distal section shorter; penis with single dense cornutus, apical cornutus less dense.
Range. Spain, Portugal and S France.

130. *Nordmannia esculi,* C Spain: **a,** genitalia; **b,** penis.

N. e. mauretanica Staudinger 1892.
Genitalia. Indistinguishable.
Range. N Africa.

NORDMANNIA ACACIAE F. 1787   CN unknown

FG p. 235; Pl. 50

Genitalia. Short, wide, labides widely separated; falces long, horizontal;

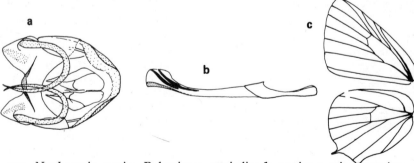

131. *Nordmannia acaciae,* Bulgaria: **a,** genitalia; **b,** penis; **c,** wing venation.

valves short, bases wider; penis with two dense cornuti and single ventral cornutus less dense.
Range. S Europe to about 48°N in France, rising to 51°N in Germany, and extending eastwards to Greece; further east, distribution uncertain.

Genus **STRYMONIDIA** Tutt 1908   TS: *Thecla thalia* Leech
Description. Upf with ♂ sex-brand near costa. Unh white pd line firmly marked. The typical species is not available for examination and generic characters cannot be defined. The name is used conventionally for *S. w-album*, *S. spini* and *S. pruni*, which show little resemblance in external features to *S. thalia*.

STRYMONIDIA SPINI   D. & S. 1775   CN unknown
FG p. 236; Pl. 50
Genitalia. Like *S. w-album*; labides closer together, falces shorter; valve wider; penis in side view with two densely chitinised cornuti, terminal ventral cornutus less dense.
Range. S and C Europe to about 55°N, widely distributed in W Asia. Absent from Mediterranean islands.
Early stages. Ovum compressed, regularly pitted and bearing short, stiff hairs. Larva with honey gland, hairy. Pupa smooth. Larval food plants *Rhamnus* spp.

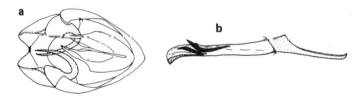

132. *Strymonidia spini*, Abruzzi, C Italy: **a,** genitalia; **b,** penis.

STRYMONIDIA W-ALBUM   Knoch 1782   CN unknown
FG p. 237; Pl. 50
Genitalia. Short, falces oblique; valve slender; penis with three cornuti, all densely chitinised.

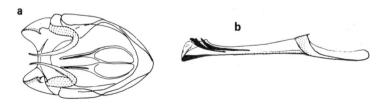

133. *Strymonidia w-album*, Rome: **a,** genitalia; **b,** penis.

Range. N Spain and C Europe including Sicily, northwards to 60°N including S England and S Scandinavia, across Siberia and Ussuri to Japan.
Early stages. Ovum compressed, domed, shell smooth. Larva with honey-gland. Pupa smooth, very wide. Larval food plants Wych Elm (*Ulmus montana*) and Common Elm (*Ulmus campestris*).

STRYMONIDIA PRUNI L. 1758   CN 23   FG p. 237; Pl. 50
Genitalia. Short, falces oblique; valves relatively wide, distal section short; penis with long, dense dorsal cornutus and another much shorter just below it, but lacking ventral cornutus, apex of penis upturned.
Range. C and N Europe and eastwards to the Amur and Korea. Absent from boreal regions and Mediterranean area excepting N Spain.
Early stages. Ovum somewhat compressed and finely pitted. Larva without honey-gland, dorsal ridges not developed but with lateral swellings on segments 2–5. Pupa with dorsal tubercles on each abdominal segment and a deep sulcus behind thorax. Larval food-plants *Prunus* spp.

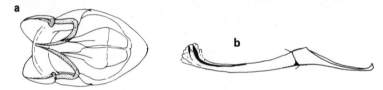

134. *Strymonidia pruni,* Switzerland: **a,** genitalia; **b,** penis.

Note. In this species the characters of larva and pupa are unusual. On this account Malicky (1969) has suggested removing *S. pruni* to the genus *Fixsenia* Tutt 1907, of which *F. herzi* Fixsen is the type species. In external characters the butterflies show little resemblance. The early stages of *F. herzi* have not been described as far as is known.

Genus **CALLOPHRYS** Billberg 1820   TS: *Papilio rubi* L.
Description. Ups reddish to dark brown, unmarked, upf ♂ sex-brand present near costa; hw lacking tail but anal lobe sometimes present; unh bright green with few markings; sexes similar. *Legs* ♂ fore-tibia slightly dilated in distal third.
Genitalia. Like *Nordmannia*; falces more robust; valves larger, extending beyond tegumen, without clearly defined distal section and incompletely enclosed within the vinculum; penis very long, slender, with two lightly chitinised cornuti finely toothed apically.

CALLOPHRYS RUBI L. 1758   CN 23   FG p. 238; Pl. 50
Genitalia. Described above.
Range. From N Africa and Europe eastwards through Asia Minor and Siberia to Amurland; closely related species or subspecies occur in N America.

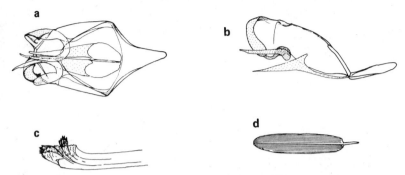

135. *Callophrys rubi*, S Spain: **a,** genitalia, dorsal view; **b,** genitalia, side view; **c,** penis apex enlarged to show cornuti; **d,** androconial scale.

CALLOPHRYS AVIS Chapman 1909   CN unknown
FG p. 238; Pl. 50

Genitalia. Like *C. rubi* but slightly wider, falces and valves more robust.
Range. SE France, local in Alpes Maritimes, Var and E Pyrenees. Spain and Portugal. N Africa.

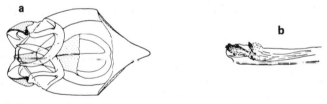

136. *Callophrys avis*, Tunisia, dorsal view; **a,** genitalia; **b,** penis apex enlarged.

Genus **TOMARES** Rambur 1839   TS: *Papilio ballus* F.
Description. Palpi very short, porrect, obscured by frontal hair-tuft. Antennal club elongate, slender. *Legs* greatly modified, in both sexes fore-tibia lacking spurs but with strong anterior tibial spine, middle- and hind-tibiae with paired spurs and paired spines, femora swollen, tibiae short. *Venation.* Fw with 11 veins, small sex-brands present at fork of v3–v4 and at fork of v7–9; v6 stalked with v7.
Genitalia. See *T. ballus* below.

TOMARES BALLUS F. 1787   CN unknown FG p. 239; Pl. 52
Genitalia. Like *Callophrys*, falces more slender; valves with short basal section and tapering rapidly to acicular apices, which project caudad beyond the tegumen; penis very long, slender, with two rather ill-defined cornuti.
Range. SE France, Spain and Portugal. N Africa from Morocco eastwards to Tripolitania and Egypt.

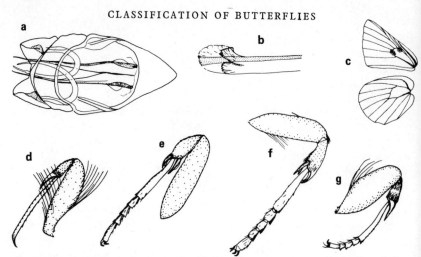

137. *Tomares ballus,* S France: **a,** genitalia; **b,** penis apex; **c,** wing venation; **d,** ♂ fore-leg; **e,** ♂ middle-leg; **f,** ♂ hind-leg; **g,** ♀ fore-leg.

TOMARES NOGELII Herrich-Schäffer 1851 CN unknown
FG p. 28

Genitalia. Like *T. ballus*; falces rather more massive; basal section of valve shorter, oval, distal section aciculate.

Range. Bessarabia, Asia Minor and Transcaucasus. Recorded by Caradja from Tulcea in northern Dobrogea, but no recent records. (*T. n. dobrogensis* Caradja 1895.)

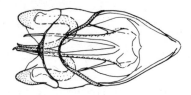

138. *Tomares nogelii,* N Turkey: genitalia, penis removed.

TOMARES MAURETANICUS Lucas 1849 CN unknown
FG p. 239; Pl. 52

Genitalia. Differ considerably from *T. ballus*, labides more slender and widely separated, falces slender; basal section of valve well-defined, almost half total length; penis with long terminal cornutus.

Range. Morocco, Algeria and Tunisia.

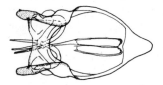

139. *Tomares mauretanicus,* Morocco: genitalia, penis removed.

Subfamily POLYOMMATINAE Swainson 1827

Description. With about 70 species this is the largest group of Lycaenidae occurring in Europe and N Africa. ♂ ups usually blue, rarely brown; ♀ brown, often suffused with blue. In both sexes uns markings consist of small dark spots arranged in transverse rows in a standard pattern which is characteristic. A common marking is a row of red submarginal lunules on one or both wings, usually present uns, more rarely on both surfaces. External characters are so uniform that genera are based chiefly upon features of the male genitalia. *Eyes* smooth or hairy. *Palpi* slender, usually porrect. *Antennae* slender with well marked fusiform or cylindrical club. *Venation.* Fw with 10 or 11 veins, v9 constantly absent, v11 more or less anastomosed with v12 in some genera; in hw precostal vein absent, a filamentous tail occasionally present. *Androconial scales* on upf very common, usually very small, round or oval, striated with characteristic ridges.

Genitalia. Uncus developed only in Everini, small saccus present only in Scolitantidini; in other respects structure varies very little throughout the subfamily, with consequent difficulty in defining tribes and genera; labides connected by narrow chitinous isthmus (tegumen?); the rami of the vinculum expanded dorsally to fuse with the labides; furca V-shaped with short basal pedicle; penis often short, sometimes relatively very small. Many tribes and genera have extensive Holarctic or world-wide distributions, so that their relationships may be most complicated.

Early stages. Ovum compressed (discoid) with elaborate minute reticulations and pits. Larva onisciform, often feeding inside flowers or seed-pods of food-plants which are usually small Leguminosae such as *Lotus*, *Onobrychis* etc. So far as known all species hibernate as small larvae in first or second instar. Many lowland species are double-brooded. In these features Polyommatinae differ greatly from Theclinae and Strymoninae which feed upon forest trees and which fly uniformly in a single brood.

References. Forster 1938. Beuret 1957.

Key to tribes of Polyommatinae

1 Uncus present . . . . Everini
   Uncus not present **2**

2 Medial margin of valve incised near apex . . Scolitantidini (part)
   Margin of valve not incised **3**

3 Tegumen and vinculum fused together . . . . Celastrini
   Vinculum well defined **4**

4 Penis large, flask-shaped . . . . . . Zizeerini
   Penis not flask-shaped **5**

5 Fringes strongly chequered black and white . Scolitantidini (part)
   Fringes not chequered **6**

6 Uns postdiscal and marginal markings of round dark spots in standard
pattern . . . . Polyommatini
Uns markings irregular, variable, oblique stripes and dark spots Lampidini

Note. Turanana panagaea Herrich-Schäffer is aberrant and difficult to
place; it agrees best with the Scolitantidini.

Tribe LAMPIDINI Tutt 1907

Description. Small or very small species, often with filamentous tail on
hw at v2; uns marked with pale oblique stripes; unf base pale to white, a
dark streak below costa is a frequent tribal character. Many species occur
in tropical Asia and Africa, of which five fly in N Africa, two in S Europe
and one is cosmopolitan. *Venation.* V11 variable.
Reference Stempffer 1967.

Key to genera of Lampidini

1 Valve with harpe . . . . *Tarucus*
Valve without harpe **2**

2 Apex of penis blunt, short . . . . . . *Lampides*
Apex of penis elongate, tapering, bifid **3**

3 Hw tailed . . . . *Syntarucus*
Hw not tailed . . . . *Cyclyrius*

Genus **TARUCUS** Moore 1881   TS: *Hesperia theophrastus* F.
Description. Uns ground-colour white. *Androconial scales* scanty, oval.
Eyes smooth. *Palpi* very slender, terminal segment almost half as long as
middle segment. *Legs* and *feet* with usual Lycaenid characters. *Venation.*
In fw V11 shortly anastomosed with v12.
Genitalia. In side view labides narrow, drooping, falces long, sharply
curved, directed backwards; rami of furca slender on short pedicle;
valve with harpe showing good specific characters; penis relatively large,
tapering to pointed apex.

Reference. Bethune Baker 1917. Stempffer 1967.

TARUCUS THEOPHRASTUS F. 1793   CN unknown
FG p. 251; Pl. 53
Genitalia. Valve tapers gradually to pointed apex armed with three small
apical spines, harpe small, about half the length of valve.
Range. Africa and W Asia. Occurs also in S Spain.

140. Tarucus theophrastus, Morocco: a, genitalia; b, valves.

116

TARUCUS BALKANICUS Freyer 1844 CN 24

FG p. 252; Pl. 53

Genitalia. Valve roughly oval tapering abruptly to pointed apex, harpe longer, densely chitinised and sharply pointed, lying flat upon the inner surface.

Range. Coastal regions of Mediterranean from Africa to Lebanon, Asia Minor and N Iran.

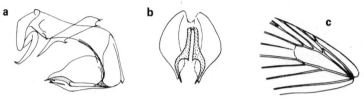

141. *Tarucus balcanicus,* Dalmatia: **a,** genitalia; **b,** valves; **c,** wing venation.

TARUCUS ROSACEUS Austaut 1885 CN unknown

FG p. 252; Pl. 13

Genitalia. Like *T. theophrastus* but valve apices turn outwards, harpes gently curved, almost as long as valves.

Range. N Africa including many desert oases. W Asia, widely distributed.

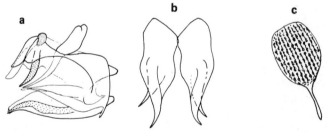

142. *Tarucus rosaceus,* Algeria: **a,** genitalia; **b,** valves; **c,** androconial scale.

Note. The genitalia of *Tarucus* are small and fragile, but it is not difficult to identify with them the three species that occur in the region. Viewed from below the valve shapes are easily seen in the intact genitalia. Viewed from the side they are also distinctive; the organs of *T. theophrastus* in particular, are easily identified by the terminal bristles. Superficially *T. balkanicus* is not difficult to distinguish from *T. rosaceus* by ups wing markings.

Reference. Stempffer 1967.

Genus **SYNTARUCUS** Butler 1881   TS: *Papilio pirithous* L.
Description. Eyes hairy. *Palpi* terminal segment about one-third the length of middle segment. *Legs* small anterior spine on front tibia only. *Venation.* In fw VII runs free, hw tailed at v2.
Genitalia. See *S. pirithous* below.

SYNTARUCUS PIRITHOUS   L. 1767   CN 24

FG p. 250; Pl. 53

Genitalia. Labides widely separated, large in side view, falces short, slender, tapering and almost straight; valves firmly united basally, tapering to pointed apices, harpes absent; stalk of furca short; penis relatively massive with prominent hook-shaped dorsal cuneus, and terminating in slender twin processes.
Range. N Africa and eastwards to Egypt, Lebanon, Asia Minor and S Europe, especially the Mediterranean coasts and extending northwards to southern Alpine slopes, more rarely to Germany etc. Has been taken in England.

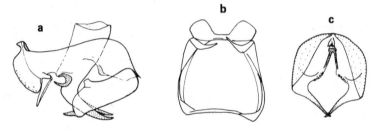

143. *Syntarucus pirithous,* S Italy: **a,** genitalia, penis *in situ*; **b,** labides and falces; **c,** valves.

Genus **CYCLYRIUS** Butler 1897
   TS: *Polyommatus webbianus* Brullé
Fringes chequered; hw without tail on v2; unf gc brown with dark, pale ringed spots; unh white pd band prominent. Closely related to *Syntarucus.* The characters are those of the single known species *C. webbianus.*

CYCLYRIUS WEBBIANUS   Brullé 1840   CN unknown

FG p. 251; Pl. 52

Description. Eyes hairy. *Palpi* slightly ascending, terminal segment one-third the length of middle segment. *Legs* not modified. *Venation.* Fw VII runs free.
Genitalia. In dorsal view labides widely separated, small, nodular, falces short, directed medially; valves like *S. pirithous,* medial borders deeply incised before the incurved pointed apices; penis with two small projections below the slender bifid apex.

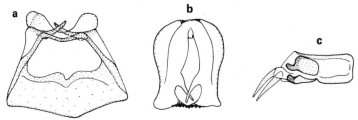

144. *Cyclyrius webbianus*, Tenerife, Canary Islands: **a,** labides and falces; **b,** valves; **c,** penis.

Range. Confined to Canary Islands, on Tenerife, Gran Canary, Gomera and La Palma.

Genus **LAMPIDES** Hübner 1819   TS: *Papilio boeticus* L.
The characters are those of *L. boeticus*.

LAMPIDES BOETICUS L. 1767   CN unknown
FG p. 250; Pl. 53

Description. Uns pale grey-brown, hw with pale transverse stripes, a round black spot in s2 is prominent on both surfaces. *Eyes* hairy. *Palpi* with short terminal segment. *Antennal* club short, cylindrical. *Legs* each leg with spurs and prominent anterior tibial spines. *Androconial scales* abundant, long, slender, length variable. *Venation.* Fw with 11 veins; v11 runs free parallel with v12; hw with short filamentous tail on v2.
Genitalia. Dorsal structures small, labides short, widely separated, falces very short, directed medially; vinculum wide dorsally, tapering to base; valves firmly united, apical process curved inwards, without harpes; penis stout, short, with two small processes below ostium.
Range. World-wide in tropical countries, widely distributed in Europe; a notable migrant, occasionally reaching England.
Early stages. Larval food plants Leguminosae, especially Senna (*Colutea*) feeding within the seed-pods.

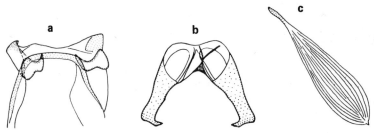

145. *Lampides boeticus,* S Spain: **a,** labides and falces; **b,** valves; **c,** androconial scale. See also fig. 108, p. 96.

Tribe EVERINI Tutt 1908

Description. Small species, hw often with filamentous tail on v2. Male ups blue or brown, uns markings almost identical in both sexes in all European species, consisting of small white-ringed dark spots on pale ground-colour. *Eyes* smooth. *Palpi* porrect, about twice as long as head, the long terminal segment exposed, slender, smoothly clothed with scales. *Venation.* Fw with 10 veins, v11 anastomosed completely with v12, which is later continued to costa.

Genitalia. Uncus present notched or with terminal beak, fused to tegumen and in dorsal view appearing as a small rectangular plate; furca well defined, the arms embracing the penis in *Cupido* so that it is not possible to extract the latter without rupturing the organs; valves firmly fused together basally, posteriorly narrow with slender falcate costal process; saccus absent; penis slender, apex spatulate and prolonged.

Key to genera of Everini

1 Uncus with deep central incision . . . . . *Azanus*
  Uncus entire **2**

2 Hw with filamentous tail on v2 . . . . . *Everes*
  Hw without filamentous tail . . . . . . *Cupido*

Genus **AZANUS** Moore 1881   TS: *Papilio ubaldus* Stoll

Description. Small butterflies of which about 20 species occur in Africa and in tropical Asia. Male ups blue with few markings; uns with complicated pattern of dark spots and striae. Hw lacking tail on v2. *Androconial scales* usually abundant. *Eyes* hairy. *Palpi* long, porrect, slender and heavily scaled, terminal segment less than quarter the length of middle segment. *Antennal* club cylindrical, about quarter the total length of antenna. *Legs* anterior tibial spines present on all legs.

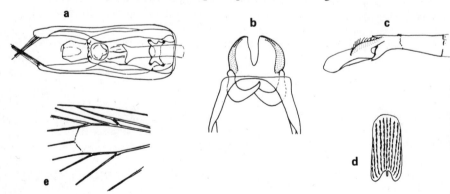

146. *Azanus jesous,* Morocco: **a,** genitalia, dorsal view; **b,** labides and falces; **c,** penis; **d,** androconial scale; **e,** venation, discal area of fore-wing.

Genitalia. Anomalous; labides represented by broad paired processes forming an uncus, projecting posteriorly.

AZANUS JESOUS Guérin 1849   CN unknown

FG p. 253; Pl. 52

Androconial scales short, wide, coarsely striated.
Genitalia. Falces directed inwards; valve long, very slender, armed with eight long terminal spines; furca pedicle very short (absent ?), rami short; terminal section of penis elongate and spatulate.
Range. Widely distributed in Africa and in tropical Asia.

AZANUS UBALDUS Stoll in Cramer 1782   CN unknown
Upf ♂ sex-brand prominent, androconial scales very narrow, length variable.
Genitalia. Like *A. jesous* but valves elongate, irregular, hairy.
Range. A desert species in Egypt and eastwards across W Asia to India and Ceylon. Recorded (teste Stempffer) from Morocco (Ben Slimane) and Tunisia (Tozeur). Both these localities are within the desert region and, strictly, are outside the scope of this book.

147. *Azanus ubaldus,* Israel: **a,** genitalia, right valve and penis removed; **b,** androconial scale.

Genus **CUPIDO** Schrank 1801   TS: *Papilio minimus* Fuessli
Description. Very small butterflies, ♂ ups usually blue without discal markings, ♀ brown; uns gc pale with dark pd spots in series, marginal markings usually absent. *Venation.* Fw VII anastomosed with V12.
Genitalia. Falces tapered gradually to apices; furca rami short embracing penis; valves with costal and apical processes. Specific characters not well defined in the genitalia.

CUPIDO MINIMUS Fuessli 1775   CN 24   FG p. 255; Pl. 53
Androconial scales abundant.
Genitalia. In dorsal view uncal beak not visible, tegumen wide; costal process of valve sharply curved; distal part of penis spatulate, slightly constricted at junction with base.
Range. From C Spain across Europe and Asia to Siberia. Absent from boreal regions, S Spain, Portugal and Mediterranean islands except Sicily.

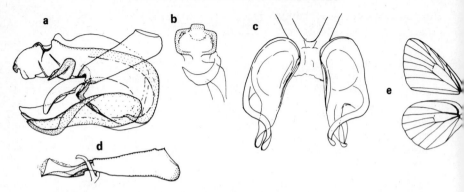

148. *Cupido minimus*, S England: **a,** genitalia; **b,** uncus, tegumen and left falx; **c,** valves attached to base of vinculum; **d,** penis, part of furca attached; **e,** wing venation.

CUPIDO OSIRIS   Meigen 1829   CN 24   FG p. 258; Pl. 53
Genitalia. Like *C. minimus*; in dorsal view uncal beak scarcely visible; costal process of valve as in *C. minimus* but less sharply curved; penis as in *C. minimus*.
Range. From S and C Europe including Spain eastwards to C Asia.

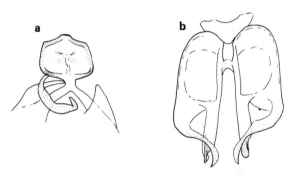

149. *Cupido osiris,* Hautes Alpes: **a,** uncus and tegumen with right falx; **b,** valves.

Note. Beuret 1957 figures a dorsal view of genitalia showing a sharply pointed uncus. In specimens from Digne, C Italy and Ankara, the uncus is scarcely visible in this view, as shown above.

CUPIDO LORQUINII   Herrich-Schäffer 1847   CN unknown
                                                FG.p. 259; Pl. 53
Genitalia. Like *C. minimus*; apical process of valve slightly expanded, costal process slender; penis as in *C. minimus*.

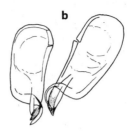

150. *Cupido lorquinii*, Morocco: **a**, uncus and tegumen with falces; **b**, valves.

Range. Morocco, Algeria, S Spain, S Portugal, especially in coastal districts.

CUPIDO CARSWELLI   Stempffer 1927   CN unknown
FG p. 259; no figure
Genitalia. Like *C. minimus*; uncus flat, beak not visible in dorsal view; valve as in *C. lorquinii*, costal process sharply curved; penis as in *C. minimus*.
Range. Confined to small area in SE Spain (Murcia), flying in mountains at middle heights.

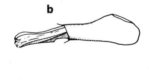

151. *Cupido carswelli*, SE Spain: **a**, uncus, tegumen and falx; **b**, penis.

Reference. Stempffer 1927.
Note. Material scarce, examination incomplete on this account.

Genus **EVERES**   Hübner 1823   TS: *Papilio argiades* Pallas
Small species resembling *Cupido* but hw with short filamentous tail at v2.
Genitalia. Like *Cupido* but beak of uncus more prominent and with specific characters; apices of falces densely chitinised and abruptly tapered; costal process of valve not closely applied to cucullus; penis not embraced by furca.

References. Lorković 1938. Courvoisier 1916.

123

EVERES ARGIADES Pallas 1771   CN 24   FG p. 254; Pl. 53

Genitalia. Uncal beak small but plainly visible in dorsal view; costal process of valve with an even curve, tapered gradually from base to pointed apex; furca as in *Cupido*; penis as in *Cupido* but constriction between apex and base less prominent.

Range. N Spain and W France and eastwards across Europe and Asia to Japan; also closely related species in N America.

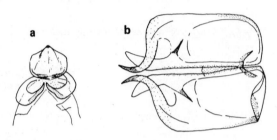

152. *Everes argiades,* Rome: **a,** uncus, tegumen and falces; **b,** valves.

EVERES ALCETAS Hoffmannsegg 1804   CN 25–26
                                                        FG p. 255; Pl. 53

Genitalia. Like *E. argiades* but beak of uncus more prominent in dorsal view; costal process of valve less curved; penis as in *E. argiades.*

Range. From C Spain across S Europe to Greece and Turkey, northwards to southern alpine slopes and across Asia Minor to C Asia.

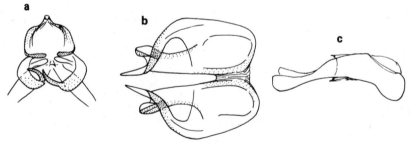

153. *Everes alcetas,* N Italy: **a,** uncus, tegumen and falces; **b,** valves; **c,** penis.

EVERES DECOLORATUS Staudinger 1886   CN 25
                                                            FG p. 254; Pl. 53

Genitalia. Like *E. argiades*; uncal beak more prominent; costal process of valve twisted, curve not even and regular; penis as in *E. alcetas.*

Range. SE Europe, Austria and Balkan countries including N Greece, to about 47°N and westwards to Mt. Nanos in Slovenia.

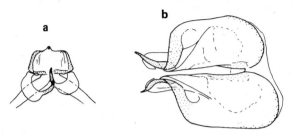

154. *Everes decoloratus,* Croatia, N Yugoslavia: **a,** uncus, tegumen and falces; **b,** valves.

Tribe ZIZEERINI Chapman 1910

Description. Very small butterflies widely distributed in tropical Africa, Asia and Australia. Few species known. *Eyes* smooth. *Palpi* porrect, slender, terminal segment short. *Legs* not modified. *Venation.* Fw VII anastomosed shortly with V12 and continued to costal margin near apex. *Genitalia.* Labides moderately separated, falces long, curved; penis relatively large, flask-shaped, with long terminal spine.

Genus **ZIZEERIA** Chapman 1910   TS: *Polyommatus karsandra* Moore *Genitalia.* Valve strap shaped with small terminal teeth

ZIZEERIA KNYSNA Trimen   CN unknown   FG p. 253; Pl. 54
Two subspecies, genitalia differing slightly.

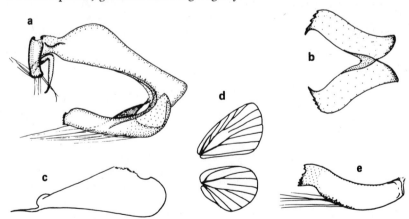

155. *Zizeeria knysna knysna,* Morocco: **a,** genitalia, penis removed; **b,** valves; **c,** penis; **d,** wing venation. *Z. k. karsandra,* Iran: **e,** valve.

Z. k. knysna Trimen 1862.
Genitalia. In dorsal view labides elongate, falces long, very slender, curved medially; valve apex obliquely pointed.
Range. Widely distributed in Africa, extending to Canary Islands, N Africa and S Spain.

Z. k. karsandra Moore 1865.
Genitalia. Like *Z. k. knysna* but valve apex rectangular. The distinctive character seems somewhat variable.
Range. Egypt, Crete, Tunisia and Sicily, and eastwards through a vast area of Asia and Australia.

Reference. Corbet 1948.

Tribe CELASTRINI Tutt 1908
The characters are those of the genus *Celastrina* Tutt.
A small isolated group, well represented in SE Asia, with a single species occurring in N Africa and Europe.

Genus **CELASTRINA** Tutt 1906   TS: *Papilio argiolus* L.
Description. Eyes hairy. *Palpi* slender, porrect. *Antennal* club oval, abrupt.
Venation. Fw with 11 veins, vII running free.
Genitalia. Structure unusual; labides and vinculum fused together forming a broad plate extending to articulation with valve which is conspicuous; furca prominent, rather stout; penis with wide base tapering to curved pointed apex.

CELASTRINA ARGIOLUS L. 1758   CN 25   FG p. 259; Pl. 52
Genitalia. Falx probably represented by a small pointed process at lower angle of tegumen; valve slender posteriorly with several long bristles arising from a point near the centre of the costal margin and directed posteriorly.

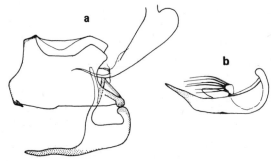

156. *Celastrina argiolus*, S England: **a,** genitalia, penis *in situ*; **b,** valve.

Range. Widely distributed from N Africa and Europe, excepting boreal regions, across Asia to Japan; further in N America from coast to coast and southwards to New Mexico. Absent from NW Scandinavia.

Early stages. Larval food plants various shrubs and small trees. Associated with ants (*Lasius*). Hibernation as pupa, flying usually in two annual broods.

Tribe SCOLITANTIDINI Tutt 1909

Description. Butterflies of small to medium size, ♂ ups blue, with, or more often without, black discal markings, wing borders black. Species variable, one group with fringes strongly chequered black and white, in the other group fringes white or grey, sometimes feebly chequered. Both groups are conventionally included in the tribe Scolitantidini Tutt (Glaucopsychini Hemming 1931). On inspection the relationship is not obvious but in the genitalia the dorsal structures are similar in both groups although the valves and penes are most variable. The tribe is widely distributed across the temperate areas of the Holarctic Region. *Eyes* smooth or with few scanty hairs. *Palpi* porrect, middle segment hairy beneath, terminal segment smooth, almost half as long as middle segment. *Antennal* club slender. *Venation.* Fw with 11 veins; v11 runs free parallel with v12, stalk of v7+8 arises before or at (*Maculinea*) end of cell.

Genitalia. In dorsal view labides widely separated, falces well developed, directed posteriorly or medially, valves at their bases firmly joined, very variable, inner border usually incised near apex in *Glaucopsyche* and *Maculinea* forming a narrow terminal tooth, absent in *Pseudophilotes* and near allies; a short saccus present in some species; penis short and stout.

Early stages. Often with symbiotic associations with ants.

Note. The genus *Philotes* Scudder, TS. *Lycaena sonorensis* Felder & Felder, is not appropriate for the European species *baton* and *abencerragus* which are placed now in the genus *Pseudophilotes* Beuret 1958.

Key to Genera

1 Ups fringes strongly chequered . . *Scolitantides, Pseudophilotes*
  Ups fringes entire or weakly chequered **2**

2 Upf with discal markings in one or both sexes . . . *Maculinea*
  Upf without discal markings **3**

3 Valve structure complicated, large species . . . *Iolana*
  Valve structure simple **4**

4 Unf pd spots in regular series . . . . . *Glaucopsyche*
  Unf pd spot in s3 large, out of line . . . . . *Turanana*

Note. In *Maculinea alcon* ♂ ups discal spots absent; in *Maculinea nausithous* ♀ ups plain brown.

Genus **PSEUDOPHILOTES** Beuret 1958
  TS: *Papilio baton* Bergsträsser
Very small butterflies, fringes chequered black and white; uns strongly marked with dark spots on pale gc.
Genitalia. Compact, falces small, directed medially; valve variable; penis stout, relatively large.

References. Beuret 1958. Hemming 1929.

PSEUDOPHILOTES BATON   Bergsträsser   CN 24
                                          FG p. 267; Pl. 53
Androconial scales abundant, round or slightly oval or elongate, variable. Three subspecies, genitalia similar in two.
Range. From Portugal across Europe and Asia to Iran and Himalaya Mts.

P. b. baton Bergsträsser 1779.
Androconial scales almost round.
Genitalia. Distal section of valve elongate, apex turned downwards and with sharp tooth about mid-point of lower border.
Range. W Europe including France with Pyrenees and N Spain, Switzerland and Italy to about 48°N.

P. b. panoptes Hübner 1813.
Genitalia. Indistinguishable. *Androconial scales* oval or elongate, slightly variable.
Range. S Portugal and S Spain.

P. b. schiffermuelleri Hemming 1929.
Genitalia. Valve lacks the elongate distal section, terminates just beyond the inferior tooth.
Range. SE Europe including Austria and Yugoslavia.

Note. P. b. baton and *P. b. schiffermuelleri* are considered distinct species by most authors, and it is necessary to explain their treatment here as subspecies. The two forms appear to be completely allopatric and vicarious, with *P. b. baton* replacing *P. b. schiffermuelleri* in W Europe, and a subspecific relationship is strongly suggested on this account. The butterflies cannot be distinguished by external examination; identification depends upon the characters of the valves, with a single short posterior process (*schiffermuelleri*) or with an additional long posterior process (*baton*). Their intimate relationship is clearly indicated by the existence of intermediate forms, as pointed out by the late H. Beuret (1957). Valves with the posterior process reduced have been found in N Italy at Arquata Scrivia (Alessandria) fig. 157e; at Orvieto (Umbria) and near Trieste, suggesting an unstable population in this part of Italy. All these specimens were associated with others having genitalia of typical *baton*. A valve with the posterior process reduced, similar to fig. 157l, is illustrated by Hemming in his original article, and is specified by him as holotype of

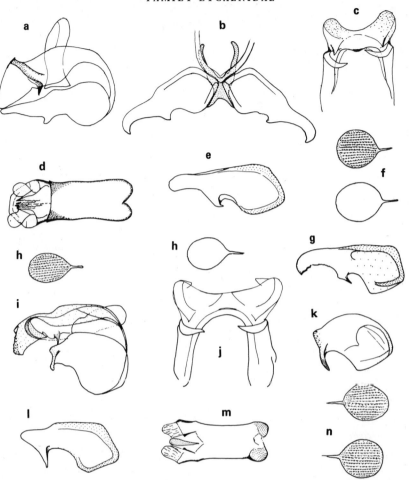

157. *Pseudophilotes baton baton,* S France: **a,** genitalia; **b,** valves; **c,** tegumen and falces; **d,** penis, ventral view. C Italy: **e,** valve, distal process reduced; **f,** androconial scales. *P. b. panoptes,* C. Spain: **g,** valve; **h,** androconial scales. *P. b. schiffermuelleri,* Bulgaria: **i,** genitalia, side view; **j,** labides and falces; **k,** valve. N Italy: **l,** valve, distal process partly developed; **m,** penis, ventral view. Macedonia: **n,** androconial scales.

P. vicrama schiffermuelleri. Unfortunately, little material is available for examination from the indicated frontier area. Material variation in dorsal structures has not been seen by the author in specimens from various localities as far east as Iran, nor has it been possible to confirm the difference in shapes of androconial scales described by Hemming in the article referred to.

PSEUDOPHILOTES ABENCERRAGUS   Pierret 1837.

CN unknown   FG p. 270; Pl. 53

Androconial scales scanty, elongate oval.

Genitalia. Like *P. baton* but valve very short, almost square, with two nearly equal triangular processes.

Range. Morocco, Algeria, Tunisia, Tripolitania, Egypt, Jordan. Spain and Portugal.

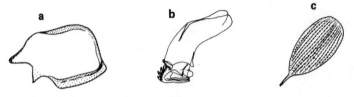

158. *Pseudophilotes abencerragus,* S Spain: **a,** valve; **b,** penis, side view; **c,** androconial scale.

Genus **SCOLITANTIDES** Hübner 1823   TS: *Papilio orion* Pallas

Closely allied to *Pseudophilotes* Scudder and with similar markings; unh orange-red submarginal spots very brilliant. *Genitalia* described below.

SCOLITANTIDES ORION   Pallas 1771   CN 23 FG p. 271; Pl. 53

Male lacks androconial scales.

Genitalia. Like *Pseudophilotes*; labides well defined, falces longer, turned inwards; valve elongate, posterior margin rounded; furca long and slender; penis short, stout, entering vertically behind tegumen.

Range. E Spain and C France in very localised colonies and across Europe, to C Asia and Japan.

Early stages. Larval food plants *Sedum.*

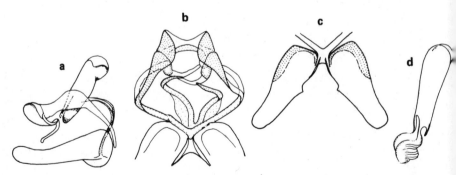

159. *Scolitantides orion,* Bolzano, S Tirol: **a,** genitalia; **b,** tegumen and falces; **c,** valves; **d,** penis.

SCOLITANTIDES BAVIUS Eversmann CN 24
FG p. 270; Pl. 53

Androconial scales abundant, elongate oval. Two subspecies with differing genitalia.

S. b. bavius Eversmann 1832.
Genitalia. Like *S. orion*, labides well defined; valve elongate, slightly expanded distally, terminating in a wide, incurved and truncate costal process; penis as in *S. orion*.
Range. Occurs in Europe in Greece, Rumania and Hungary, further Asia Minor, S Russia and Caucasus.

S. b. fatma Oberthur 1890.
Genitalia. Like *S. b. bavius* but valve narrow, tapering rather abruptly to a point, apex incurved, dorsal structures and penis as in *S. b. bavius*.
Range. Morocco, Algeria, in Middle Atlas.

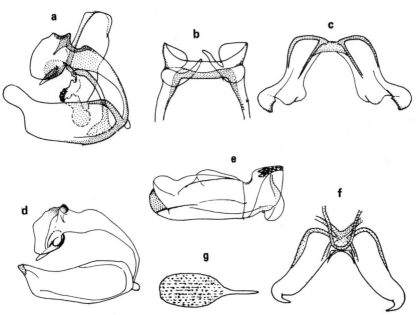

160. *Scolitantides bavius bavius,* Asia Minor: **a,** genitalia; **b,** labides and falces; **c,** valves. *S. b. fatma,* Middle Atlas, Morocco: **d,** genitalia; **e,** penis; **f,** valves; **g,** androconial scale.

Genus **GLAUCOPSYCHE** Scudder 1872
TS: *Lycaena lygdamus* Doubleday
Description. Small butterflies, ♂ ups blue with wing-borders dark, otherwise unmarked; ♀ ups brown, often suffused with blue; unf pd spots

present, often enlarged in s2 and s3; marginal markings uns reduced or absent. The genus has an extensive Holarctic distribution. *Androconial scales* round. *Eyes* hairy. *Palpi* porrect, terminal segment short. *Legs* anterior tibial spines reduced or absent.

Genitalia. Penis shorter than valve, apical structure elaborate.

GLAUCOPSYCHE ALEXIS Poda 1761   CN 23

FG p. 262; Pl. 53

Genitalia. Terminal tooth of valve narrow, tapering, about half the width of valve.

Range. From N Africa and W Europe across Russia and C Asia to Amurland.

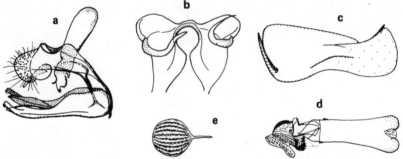

161. *Glaucopsyche alexis,* SE France: **a,** genitalia; **b,** labides and falces; **c,** valve; **d,** penis, dorsal view; **e,** androconial scale.

GLAUCOPSYCHE MELANOPS Boisduval 1828   CN 23

FG p. 262; Pl. 54

Genitalia. Like *G. alexis*; valve longer, narrow, terminal incision very small, a shallow notch on inner margin; a small saccus is present.

Range. N Africa. Spain and SE France including E Pyrenees.

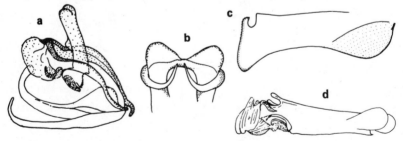

162. *Glaucopsyche melanops,* S Spain: **a,** genitalia; **b,** tegumen and falces; **c,** valve; **d,** penis, side view.

Note. Hemming (1931) has proposed a new genus *Apelles* for this species. It does not appear to the writer that this action is necessary.

Genus **MACULINEA** van Ecke 1915   TS: *Papilio alcon* D. & S.
Description. Butterflies of middle size, ♂ ups blue with or without black discal markings, ♀ more heavily marked. The genus is closely related to *Glaucopsyche*, differing chiefly in the arrangement of markings. *Andro-conial scales* oval. *Eyes* smooth. *Venation.* In fw stalk of v7+8 arises at end of cell.
Genitalia. Like *Glaucopsyche*; falces well developed, directed inwards and backwards; valve oblong, horizontal, incised medially before apex; furca conspicuous, rami short.

References. Frohawk 1924. Bernardi 1947B, 1951.

MACULINEA ALCON D. & S.   CN 23   FG p. 263; Pl. 54
Range through N Spain and C Europe to Caucasus and C Asia. Two subspecies with similar genitalia.

M. a. alcon D. & S. 1775.
Genitalia. In dorsal view terminal spine of valve short.
Range. From N Spain and France across C Europe, northwards to Denmark, east to Rumania, Balkans and Greece.

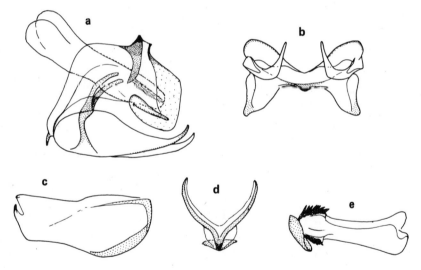

163. *Maculinea alcon alcon,* Bavaria: **a,** genitalia; **b,** labides and falces; **c,** valve; **d,** furca; **e,** penis, side view.

M. a. rebeli Hirschke 1904.
Wing markings give subspecific characters, but development of these is variable, especially constant and well developed in mountain races, per-haps the extreme phase of a cline (ecological).

133

Range. Occurs in various localities, more frequently than nominate race.

Reference. Chapman 1919.

Note. A side view of entire genitalia is shown for this species, but this view is not repeated for the three species following as structure in all is so similar.

MACULINEA ARION L. 1758   CN 23   FG p. 264; Pl. 54
Genitalia. Like *M. alcon*; terminal spine of valve long, oblique.
Range. W Europe including Spain across Russia and Siberia to China.

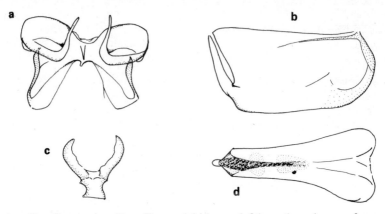

164. *Maculinea arion,* Engadin: **a,** labides and falces; **b,** valve; **c,** furca; **d,** penis, dorsal view.

MACULINEA TELEIUS Bergsträsser 1779   CN unknown
                                            FG p. 265; Pl. 54
Genitalia. Like *M. alcon*; terminal spine of valve strong, at right-angle to valve costa.
Range. France, across temperate Europe and Asia to Japan.

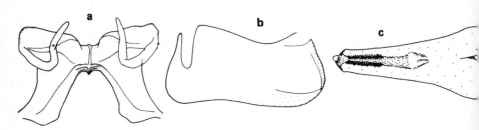

165. *Maculinea teleius,* Bavaria: **a,** labides and falces; **b,** valve; **c,** penis, dorsal view.

MACULINEA NAUSITHOUS Bergsträsser 1779   CN unknown

FG p. 266; Pl. 54

Genitalia. Like *M. alcon*; valve slightly curved, terminal spine long, oblique.

Range. N Spain and France across C Europe to Ural Mts. and Caucasus, occurring in widely scattered colonies.

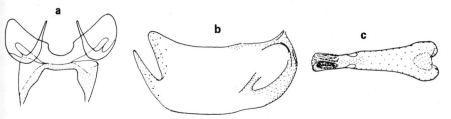

166. *Maculinea nausithous,* Poland: **a,** labides and falces; **b,** valve; **c,** penis, dorsal view.

Genus **IOLANA** Bethune Baker 1914
   TS: *Lycaena iolas* Ochsenheimer
Markings very simple, resembling *Glaucopsyche. Eyes* hairy. *Androconial scales* oval.
Genitalia. Labides narrow, falces robust, scarcely tapered; vinculum with small bilobed saccus; valve hemispherical with single posterior process; penis stout with two small terminal points.

IOLANA IOLAS Ochsenheimer 1816   CN 22 FG p. 266; Pl. 53
Genitalia. Described above.
Range. Algeria. Spain and eastwards across S Europe, in very localised colonies, more common in W Asia.

Reference. Hemming 1931.

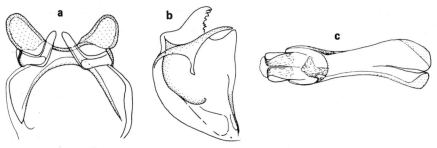

167. *Iolana iolas,* Macedonia: **a,** labides and falces; **b,** valve; **c,** penis, ventral view.

Genus **TURANANA** Bethune Baker 1916
TS: *Lycaena cytis* Christoph
Small species in which the distinctive character is the black spot unf in s3 which is displaced distally. *Genitalia* as in *Scolitantides*.

TURANANA PANAGAEA Herrich-Schäffer 1851   CN 24
FG p. 263; Pl. 52
Genitalia. Tegumen wide; valve elongate, apex rounded; furca short, slender; penis short and stout.
Range. S Greece (Taygetus Mts.) and through Asia Minor and Lebanon to Iran and Turkestan.

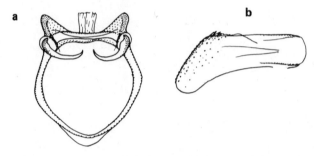

168. *Turanana panagaea*, Lebanon: **a,** labides and falces; **b,** valve.

Tribe POLYOMMATINI Swainson 1827
By far the most extensive Lycaenid tribe in the region, including several small groups of closely related, possibly imperfectly differentiated species. *Description*. Ups markings variable, ♂ usually blue, rarely brown, ♀ brown, often with blue basal ups suffusions which may vary greatly in individuals from the same colony. On unh there are characteristic markings of dark spots in a pd series and red submarginal lunules well developed in almost all species. *Eyes* smooth or hairy. *Palpi* porrect, middle segment clothed beneath with long hair, terminal segment more exposed, long and slender. *Antennal club* narrow, about quarter total length. *Legs* anterior tibial spine often present on front and middle legs in both sexes, more rarely hind-legs also spined. *Androconial scales* upf usually present. *Venation*. Fw with 11 veins, v8 and v9 arise from cell-end on a common stalk; vII and vI2 do not touch; hw never tailed.
Genitalia. Fragile, in dorsal (A–P) view labides pointed, falces slender; valves elongate, vertical, structure simple, usually with hooked costal process, bases firmly joined together and loosely attached to base of vinculum, widely separated from dorsal structures; furca very long, rami often filiform and in most species appear to support the long vinculum

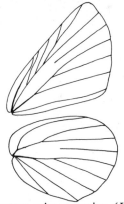

169. POLYOMMATINI, wing venation (*Lycaeides idas*).

without obvious connection with the small penis. Penis very small, straight or slightly curved, situated far above the valves.· Generic and specific characters usually shown best by dorsal (A–P) views of labides and falces and by the shape of the penis (Chapman 1910(2)).

Early stages. Ovum round, compressed, regularly embossed over top and sides with small pits in a reticulate pattern. Larva onisciform. Pupa short, stout, abdominal segments rigid, usually pubescent, lying unattached upon the soil. Favourite food plants include *Lotus*, *Onobrychis*, *Thymus* etc., young larvae often feeding inside flowers or seed-pods, hibernating as larvae. Many species produce two or more annual broods in warm areas, but single broods in N Europe.

The sixteen genera recognised in this book, mostly based upon rather insignificant characters, fall naturally into four groups, determined by genitalia characters, by the hairiness, or the reverse, of the eyes, and the presence or absence unf of a basal cell-spot.

References. Chapman 1910(2), 1916. Tutt 1908. Forster 1938.

Key to genera of Polyommatini

1	Eyes smooth	**2**
	Eyes hairy	**11**
2	Unf cell-spot present	*Agriades*
	Unf cell-spot absent	**3**
3	Fw 8–9mm, unh black marginal spots in s2, s3, s4 . .	*Freyeria*
	Fw 12mm or more, unh not so marked	**4**
4	Unh pd series of spots broken at s6	**5**
	Unh pd series of spots in regular curve	**6**

5 Unh spots numerous, black ringed white . . . *Aricia*
Unh spots scanty, white, black pupils minute if present . *Albulina*

6 Unh with short white discal stripe along v4 . . . **7**
Unh without short white discal stripe **8**

7 ♂ ups brown . . . . *Eumedonia*
♂ ups blue, wing borders brown . . . . . *Pseudoaricia*

8 Unh with single conspicuous orange anal spot . . *Vacciniina*
Unh with complete series of orange marginal spots . . **9**

9 ♂ ups brown . . . . *Kretania*
♂ ups blue **10**

10 In dorsal view falces straight . . . . . . *Plebejus*
In dorsal view falces curved to a semi-circle . . . *Lycaeides*

11 Eyes hairy **12**

12 Unf without spot in cell **13**
Unf with spot in cell **15**

13 Uns marginal markings vestigial or absent . . . *Cyaniris*
Uns marginal markings present in usual pattern . . **14**

14 Unh often with white stripe along v4; CN usually below 100 *Agrodiaetus**
Unh without white stripe along v4; CN 134 or over . *Plebicula*

15 In dorsal view apex of penis not bulbous . . . *Polyommatus*
In dorsal view apex of penis bulbous **16**

16 Outer margin of hw entire . . . . . . *Lysandra*
Outer margin of hw scalloped near anal angle . . . *Meleageria*

*The species *coelestina* Eversmann and *ellisoni* Pfeiffer are anomalous. Eyes are not hairy although by genitalia both species belong to the *Agrodiaetus* group.

Genus **FREYERIA** Courvoisier 1920
    TS: *Lycaena trochylus* Freyer
The characters are those of the species *F. trochylus* Freyer.

FREYERIA TROCHYLUS Freyer 1844   CN 23 FG p. 271; Pl. 53
One of the smallest butterflies known. Ups brown, unh with two or three large marginal black spots. Sexes similar.

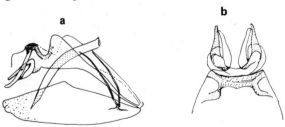

170. *Freyeria trochylus,* Lebanon: **a,** genitalia; **b,** tegumen and falces.

Genitalia. Like *P. argus*; in side view dorsal structures relatively large; labides rather long, falces protrude behind labides; vinculum oblique at about 45°; valve short, apex blunt, terminal hook not well developed; penis slender, elongate, curved, tapering to pointed apex.

Range. In Europe, only in the extreme SE in Greece, Turkey and Crete. Widely distributed in tropical and subtropical Asia and Africa.

Genus **PLEBEJUS** Kluk 1802   TS: *Papilio argus* L.

Genitalia. In side view labides narrow, falces vertically curved to appear posteriorly behind and above apices of labides; penis short, slightly curved near apex; in dorsal view labides tubular, sinuous, apices turned outwards, falces appear very narrow, straight. Genitalia very similar in all species, specific characters rarely obvious, best seen when present in minor features of the labides. The dorsal structures usually give most information when mounted to show an A–P view. Apparent differences in valve shapes are less reliable as they can be caused by slight variation due to movement during mounting, or to pressure.

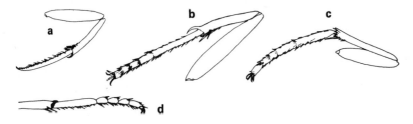

171. Genus *Plebejus*, legs (*Plebejus argus*): **a,** ♂ fore-leg; **b,** ♂ middle-leg; **c,** ♂ hind-leg; **d,** ♀ fore-tarsus.

PLEBEJUS ARGUS L.   CN 23   FG p. 276; Pl. 55

Tibial spines present in both sexes on front and middle legs.

Genitalia. Furca with long central process arising from base; valve apex bordered with 7–8 long teeth. To display these the valve must be pressed flat to unfold posterior flap. Range beyond Europe extends to C Asia and Siberia. Four European subspecies defined by external characters, genitalia similar in all.

P. a. argus L. 1758.

Genitalia. Described above.

Range. S Sweden, extending, in lowland localities and slightly different forms, widely across Europe, absent from many Mediterranean islands.

P. a. aegidion Meisner 1818.

Range. Occurs at high altitudes in Alps etc.

P. a. corsicus Bellier 1862.

Range. Occurs on Corsica and Sardinia.

P. a. hypochionus Rambur 1858.
Range. Occurs in S Spain.
References. Forster 1936. Beuret 1961.

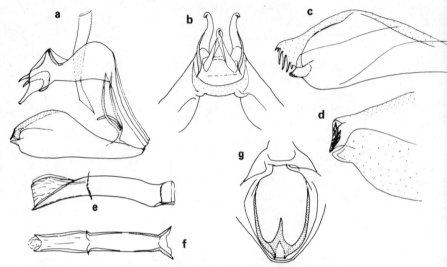

172. *Plebejus argus hypochionus,* S Spain: **a,** genitalia; **b,** labides and falces; **c,** valve, apical teeth displayed; **d,** valve apex, teeth fold retracted; **e,** penis, side view; **f,** penis, dorsal view. C Pyrenees: **g,** furca within vinculum.

PLEBEJUS PYLAON   Fischer de Waldheim 1832   CN 19
FG p. 275; Pl. 54

Range. S Europe and widely through W Asia and S Russia to Iran.
Genitalia. Like *P. argus* but furca lacks central process; apex of valve rounded, without marginal teeth. Three European subspecies with similar genitalia.

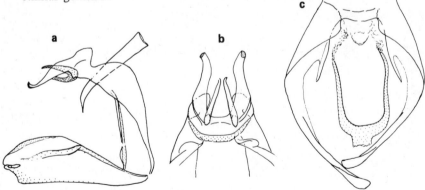

173. *Plebejus pylaon trappi,* Valais, Switzerland: **a,** genitalia; **b,** tegumen and falces; **c,** furca within vinculum.

P. p. sephirus Frivaldsky 1835.
Range. Occurs in Bulgaria and Greece.

P. p. trappi Verity 1927.
Range. Occurs very locally in S Switzerland.

P. p. hespericus Rambur 1839.
Range. Occurs in C and S Spain; male coloration varies in different colonies.
Genitalia. Indistinguishable in all. Correct grade of these different phenotypes uncertain, considered specifically distinct by some authors.
Reference. Agenjo 1967.

PLEBEJUS MARTINI Allard 1867 CN unknown FG p. 274; Pl. 55
Genitalia. Like *P. p. sephirus*, valve apex rounded.
Range. Morocco and Algeria, not recorded from Tunisia.

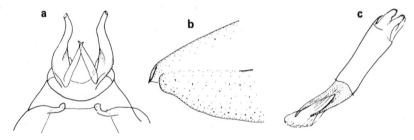

174. *Plebejus martini,* Algeria: **a,** tegumen and falces; **b,** valve apex; **c,** penis.

PLEBEJUS VOGELII Oberthur 1920
CN unknown FG p. 274; Pl. 55
Genitalia. Like *P. p. sephirus*; in dorsal view labides shorter, more sharply curved; apex of valve as in *L. p. sephirus*, rounded; penis slender, vesica partly exposed.
Range. Only known from Taghzeft Pass, Middle Atlas, Morocco.

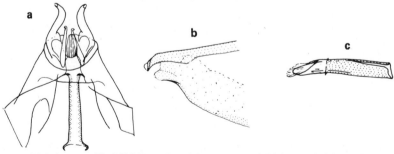

175. *Plebejus vogelii,* Middle Atlas, Morocco: **a,** labides and falces; **b,** valve apex; **c,** penis.

Genus **LYCAEIDES** Hübner 1823.   TS: *Papilio idas* L.
Fore-legs without tibial spines.
Genitalia. Like *Plebejus*; in side view labides shorter, wider, falces curved in horizontal plane, appearing below and almost parallel with lower margins of labides; in dorsal view labides tubular, bases wide, apices pointed, turned inwards, falces evenly curved; valve rather wide, apex pointed, terminal hook short, variable, flap with very small teeth; penis slender lateral zonal ribs prominent.

LYCAEIDES IDAS L.   CN 24   FG p. 277; Pl. 54, 55
Genitalia. In dorsal view proximal and distal parts of falces about equal in length.
Range. Very extensive; all continental Europe, Corsica, Sardinia, and eastwards across Asia to Altai Mts., probably to Ussuri and perhaps represented in N America. Six subspecies, five with similar genitalia.

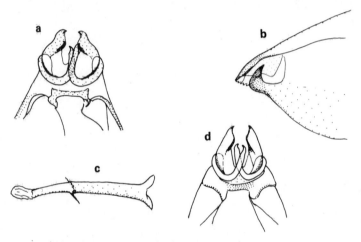

176. *Lycaeides idas idas,* N Italy: **a,** labides and falces; **b,** valve apex. *L. i. bellieri,* Corsica: **c,** penis. *L. i. laponicus,* Norway: **d,** labides and falces.

L. i. idas L. 1761.
Range. S Sweden. With minor local variation in many areas of Europe.

L. i. bellieri Oberthur 1910.
Range. Corsica and Sardinia.

L. i. calliopis Boisduval 1832.
Range. SE France, Alpes Maritimes etc. Associated with food plant *Polygonum.*

L. i. haefelfingeri Beuret 1935.
Range. Alps of Savoie and Switzerland, at high altitudes.

L. i. magnagraeca Verity 1925.
Range. S Balkans, (N Iran?). Perhaps specifically distinct.

L. i. lapponicus Gerhard 1853.
Genitalia. Labides more elongate (constant?).
Range. Fennoscandia, boreal regions.

LYCAEIDES ARGYROGNOMON   Bergsträsser 1779   CN 24
FG p. 279; Pl. 54

Genitalia. Like *L. idas*; in dorsal view falces longer, almost reaching apices of the slightly stouter labides.
Range. From France in local colonies across S and C Europe and Asia to the Amur, represented in N America by *L. scudderi* Edwards.

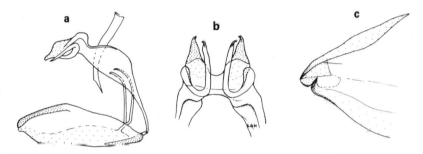

177. *Lycaeides argyrognomon,* N Italy: **a,** genitalia; **b,** labides and falces; **c,** valve apex.

Note. The involved nomenclature of this and of related species *L. idas* and *Plebejus argus* was finally settled by the I.C.Z.N. in their Opinion dated 1954, No. 269, wherein figure 23 on Plate 8 in the paper by Reverdin & Chapman was specified as illustrating the genitalia of *L. argyrognomon* Bergsträsser; figure 1 on Plate 20 in Tutt, British Lepidoptera vol. 10 was specified as illustrating the genitalia of *Plebejus argus*; and figure 7, Plate 3 in Oberthur, Lep. Comp. vol. 14 was specified as illustrating the genitalia of *Lycaeides idas* L.

References. Reverdin & Chapman 1917.

Genus **ARICIA** Reichenbach 1817   TS: *Papilio agestis* D. & S.
Unh pd spot in s6 displaced basally causing a gap in the series.
Genitalia. In side view dorsal structures large; in dorsal view labides with narrow medial expansions, falces small; valve narrow, apical hook prominent; penis distinctive, gently curved, tapering to pointed apex, zonal rib prominent.

143

ARICIA AGESTIS D. & S.   CN 24   FG p. 281; Pl. 55
Androconial scales absent. Two subspecies, genitalia differing slightly.

A. a. agestis D. & S. 1775.
Genitalia. In dorsal view falces about one-third the length of labides.
Range. Widely distributed in Europe from Pyrenees northwards and east-
wards, including S England, Denmark, S Norway and S Sweden and in
Mediterranean islands excepting Balearic islands. In Asia range extends
across Turkey and Lebanon to Iran.

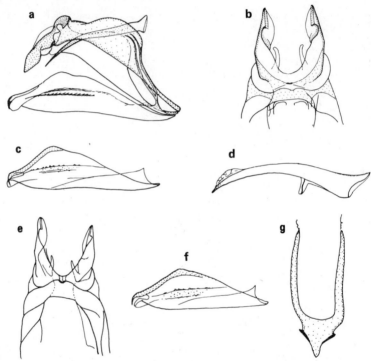

178. *Aricia agestis agestis,* Valais, Switzerland: **a,** genitalia; **b,** labides and
falces; **c,** valve; **d,** penis with zonal rib. *A. a. cramera,* S Spain: **e,** labides and
falces; **f,** valve. Morocco: **g,** furca.

A. a. cramera Eschscholtz 1821.   FG p. 283; Pl. 55
Genitalia. Like *A. a. agestis,* but falx shorter and smaller, about quarter
the length of labides.
Range. Canary Islands, N Africa, Portugal, Spain northwards to river
Ebro and in Balearic Isl. The two subspecies are probably indistinguishable by external characters and it is not known whether their distributions
overlap. In both, the series of orange submarginal spots ups is almost or
quite complete on each wing. The known distributions suggest that *A. a.*

cramera is replaced by *A. a. agestis* from the Pyrenees northwards, in a pattern that recalls *M. j. hispulla* and *M. j. jurtina.*

ARICIA ARTAXERXES F. CN unknown FG p. 282; Pl. 55
Androconial scales absent. The white discal spot upf in *A. a. artaxerxes* is due to a recessive gene established locally in the Scottish Highlands, which occurs occasionally far more widely (Jarvis 1962). The name has priority and is therefore the valid name of the complex which includes the widely distributed *A. a. allous* Geyer, probably also *A. a. montensis* Verity, with *A. a. artaxerxes* F. as nominate subspecies.
Genitalia. Like *A. agestis* D. & S., indistinguishable.
Range. Mountains of N Africa and Europe and at lower altitudes in northern localities to 70°N in Fennoscandia, further across Russia to the Altai Mts., but eastern distribution not well defined. Four subspecies, genitalia slightly variable.

A. a. artaxerxes F. 1793.
Range. Occurs with constant characters only in Scotland, occasional in some colonies of *A. a. inhonora* in N England.

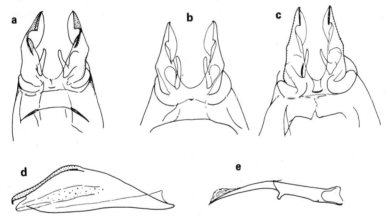

179. *Aricia artaxerxes artaxerxes,* Scotland: **a,** labides and falces. *A. a. allous,* Switzerland: **b,** labides and falces. *A. a. montensis,* S Spain: **c,** labides and falces; **d,** valve; **e,** penis.

A. a. inhonora Jachontov 1909.
Similar to above without white discal spot upf.
Range. Fennoscandia, N England, E Russia etc., subspecific name perhaps inappropriate.

A. a. allous Geyer 1837. CN 23
Range. Widely distributed at subalpine levels in mountains of C Spain, Pyrenees, Alps and Balkans to Greece.

A. a. montensis Verity 1928.

Genitalia. Labides relatively longer when compared with *A. a. allous.*

Range. N Africa, S Spain, less frequent in C Spain where large size is less constant, rather rarely in SW Alps; seen also from Balkans, Denmark (Tornby) and Poland. In some series the character of long labides is inconstant, occurring among other specimens with features closer to *A. a. allous.* As a character 'long' labides is a matter of degree and consequently often equivocal. The precise taxonomic rank of *A. a. montensis* remains uncertain. In Spain and in the SW Alps the form appears to be an extreme phase of a clinal series with *A. a. allous.*

Note 1. Forms of the *allous-montensis* series have not been seen from W Asia although in Lebanon, Turkey, and in Iran and Kurdistan *A. agestis* is a common mountain butterfly occurring up to 2,500m.

Note 2. *A. agestis* D & S. and *A. artaxerxes* F. are considered specifically distinct but identification may be difficult since the genitalia do not show constant differences and the wing markings are variable. The matter has been investigated by Jarvis and Hoegh-Guldberg in laborious experiments, cross-breeding *A. agestis* from S England with *A. artaxerxes* forms from Denmark and N England. Since it is not possible to carry young larvae through their normal winter hibernation, the experiments have to be carried out under special conditions, using constant artificial light and heat to suppress hibernation, when development is continuous with emergence of imagines in late autumn or winter. In spite of difficulties, a cross of *artaxerxes* ♂ (Durham) with *agestis* ♀ (Winchester) was maintained for two generations (i.e. F_1 and F_2 both raised successfully.) Another cross between *agestis* ♂ (Winchester) × *artaxerxes* ♀ (Danish) was successful in F_1 but there was high pupal mortality in F_2, due perhaps to severe weather conditions with frost which interfered with maintenance of correct temperature. Many other breeding results are recorded.

In summarising results, Jarvis states that British *A. a. artaxerxes* cross successfully with Danish specimens, but crossed with *A. agestis* from S England results were less satisfactory, usually with high mortality and other features suggesting genetic imbalance in F_2, if not also in F_1. Examination of the very complete reports of these experiments suggests that close relationship exists between *A. artaxerxes* and *A. agestis.* This is especially true in Britain where crossings produced viable families to F_2, in spite of the unnatural conditions of the experiment. The situation in other parts of Europe has not been examined.

References. Jarvis 1962 (1963), 1966. Hoegh-Guldberg 1961, 1966, 1968. Beuret 1960. Hoegh-Guldberg & Jarvis 1969. Lorković & Sijarić 1967. Kaaber & Hoegh-Guldberg 1961.

ARICIA MORRONENSIS Ribbe 1910   CN unknown

                                                  FG p. 284; Pl. 55

Androconial scales absent; ups brown.

Genitalia. Very small; in dorsal view labides wider than those of *A. agestis,*

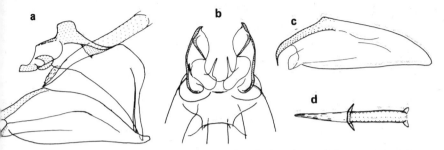

180. *Aricia morronensis,* S Spain: **a,** genitalia; **b,** labides and falces; **c,** valve; **d,** penis.

falces slender, short, straight; penis as in *A. agestis,* zonal rib present.
Range. A mountain species confined to Spain south of the Pyrenees.

ARICIA ANTEROS   Freyer 1839   CN 23   FG p. 285; Pl. 55
Androconial scales present; ups blue.
Genitalia. In side view labides horizontal, medial expansions prominent below the apices; in dorsal view labides short, pointed, falces straight, short; penis as in *A. agestis* but zonal membrane weakly chitinised.
Range. S Balkans, Turkey, Lebanon to N Iran.
Beuret has proposed a new genus *Ultraricia* 1959 for this species on account of the presence of androconial scales, blue ups, and genitalia characters. It does not appear to the writer that generic distinction is necessary.

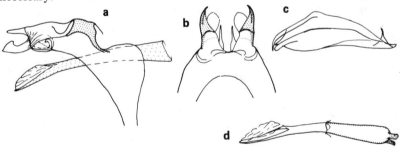

181. *Aricia anteros,* Greece: **a,** dorsal structures and penis; **b,** labides and falces; **c,** valve; **d,** penis.

Genus **PSEUDOARICIA** Beuret 1959
   TS: *Polyommatus nicias* Meigen
Unh pd spot in s6 not displaced.
Androconial scales present; ♂ ups blue.
Genitalia. In side view labides narrow, horizontal; in dorsal view labides very elongate, narrow, falces very small; penis as in *A. agestis,* zonal rib prominent.

PSEUDOARICIA NICIAS Meigen 1830   CN 23 FG p. 285; Pl. 55
Genitalia. Described above.
Range. E Pyrenees, W Alps, Finland and eastwards to Russia and Altai
Mts., widely distributed but always local.

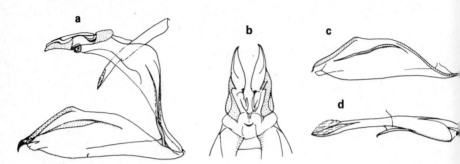

182. *Pseudoaricia nicias,* Hautes Alpes, S France: **a,** genitalia; **b,** labides and
falces; **c,** valve; **d,** penis.

Genus **EUMEDONIA** Forster 1938   TS: *Papilio eumedon* Esper
Closely related to *Agriades* and to *Aricia*; unh pd spots in regular series.
Androconial scales absent.
Genitalia. See *E. eumedon.*

EUMEDONIA EUMEDON Esper 1780   CN 24 FG p. 281; Pl. 56
Genitalia. In side view labides short, falces well developed with apices
appearing behind labides; dorsum of vinculum strongly humped; in

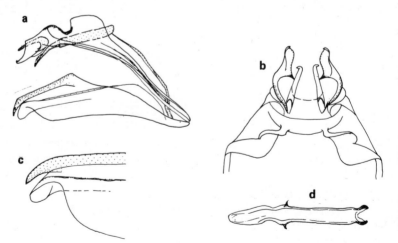

183. *Eumedonia eumedon,* Engadin, Switzerland: **a,** genitalia; **b,** labides and
falces; **c,** valve apex; **d,** penis.

dorsal view labides tubular, lacking lamellar expansions, slightly sinuous, apices pointed and turned inwards; falces long, slender, straight; penis small, tapering as in *Aricia,* zonal ribs well developed.

Range. Widespread in Europe including Sicily and Balkans and across Asia Minor to Amurland. Absent from Mediterranean islands except Sicily, C and S Spain, Portugal and Britain.

Genus **VACCINIINA** Tutt 1909   TS: *Papilio optilete* Knoch
The few known species are small butterflies, ♂ ups violet blue, unmarked; ♀ brown or with blue basal areas upf. The species have an extensive distribution across the boreal and mountainous regions of Europe, Asia and N America where the food plant *Vaccinium* grows.

VACCINIINA OPTILETE   Knoch 1781   CN 24 FG p. 279; Pl. 55
Genitalia. In side view dorsal structures small, labides short, falces curved vertically and protruding behind the labides; terminal costal hook of valve stout with blunt apex; penis slender, apex angled downwards; in dorsal view labides short, wide and evenly curved, apices only slightly spatulate; falces slender, long, extending to apices of labides.
Range. Arctic and sub-arctic regions of Europe and Asia and on most of the higher mountains in Europe and in C Asia. Widely distributed in N America in mountainous districts of Yukon and Alaska (*Lycaena yukona* Holland).

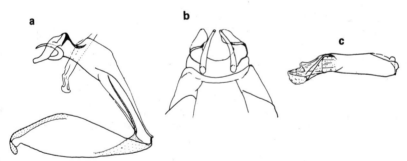

184. *Vacciniina optilete,* Valais, Switzerland: **a,** genitalia; **b,** labides and falces; **c,** penis.

Genus **ALBULINA** Tutt 1909   TS: *Papilio orbitulus* de Prunner
Unh ground-colour pale grey marked with white spots, submarginal series absent.
Genitalia. In side view falces curved in vertical plane, short with wide base, labides short; in dorsal view labides wide, spatulate, falces almost straight; penis straight, rather short.

ALBULINA ORBITULUS de Prunner 1798   CN 23

FG p. 286; Pl. 55

Genitalia. Described on p. 149

Range. C Europe from Basses Alpes to Gr. Glockner, flying at high altitudes. Norway, only in southern mountains. Altai Mts. and Himalaya Mts. to Tibet, as subspecies or closely related species.

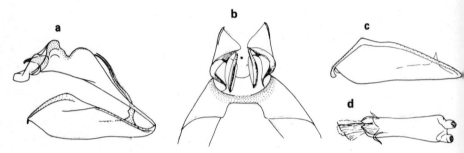

185. *Albulina orbitulus,* Switzerland: **a,** genitalia, penis removed; **b,** labides and falces; **c,** valve; **d,** penis.

Genus **AGRIADES** Hübner 1822   TS: *Papilio glandon* de Prunner Small butterflies, unh with irregular markings and white spots with or without black pupils, pd series displaced distally or fused with marginal markings and usually with wide space between spots in s5 and s6.
Genitalia. In dorsal view labides tubular, apices blunt, turned outwards; in side view falces vertical, apices protruding behind labides.

AGRIADES GLANDON   de Prunner CN 24   FG p. 286; Pl.56

Genitalia. Like *P. argus*; in side view labides short, apices slightly up-turned; valve with long apical hook; penis short, stout, with membranous apical extension; furca straight or nearly so. Three subspecies defined by wing-markings, all with similar genitalia.

A. g. glandon de Prunner 1798.
Range. Pyrenees and Alps, flying at high altitudes.

A. g. zullichi Hemming 1933.
Range. Confined to Sierra Nevada, flying at 3,000m or over.

A. g. aquilo Boisduval 1832.
Range. Norway, not south of 66°N. Closely related subspecies or species occur in E Asia and in N America.
Early stages. A. g. glandon, larval food plants Primulaceae (blossoms). *A. g. aquilo,* larval food plant *Astragalus alpinus.*

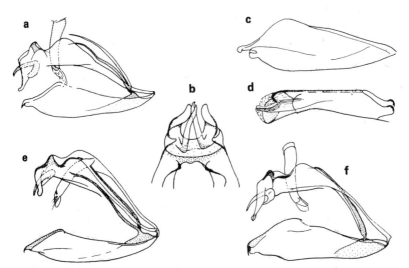

186. *Agriades glandon glandon*, Switzerland: **a,** genitalia; **b,** labides and falces; **c,** valve; **d,** penis. *A. g. zullichi*, Sierra Nevada, S Spain: **e,** genitalia. *A. g. aquilo*, arctic Norway; **f,** genitalia.

Note. A. g. aquilo was described by Boisduval with the localities North Cape, Siberia, Altai Mts. and Labrador. Staudinger 1871 includes the name in his catalogue with the single locality Labrador, without mentioning the other localities referred to by Boisduval. The first conventional specification of the type locality so far identified appears in Aurivillius 1888, in which *L. aquilo* is recorded as a species from Arctic Europe, and is compared with *L. orbitulus* (i.e. *glandon* Prunn.) from the Alps and *L. franklinii* from Labrador. The name is used here for the arctic European butterfly for this reason.
References. Staudinger 1871. Aurivillius 1888.

AGRIADES PYRENAICUS   Boisduval   CN unknown
FG p. 290; Pl. 56

♂ ups silver-blue, upf outer marginal border narrow.
Genitalia. Like *A. glandon*, in side view labides slightly more slender, furca oblique, rami angled at junction of middle and upper thirds; penis as in *A. glandon*. Three subspecies with similar genitalia.

A. p. pyrenaicus Boisduval 1840.
Range. Confined to Hautes Pyrénées.
Early stages. Larval food plant *Androsace villosa* (Pyrenees).

A. p. asturiensis Oberthur 1910.
♂ upf veins lined dark.
Range. Only known from Picos de Europa, Cantabrian Mts., N Spain.

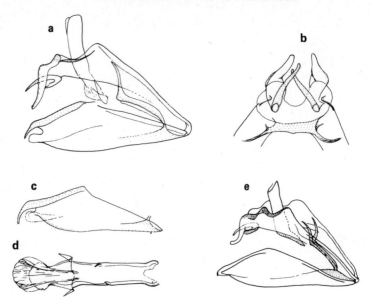

187. *Agriades pyrenaicus pyrenaicus,* Hautes Pyrénées: **a,** genitalia; **b,** labides and falces; **c,** valve; **d,** penis. *A. p. dardanus,* Herzegowina: **e,** genitalia.

A. p. dardanus Freyer 1844.
Smaller, uns black markings reduced.
Range. Yugoslavia, very local, known only from a few high mountains in Herzegowina (Cvrstnića etc.).

Genus **CYANIRIS** Dalman 1816   TS: *Papilio semiargus* Rottemburg
Uns marginal markings vestigial or absent.
Genitalia. In side view labides slender, falces well developed, projecting beyond labides; penis short, straight, distal section very short but with membranous extension; the terminal dorsal process described by Chapman 1910(A) may be difficult to recognise.

CYANIRIS SEMIARGUS Rottemburg 1775   CN 24
FG p. 290; Pl. 55
Genitalia. Described above; in side view dorsal expansion of vinculum not prominent.
Range. Morocco and throughout temperate Europe eastwards to Mongolia. Absent from Britain (extinct ?), rare in NW Europe.

CYANIRIS ANTIOCHENA Lederer 1862   CN 24 FG p. 291; Pl. 55
Genitalia. Like *C. semiargus,* dorsal expansion of vinculum slightly wider.
Range. Distributed in Asia Minor, Lebanon, Iraq and S Greece.

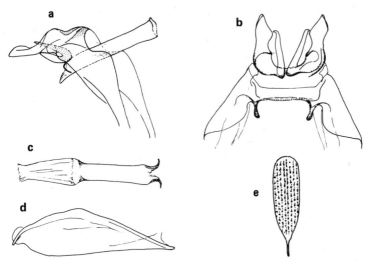

188. *Cyaniris semiargus,* Switzerland: **a,** dorsal structures; **b,** labides and falces; **c,** penis, dorsal view; **d,** valve; **e,** androconial scale.

C. a. helena Staudinger 1862.

Genitalia. Described on p. 152.

Range. Greece, Peloponnesus, Mt. Taygetos, Mt. Chelmos etc.

Reference. Tutt 1909.

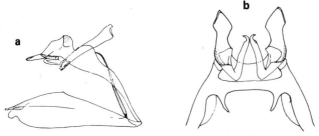

189. *Cyaniris antiochena helena,* S Greece: **a,** genitalia; **b,** labides and falces.

Genus **KRETANIA** Beuret 1959   TS: *Lycaena psylorita* Freyer

Small brown species, uns orange marginal lunules more or less developed; *Androconia* abundant. *Eyes* smooth.

Genitalia. In side view like *A. glandon*; labides short, tapering to upturned apices, falces slender, oblique; in dorsal view medial expansions of labides small; penis short, distal section very short, zonal membrane not chitinised.

KRETANIA PSYLORITA Freyer 1845   CN unknown
FG p. 280; Pl. 56
Genitalia. In dorsal view labides wide basally, apices pointed, turned inwards.
Range. Confined to Crete on Mt. Ida.

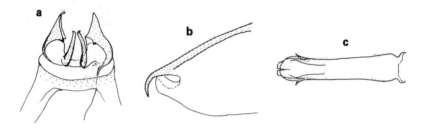

190. *Kretania psylorita,* Crete: **a,** labides and falces; **b,** valve apex; **c,** penis.

KRETANIA EURYPILOS Freyer 1852   CN 20 FG p. 280; Pl. 13
Genitalia. Like *K. psylorita* in dorsal view labides longer and narrower, falces shorter; penis as in *K. psylorita.*
Range. Widely distributed in W Asia; reported from Greece (Peloponnesus).

Reference. Rebel 1902.

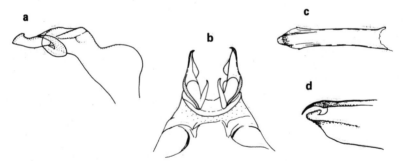

191. *Kretania eurypilos,* N Turkey: **a,** dorsal structures; **b,** tegumen and falces; **c,** penis; **d,** valve apex.

The following genera *Agrodiaetus, Plebicula* and *Lysandra* are fairly well defined by markings, but anatomical characters are so uniform that it is not possible to confirm these groups by genitalia. In the Lycaenidae acceptable generic groups are determined by anatomical features, especially of the genitalia, and by this standard the following series forms a single large genus (*Agrodiaetus*), but division is required for convenience. Forster has pointed out (1938) the difficulties, but he did accept *Lysandra* with generic status. At the same time it should be recognised that these genera, *Lysandra* and *Plebicula*, based entirely upon wing markings, do not conform with other Lycaenid genera on this account. They do not qualify for full generic rank and are better graded as subgenera.

Genus **AGRODIAETUS** Hübner 1822   TS: *Papilio damon* D & S.
Description. Ups marginal markings absent in males, often absent or poorly defined in females; unf lacking basal cell spot; unh with white stripe along v4 (rarely absent); fringes white. *Legs* anterior tibial spines present on front and middle legs in both sexes. *Eyes* hairy.
Genitalia. In side view dorsal structures massive, falces well developed, usually projecting behind labides, dorsal expansion of vinculum prominent; penis small with membranous apical expansion; in dorsal view labides spatulate with medial expansions, apices pointed and curved inwards, falces about half the length of labides; apex of penis expanded laterally to appear round or oval ('bulbous'). CN usually under 100.

The numerous species, which are distributed throughout the Mediterranean subregion, include forms almost or quite indistinguishable by external characters or genitalia, but with differences in chromosomal numbers (karyotype) in geographically localised races, which are accepted here with specific rank. These situations have been studied especially by H. de Lesse.

References. de Lesse 1960(A) etc. Forster 1956–60, 1961.

AGRODIAETUS DAMON D. & S. 1775   CN 45 FG p. 294; Pl. 57
Genitalia. Described above.
Range. From C Spain locally through temperate Europe to the Caucasus, Altai and Changai Mts. and Thian Shan.

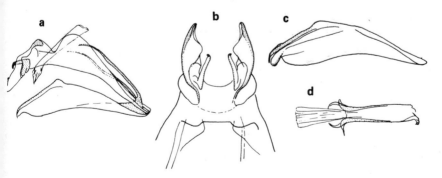

192. *Agrodiaetus damon*, Engadin, Switzerland: **a,** genitalia; **b,** labides and falces; **c,** valve; **d,** penis, dorsal view.

AGRODIAETUS DOLUS   Hübner   CN 123–125 FG p. 294; Pl. 57
Genitalia. Like *A. damon.*
Range. S France and C Italy in scattered colonies. Represented in Asia by closely related species. Two subspecies with similar genitalia.

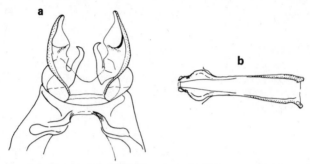

193. *Agrodiaetus dolus,* SE France: **a,** labides and falces; **b,** penis.

A. d. dolus Hübner 1823.
Ups gc pale blue.
Range. S France and NE Spain (Catalonia).

A. d. virgilius Oberthur 1910.
Ups gc almost white, slightly variable in tone.
Range. Peninsular Italy, very local.

Reference. de Lesse 1966.

AGRODIAETUS AINSAE   Forster 1961   CN 108
FG p. 295; no figure
Genitalia. Like *A. damon.*
Range. NE Spain near Jaca, Ainsa etc.

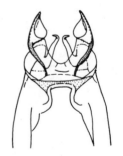

194. *Agrodiaetus ainsae,* NE Spain: labides and falces.

195. *Agrodiaetus pseudovirgilius,* Burgos, N Spain: labides and falces.

AGRODIAETUS PSEUDOVIRGILIUS de Lesse   CN 108
Not included in FG

Genitalia. Like *A. damon.*
Range. N Spain near Burgos. Described as a subspecies of *A. dolus,* but correct taxonomic rank uncertain.

AGRODIAETUS RIPARTII   Freyer 1830   CN 90
FG p. 296; Pl. 57

Upf with furry sex-brands.
Genitalia. Like *A. damon*
Range. SE France, N Italy at Ulzio in Piedmont, Balkans and Asia Minor.

References. de Lesse 1960B. 1961B.

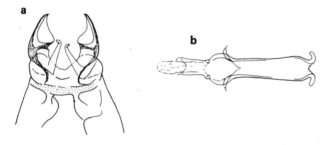

196. *Agrodiaetus ripartii,* Piedmont, N Italy: **a,** labides and falces; **b,** penis.

AGRODIAETUS ADMETUS   Esper 1785   CN 80 FG p. 295; Pl. 57
Upf with furry sex-brand.
Genitalia. Like *A. damon.*
Range. SE Europe and Asia Minor.

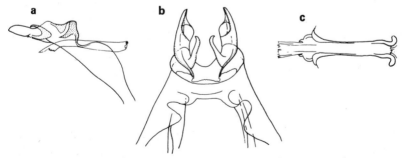

197. *Agrodiaetus admetus,* Yugoslav Macedonia: **a,** dorsal structures; **b,** labides and falces; **c,** penis.

AGRODIAETUS FABRESSEI Oberthur 1910   CN 90

FG p. 296; no figure

Distinguished from *A. admetus* by chromosome number and karyotype.
Genitalia. Like *A. damon*, labides slightly more elongated.
Range. N and C Spain.

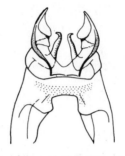

198. *Agrodiaetus fabressei,* C Spain: labides and falces.

AGRODIAETUS AMANDA Schneider 1792   CN 22–24

FG p. 302; Pl. 56

Genitalia. Like *A. damon* but in side view labides appear longer and in
dorsal view wider and more sharply curved; penis large.
Range. Widely distributed from Morocco and S Spain to Sweden and
eastwards to S Russia, Lebanon, Iran.

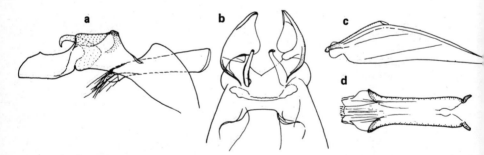

199. *Agrodiaetus amanda,* Switzerland: **a,** dorsal structures; **b,** labides and
falces; **c,** valve; **d,** penis.

AGRODIAETUS COELESTINA Eversmann 1843   CN unknown

FG not included

Genitalia. Like *A. damon.*
Range. Armenia, S Russia, Asia Minor and Greece (Peloponnesus).

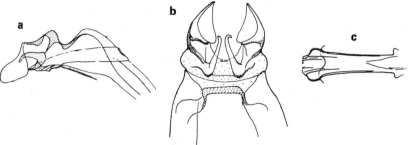

200. *Agrodiaetus coelestina,* S Greece: **a,** dorsal structures; **b,** labides and falces; **c,** penis.

AGRODIAETUS THERSITES Cantener 1834 CN 24
FG p. 302; Pl. 56

Genitalia. Like *A. damon*, in dorsal view labides slightly narrower.
Range. Morocco and widely distributed across S Europe and W Asia to Iran.

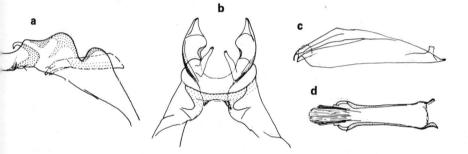

201. *Agrodiaetus thersites,* C Italy: **a,** dorsal structures; **b,** labides and falces; **c,** valve; **d,** penis.

AGRODIAETUS ESCHERI Hübner CN 23 FG p. 297; Pl. 57
Two subspecies with similar genitalia. Occurs in local colonies from Morocco across S Europe including Balkans. Recorded from Asia Minor.

A. e. escheri Hübner 1823.
♂ ups bright blue, upf narrow marginal line.
Genitalia. Like *A. damon*, labides slightly shorter and wider.
Range. Morocco, SW Europe, N and C Italy.

A. e. dalmatica Speyer 1882.
♂ ups pale blue, upf black marginal border wider.
Range. Balkans, including Dalmatia and Greece.

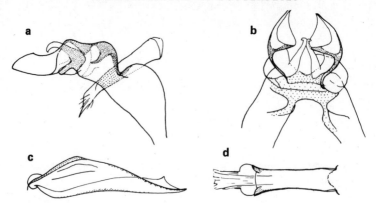

202. *Agrodiaetus escheri,* Switzerland: **a,** dorsal structures; **b,** labides and falces; **c,** valve; **d,** penis.

Genus **PLEBICULA** Higgins 1969   TS: *Papilio dorylas* D. & S.
Ups marginal markings absent in ♂, often present in ♀; unf basal cell-spot absent; unh lacking white stripe along v4 but often with white pd mark in this position; fringes white.
Genitalia. Like *Agrodiaetus.* CN 134–223
The genus now restricted as suggested by the late H. de Lesse.

PLEBICULA DORYLAS   D. & S. 1775   CN 149–151
FG p. 298; Pl. 56
Genitalia. Like *A. damon.*
Range. S and C Europe eastwards to Asia Minor.

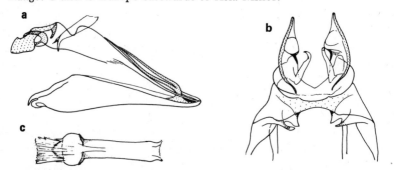

203. *Plebicula dorylas,* Switzerland: **a,** genitalia; **b,** labides and falces; **c,** penis. See also figures p. 96.

PLEBICULA GOLGUS   Hübner 1813   CN 134 FG p. 298; Pl. 56
Genitalia. Like *A. damon,* labides short.
Range. Only known at high altitudes on Sierra Nevada, S Spain.

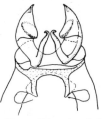

204. *Plebicula golgus,* Sierra Nevada, S Spain: labides and falces.

PLEBICULA NIVESCENS Keferstein 1851   CN 190–191
FG p. 299; Pl. 56

Genitalia. Like *A. damon.*
Range. Spain and northwards to Pyrenees (Aulus).

205. *Plebicula nivescens,* Cuenca, C Spain: labides and falces.

PLEBICULA ATLANTICA Elwes 1905   CN 223 FG p. 299; Pl. 56
Genitalia. Like *A. damon.*
Range. Morocco, in Middle and High Atlas.

Reference. de Lesse 1959B.

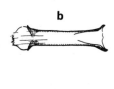

206. *Plebicula atlantica,* High Atlas, Morocco: **a,** labides and falces; **b,** penis.

Genus **LYSANDRA** Hemming 1933   TS: *Papilio coridon* Poda
Ups submarginal markings usually present in ♂ and ♀, but absent in ♂

bellargus; unf basal cell-spot present; unh lacking white stripe on v4 but often with white pd mark; fringes white chequered black. *Genitalia* like *Agrodiaetus* Hübner.

LYSANDRA CORIDON Poda 1761 CN 87–92

FG p. 306; Pl. 57

Genitalia. Labides rather elongate, similar to *P. dorylas.*
Range. Restricted to temperate Europe, locally common from C Spain to Greece. Occurs in several colour-forms, see Note below.

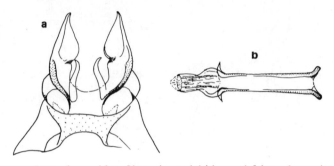

207. *Lysandra coridon*, Slovenia: **a,** labides and falces; **b,** penis.

Note on distribution of *L. coridon* and its named forms.
A close study of the complicated taxonomic situations presented by this species has been made by de Lesse, and his conclusions are accepted in this book. Minor geographical variation appears in many localities, and in Spain local colour forms occur which must rank as major subspecies. These are the slightly violet-tinted *L. c. caelestissima* Verity of C Spain with CN 87, and the bright blue *L. c. asturiensis* Sagarra and related races with CN 87–88, rather widely distributed northwards and extending into the Cantabrian Mts., but only south of the Pyrenees. In the Pyrenees and throughout W Europe including Britain, the ground-colour is paler blue-grey and the CN constant at 88, but CN 87 only in *L. c. sibyllina* Verity restricted to C Italy and Florence. Further east in the Alto Adige de Lesse found colonies with CN 89. In Slavonia and in other areas of N Yugoslavia the CN rises to 90, with CN in Rumania 91 and in Bulgaria 92. There is cohabitation in C and N Spain with *L. albicans* in its various forms, and in N Spain also with *L. hispana* H.-S. It is noteworthy that external characters show definable subspecific variation in the western races, which does not correspond with the changes in chromosome counts. It has been found that these variants are constant within a given colony, so that the absence of cohabitation is a striking feature. This complicated picture is shown best on the accompanying map which the late Monsieur de Lesse kindly allowed the author to reproduce in this book. The genitalia do not show subspecific characters.

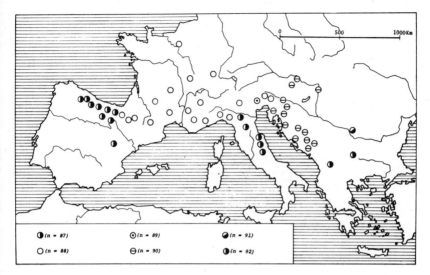

Map showing geographical variation in chromosome numbers in *Lysandra coridon*, drawn by the late H. de Lesse.

References. de Lesse 1960(A), 1970(A). 1969. Agenjo 1956.

LYSANDRA HISPANA Herrich-Schäffer 1852   CN 84
FG p. 307; Pl. 57

This double-brooded species resembles *L. coridon* very closely.
Genitalia. Like *A. damon* and *L. coridon*.
Range. NE Spain and SE France and eastwards to Florence, widely distributed especially in coastal districts.

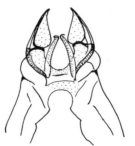

208. *Lysandra hispana*, S France: labides and falces.

LYSANDRA ALBICANS Herrich-Schäffer 1851   CN 82
FG p. 307; Pl. 13, 57

Genitalia. Like *A. damon* and *L. coridon*.
Range. Morocco (very local) and Spain.

163

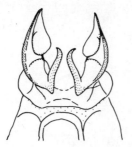

209. *Lysandra albicans,*
S Spain: labides and falces.

LYSANDRA BELLARGUS   Rottemburg 1775   CN 45

FG p. 309; Pl. 57

Genitalia. Like *A. damon* and *P. coridon,* but in dorsal view labides more slender, medial expansions reduced.
Range. S and C Europe and eastwards across Russia to Iraq and Iran. Absent from Ireland, Mediterranean islands and S Greece (Peloponessus).

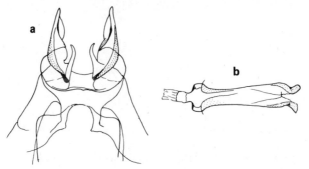

210. *Lysandra bellargus,* Pyrenees: **a,** labides and falces; **b,** penis.

LYSANDRA PUNCTIFERA   Oberthur 1876   CN 24

FG p. 309; Pl. 57

Genitalia. Like *A. damon* and *L. bellargus,* labides slender.
Range. Confined to Morocco and Algeria.

211. *Lysandra punctifera,* Morocco: **a,** labides and falces; **b,** penis.

Genus **MELEAGERIA** Sagarra 1925   TS: *Papilio daphnis* D. & S.
Outer margin of hw distinctly scalloped near anal angle.
Genitalia. Like *Agrodiaetus*, apical lateral expansions of penis little
developed.

MELEAGERIA DAPHNIS D. & S. 1775   CN 23–24
FG p. 303; Pl. 56, 57
Genitalia. Described above.
Range. S France and eastwards in localised colonies across S Europe, with
closely related subspecies and species in Asia Minor, Lebanon and Iran.

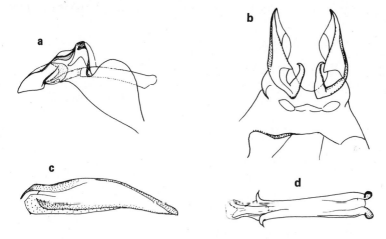

212. *Meleageria daphnis*, S France: **a,** dorsal structures; **b,** labides and falces;
c, valve; **d,** penis.

Genus **POLYOMMATUS** Kluk 1801   TS: *Papilio icarus* Rottemburg
Uns usual wing markings complete including basal, postdiscal, submarginal and marginal series of spots. *Legs* tibial anterior spine present
on front and middle legs.
Genitalia. In dorsal view like *Agrodiaetus* but penis straight, lacking
apical lateral expansions, with membranous extension and conical apical
cap.

POLYOMMATUS ICARUS Rottemburg 1775   CN 23
FG p. 310; Pl. 4, 55
Genitalia. Described above.
Range. Canary Islands, N Africa, Europe including Mediterranean islands,
and across Asia to Pacific coast.

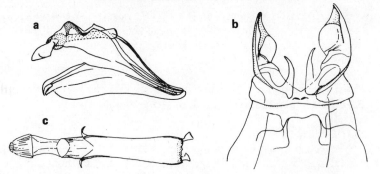

213. *Polyommatus icarus*, Bavaria: **a,** genitalia; **b,** labides and falces; **c,** penis.

POLYOMMATUS EROIDES   Frivaldsky 1835   CN 23
FG p. 310; Pl. 56

Genitalia. Like *L. icarus*; in dorsal view labides shorter, wider, more regularly curved, falces slightly shorter; penis as in *P. icarus*.
Range. Poland, Czechoslovakia, Bulgaria. Reported from Asia Minor.

214. *Polyommatus eroides*, Bulgaria: **a,** labides and falces; **b,** penis.

POLYOMMATUS EROS   Ochsenheimer 1808   CN 23
FG p. 311; Pl. 56

Genitalia. Like *L. icarus*, in dorsal view labides slightly shorter, narrower, less curved than in *L. eroides*.
Range. Pyrenees, Alps, Balkan Mts. including Greece, also in C Asia.

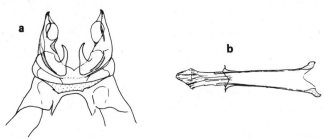

215. *Polyommatus eros*, Switzerland: **a,** labides and falces; **b,** penis.

Family **RIODINIDAE** Grote 1895

Closely related to Lycaenidae but differing in three important respects.
1. Male fore-leg greatly reduced, useless for walking.
2. A precostal vein is present in hw.
3. Male genitalia have a well developed uncus.
This extensive family is greatly developed in the American tropics. In the Old World it is represented by a few genera in tropical Asia and Africa, and in Europe by a single species of the genus *Hamearis*.

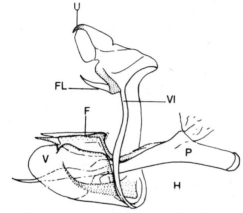

216. RIODINIDAE, male genitalia. (*Hamearis lucina*)

Genus **HAMEARIS** Hübner 1818   TS: *Papilio lucina* L.

Description. The single European species is a small butterfly, wing-margins entire, apex of fw pointed. *Eyes* hairy. *Palpi* small, slender, porrect. *Antennae* slender, club abrupt, pyriform. *Legs* ♂ foreleg with single short tarsal segment lacking claw; ♀ fore-leg small but with five tarsal segments and terminal claws; middle and hind-legs normal in both sexes, claws with pulvilli and paronychia. Androconial scales absent. *Venation.* Fw with 12 veins, v6 from apex of cell with stalk of v7–9, internal vein present; hw precostal vein directed distad; cell closed in both wings.

Genitalia. See *H. lucina.*

Early stages. Ovum subconical, surface smooth. Larva onisciform, pilose. Pupa short, abdominal segments rigid, usually suspended, fixed by cremaster to a silken pad and with a silken girdle; hibernation as pupa.

HAMEARIS LUCINA L. 1758   CN 29   FG p. 231; Pl. 14, 21

Genitalia. Uncus short, apex hooked, falces present as in Lycaenidae; valve short, apex rounded, harpe narrow, elongate; furca with dorsal and ventral plates attached to vinculum and embracing penis; penis almost three times as long as uncus+tegumen, apex pointed, caecum long; saccus absent.

Range. C Spain, S and C Europe including S England, S Sweden and eastwards to C Russia.

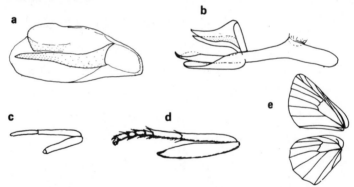

217. *Hameoris lucina,* S England: **a,** valve, showing harpe; **b,** penis and furca, composite drawing: **c,** ♂ fore-leg; **d,** ♀ fore-leg; **e,** wing venation.

Family **LIBYTHEIDAE** Boisduval 1840

Rather small butterflies related to the Nymphalidae, recognisable by the prominent tooth on the outer margin of fw and by the great length of the palpi. They are migrants, and although the number of species is not large, they have become established on every continent and on many remote islands. Their characters are those of the genus *Libythea*.

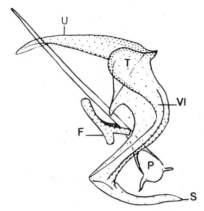

218. LIBYTHEIDAE, male genitalia. (*Libythea celtis*): side view showing uncus (U), vinculum (VI), furca (F), penis (P), saccus (S).

Genus **LIBYTHEA**   F. 1807   TS: *Papilio celtis* Laicharting
Description. Eyes smooth. *Palpi* half as long as abdomen, porrect, length of apical segment equal to that of basal+middle segments. *Antennae* less than half the length of fw, thickened gradually to blunt apex. *Legs* male fore-leg hairy, very small with single tarsal segment, useless for walking; ♀ fore-leg with claws, paronychia and pulvillus, five tarsal segments not well defined, heavily spined posteriorly. *Venation.* In fw v10 and v11 arise before end of cell, v6 from apex of cell, cell closed in both wings by vestigial veins.
Genitalia. See *L. celtis.*
Early stages. Ovum a tall oval with numerous fine ribs. Larva pilose. Pupa suspended. Imago flies in a single brood, hibernates as imago. Larval food plant *Celtis.*

LIBYTHEA CELTIS   Laicharting in Fuessli 1782   CN 31

FG p. 74; Pl. 22

Hw costa with marked dorsal bulge.

Genitalia. Uncus pointed, fused to tegumen; valve oval, terminating in a long sharply pointed apex; furca present; penis sinuous in lateral view, long and slender (slightly rotated in fig. 218).

Range. Algeria, Tunisia and S Europe and across C Asia to Japan.

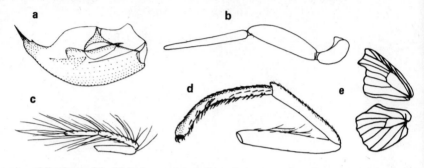

219. *Libythea celtis,* N Italy: **a,** valve; **b,** palpus; **c,** ♂ fore-leg; **d,** ♀ fore-leg; **e,** wing venation.

Family **NYMPHALIDAE** Swainson 1827

Description. In this extensive family most species are of medium or rather large size, often brightly coloured. *Eyes* smooth or hairy. *Palpi* very variable. *Antennae* usually strong, rigid, club always well defined. *Legs* ♂ fore-tarsus reduced to one to three segments, hairy; ♀ usually with five segments, four distal segments compressed and armed with strong spines; useless for walking in both sexes, middle and hindlegs normal, tibiae and tarsi armed with spines, tibiae with a single pair of spurs in both sexes; feet with pulvilli and paronychia. Among European species *androconial scales* occur only in the Argynnini, in the genus *Argynnis* and its close relatives. *Venation.* Fw with 12 veins, none swollen at the base; in either wing, cell open or closed, often by vestigial veins; fw upper dcv usually absent; hw precostal vein present.
Genitalia. Variable, valve often with harpe and complicated accessory processes.

Early stages. Ovum barrel-shaped. or cylindrical, flat-topped, with longitudinal ribs and reticulate. Larva usually with several complete rows of hairy tubercles or spines, but in *Apatura* and *Charaxes* smooth or granular, with horns on the head only. Pupa always suspended head-down by cremastral hooks without a silken girdle; except in *Apatura* and *Charaxes* it is often partly gilded.

Key to subfamilies of Nymphalidae

1 Saccus longer than valve **2**
   Saccus shorter than valve **3**

2 Furca very long, narrow, grooved . . . . Charaxinae
   Furca short, bilobed . . . . . . Apaturinae

3 Brachia present **4**
   Brachia absent **5**

4 Brachia very slender, descending . . . . Limenitidinae
   Brachia stout, parallel with uncus . . . Nymphalinae (part)

5 Hw outer margin evenly rounded **6**
   Hw outer margin angled at v4 . . . . . **7**

6 Uncus present . . . . Argynninae
   Uncus absent . . . . Melitaeinae

7 Harpe elongate . . . . . . Nymphalinae (part)
   Harpe small, triangular . . . . . . Araschniinae

Subfamily ARASCHNIINAE Grote 1897

The characters are those of the genus *Araschnia*.

Genus ARASCHNIA   Hübner 1818   TS: *Papilio levana* L.
Description. Small butterflies, fw angled at v6, hw with slight projection at v4. *Eyes* hairy. *Palpi* long, porrect, slightly hairy. *Antennae* straight, slender, club oval, abrupt. *Legs* ♂ fore-leg very small, hairy, with single long tarsal segment; ♀ fore-leg with four tarsal segments; in both sexes fore-legs lack claws, useless for walking. *Venation.* In fw basal veins slightly thickened; v10 arises from stalk of v7–9, v11 runs close to v12 with which it may fuse; fw cell closed; hw cell open.
Genitalia (*A. levana*). Fragile, uncus small, deeply bifid; valve narrow, without a harpe, apex slender, curved, costal process sharply incurved; furca short, transtilla well developed; saccus narrow; penis slender, gently curved, longer than valve.

ARASCHNIA LEVANA   L. 1758   CN 31   FG p. 89; Pl. 16
Genitalia. Described above.
Range. C and E Europe and eastwards through Asia to Korea and Japan. Absent from Mediterranean region.
Early stages. Ovum barrel-shaped with 13 feeble ribs and reticulate. Ova are laid 8–12 together, adhering end-to-end like a row of pearls, forming a short rigid rod fixed to a leaf of food-plant. Larval head with single pair of spines, thoracic and abdominal segments with seven rows of spines. Pupa with small dorsal tubercles but without cephalic prominences. The larvae feed gregariously on nettles (*Urtica*). Hibernation as pupa.

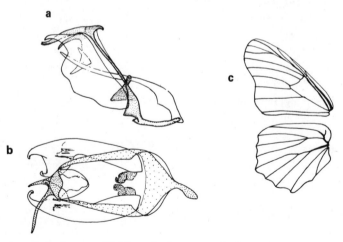

220. *Araschnia levana,* N Yugoslavia: **a,** genitalia, side view. Austria: **b,** genitalia, dorsal view; **c,** wing venation.

Subfamily NYMPHALINAE Swainson 1827

Description. Butterflies of medium or large size, wings broad, margins often dentate; sexes alike. *Eyes* hairy. *Palpi* long, porrect, terminal segment depressed. *Antennae* long, rigid, club narrow. *Legs* very hairy, especially ♂ fore-tarsus. *Venation.* Fw vio arises close to vii before apex of cell; cell closed in both wings.

Genitalia. Many unusual features; tegumen extends cephalad as a wide shelf; uncus small, with or without brachia; valve often fused to peduncle (or to vinculum) and cannot be detached without injury; arms of furca stout, prominent in side view, rising above vinculum in all genera; transtilla well defined; penis variable.

Early stages. Ovum barrel-shaped, reticulate and strongly ribbed. Larva bearing dorsal, lateral and sub-spiracular rows of branching spines. Pupa with twin cephalic prominences and dorsal tubercles. In Europe all species hibernate as imagines and reappear in spring when mating occurs and eggs are laid.

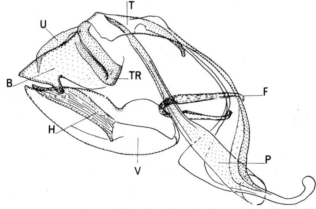

221. NYMPHALINAE, male genitalia (*Inachis io*). For explanation of lettering see p. 29.

Key to genera of Nymphalinae

1 Ups marked with peacock eyes	*Inachis*
Ups not so marked.	**2**
2 Brachia absent	*Nymphalis*
Brachia present	**3**
3 Brachia long and flexible	*Aglais*
Brachia firmly chitinised	**4**
4 Costal margin of valve with wide hiatus . . .	*Vanessa*
Costal margin of valve intact	*Polygonia*

Genus **NYMPHALIS**   Kluk 1802   TS: *Papilio polychloros* L.
Description. Large butterflies, wing margins irregular with projections on fw at veins 2 and 6, on hw at v4; bristles usually present on legs and body and base of fw. *Palpi* hairy and with long, dense bristles.
Genitalia. Uncus narrow, brachia not present, transtilla densely chitinised; valve wide with simple downturned apex, harpe long; saccus rather small; furca a strong bifid structure arising from the bases of the valves, and in side view visible above the vinculum; penis short, base massive, tapering rapidly to upturned pointed apex, ostium penis on dorsal surface.
Early stages. Larva black with paler markings, gregarious in silken nests, feeding upon forest trees.

NYMPHALIS POLYCHLOROS   L. 1758   CN 31 FG p. 84; Pl. 17
Genitalia. Described above; harpe about three-quarters the length of valve.
Range. From N Africa and W Europe across Russia and W Asia to the Himalaya Mts. Absent from boreal regions.

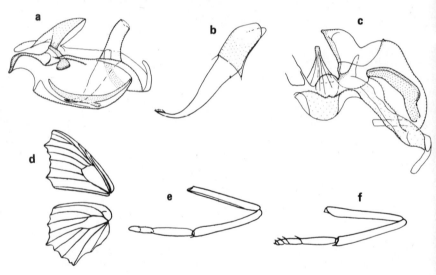

222. *Nymphalis polychloros,* N Italy: **a,** genitalia, side view; **b,** penis; **c,** genitalia spread, showing valve; **d,** wing venation; **e,** ♂ fore-leg, hair removed; **f,** ♀ fore-leg.

NYMPHALIS XANTHOMELAS   D. & S. 1775   CN 31
                                            FG p. 84; Pl. 17
Genitalia. Like *N. polychloros,* harpe wider, about half length of valve.
Range. From Austria across Europe and Asia to Himalaya Mts. and Japan.

223. *Nymphalis xanthomelas*, Iran: genitalia, penis removed.

NYMPHALIS VAUALBUM   D. & S. 1775   CN unknown
FG p. 85; Pl. 17

Genitalia. Like *N. polychloros*, terminal process of valve more elongate.
Range. From E Europe (rare) across temperate Asia and N America.

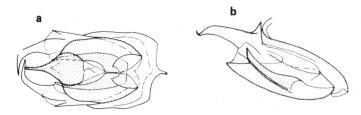

224. *Nymphalis vaualbum*, Hungary: **a,** genitalia, dorsal view; **b,** valve.

NYMPHALIS ANTIOPA   L. 1758   CN 30–31   FG p. 83; Pl. 17

Genitalia. Like *N. polychloros*, terminal process of valve slightly longer and more slender.
Range. Europe, except boreal regions, and across temperate Asia and N America. A rare migrant to Britain.

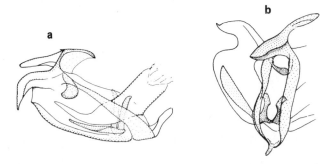

225. *Nymphalis antiopa*, N Italy: **a,** genitalia, side view; **b,** genitalia spread, penis and right valve omitted.

It is not easy to illustrate the rather complicated construction of the genitalia of the remaining species of Nymphalinae, all of which possess brachia and in which the vinculum is often incomplete. The valves cannot be detached without damage. The most instructive view of the parts is obtained by dividing the saccus, when the valves can be spread out flat to show the harpe, and the uncus and brachia can be seen clearly. Specimens prepared in this way must be mounted at once after dehydration in alcohol, when they will be sufficiently flexible to allow spreading without fracture. The preparation shows a lateral view of the valve with a dorsal view of the uncus and brachia.

Genus **INACHIS** Hübner 1818   TS: *Papilio io* L.
Resembles *Nymphalis* in habitus; bristles on palpi less coarse.
Genitalia. Uncus small, narrow, apex forked, brachia very massive; anterior shelf of tegumen wide; valve small, tapering, harpe short and stout; saccus slender, upturned, almost as long as valve, penis slender and sinuous.

INACHIS IO L. 1758   CN 31   FG p. 85; Pl. 17
Genitalia. Described above.
Range. Europe, excluding boreal regions, and across Asia to Japan.
Early stages. Egg barrel-shaped with eight strong ribs. Dorsal projections of pupa strongly developed. Larvae gregarious on nettles.

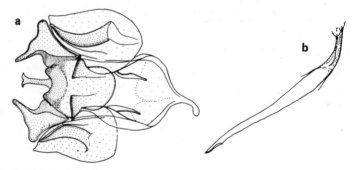

226. *Inachis io*, S England: **a,** genitalia spread showing small uncus and massive brachia; **b,** penis.

Genus **VANESSA**   F. 1807   TS: *Papilio atalanta* L.
Butterflies of medium or rather large size, brightly coloured above and with cryptic markings beneath. Wings and palpi without bristles. The genus is cosmopolitan.
Genitalia. Organs small, uncus small with short, densely chitinised brachia; valve wide, apex truncate, costal margin with deep hiatus, harpe long and slender; furca small; transtilla absent; saccus small; distal section of penis slender, tapering and curved slightly upwards.

Early stages. Larval spines shorter and more slender than those of *Nymphalis*; larvae solitary, living in shelters of rolled leaves of nettles, thistles and of other plants; pupa without cephalic projections, dorsal tubercles small.

VANESSA ATALANTA L. 1758   CN 31   FG p. 86; Pl. 17

Fw angled at v6.
Genitalia. Described above, apex of uncus cleft; valve with small ampullary process.
Range. Canary Islands, N Africa, Europe, W Asia, N America.

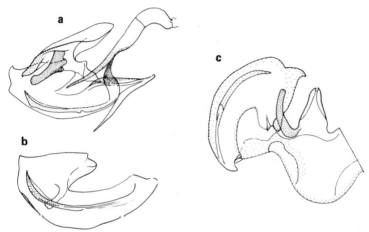

227. *Vanessa atalanta,* S England: **a,** genitalia, side view: **b,** valve; **c,** genitalia spread, right valve and penis omitted.

VANESSA INDICA   Godart 1819   CN 31   FG p. 86; Pl. 17

Genitalia. Like *V. atalanta*; uncus shortly bifid, brachia more slender; valve more elongate, harpe longer.
Range. Ceylon, India, China, Japan, Korea and Madeira and Canary Islands.

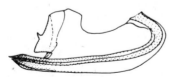

228. *Vanessa indica vulcania,* Canary Islands: valve.

V. i. vulcania Godart 1819.

Genitalia. Described above, almost indistinguishable from Indian specimens.
Range. Madeira, Canary Isles.

VANESSA CARDUI L. 1758 CN 31 FG p. 86; Pl. 17
Wing margins not angled, fw outer margin slightly concave.
Genitalia. Very small, brachia slender; valve truncate with process descending from costal margin, harpe sharply curved; penis as in *V. atalanta.*
Range. Absent from S America, otherwise cosmopolitan.

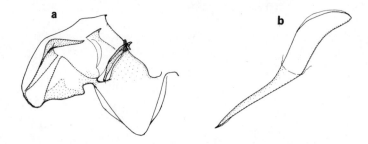

229. *Vanessa cardui,* S England: **a,** genitalia spread showing left valve and small uncus (U), right valve and penis omitted; **b,** penis.

VANESSA VIRGINIENSIS Drury 1773 CN 31 FG p. 87; Pl. 17
Wing margins not angled.
Genitalia. Like *V. cardui* but harpe longer, not angled; cuillier with two small teeth.
Range. Canary Islands. Widely distributed in N and S America.

230. *Vanessa virginiensis,* Canary Islands: **a,** valve; **b,** tegumen and uncus, dorsal view, with brachia.

Genus **AGLAIS** Dalman 1816 TS: *Papilio urticae* L.
Fw with marginal angle at v6; hw with angle at v4; wing surfaces lack bristles.
Genitalia. See *A. urticae.*

AGLAIS URTICAE L. CN 31 FG p. 87; Pl. 17
Two subspecies with similar genitalia.
Genitalia. Uncus small, apex bulbous, brachia present, long, flexible;

178

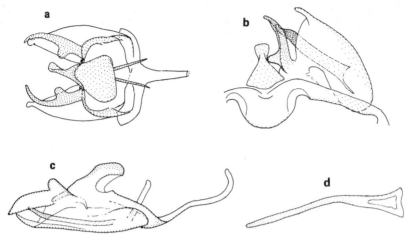

231. *Aglais urticae*, S England: **a**, genitalia, dorsal view, showing brachia **b**, genitalia spread, left valve and penis omitted; **c**, genitalia, side view; **d**, penis.

valve narrow with costal hiatus, harpe long, slender; saccus almost as long as valve; penis long, almost straight.

A. u. urticae L. 1758.
Range. All continental Europe and temperate Asia to China and Japan. Absent from Canary Islands, N Africa, Corsica and Sardinia

A. u. ichnusa Hübner 1824.
Differentiated by external wing-markings.
Range. Corsica, Sardinia.

Genus **POLYGONIA**   Hübner 1818   TS: *Papilio c-aureum* L.
Butterflies of moderate size, wing margins very irregular; fw inner margin sinuous, outer margin angled at v2 and v6; hw outer margin angled at v4 and v7; antennae almost two-thirds the length of fw.
Genitalia. In dorsal view uncus small with massive pincer-shaped brachia; vinculum well developed; valve short, harpe stout; saccus absent; penis rather short with slender apical section.
Early stages. Ovum sub-conical with ten ribs. Larval head bilobed with two hairy papillae; dorsal spines absent from segments 1–3; abdominal segments nine and ten each with two spines; larva living by itself on food plants Pellitory, Hazel, Briars etc. Pupa with prominent dorsal hump.

POLYGONIA C-ALBUM L. 1758   CN 31   FG p. 88; Pl. 16

Genitalia. Organs wide in dorsal view; valve oval, elongate, harpe curved upwards, base wide.

Range. N Africa. S and C Europe widely distributed and across Asia to Japan.

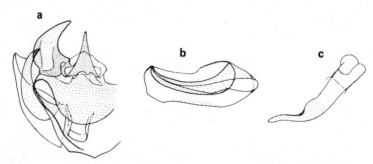

232. *Polygonia c-album,* S England: **a,** genitalia spread showing dorsal structures, right brachium and valve omitted; **b,** valve; **c,** penis.

POLYGONIA EGEA Cramer 1775   CN 31   FG p. 88; Pl. 16

Genitalia. Like *P. c-album* but less wide; in dorsal view brachia more abruptly curved; valve more elongate, harpe narrower; penis as in *c-album.*

Range. From S Europe across W Asia to Iran.

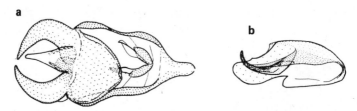

233. *Polygonia egea,* Susa, NW Italy: **a,** genitalia, dorsal view, valves and penis omitted, showing strong brachia; **b,** valve.

Subfamily ARGYNNINAE Duponchel 1844

Description. Most species ups have an almost uniform pattern of black spots and striae on fulvous gc, unh often with silver spots, ♂ upf sometimes with sex-brands. The species, which vary greatly in size, are widely distributed throughout the Holarctic Region, with a few representatives on high mountains in C Africa and in S America. *Androconial scales* when present are very slender with tufted apices, massed in sex-brands. *Eyes* smooth. *Palpi* middle segment long, swollen, clothed with hair and bristles,

apical segment small. *Antennae* very slender, rigid, club oval, abrupt.
Venation. Cell closed in both wings, dc vein in hw often vestigial.
Genitalia. Uncus well developed, usually with central membranous
lacuna; apex angularis present; valve with prominent costal process,
harpe usually absent, very small if present; penis stout, short, often
armed with spicules or larger cornuti, vesica expands above apex;
transtilla usually present.
Early stages. Ovum sub-conical with several vertical ribs. Larva with five
rows of spines or hairy warts. Pupa with dorsal, thoracic and abdominal
tubercles. Larval food plants chiefly *Viola* species; hibernation as small
larva, rarely as ovum. Most species fly in a single annual brood. Many
occur in arctic regions and at high altitudes.
In genera *Argynnis, Pandoriana, Argyronome, Mesoacidalia (Speyeria),
Fabriciana, Issoria* and *Brenthis,* outer margin of fw concave or straight,
v10 and v11 arise close together from subcostal vein near cell apex,
proximal opening of the penis partly dorsal; in the first five genera only,
upf with sex-brands along two or more veins and larval spines rather long.

References. Warren 1944. dos Passos & Grey 1945.

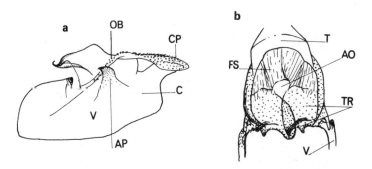

234. ARGYNNINAE: **a,** valve (*Brenthis hecate*), showing costal process (CP);
ampullary process (AP) etc.; **b,** A-P view of dorsal structures (*Mesoacidalia
aglaja*) showing membranous fultura superior (FS) with opening for the anal
gut (AO) etc. For further explanation of letters see p. 29.

Key to genera of Argynninae

1	Fw v10 arises from subcostal vein or from apex of cell		.				2
	Fw v10 arises from stalk of v7-9	.		.	.	.	8
2	Apex of uncus cleft	.	.	.	.	.	.	*Brenthis*
	Apex of uncus not cleft .	.	.	.	.	.	.	3
3	Uph black pd spots absent	.	.	.	.	.	. *Mesoacidalia*
	Uph black pd spots present	.	.	.	.	.	4
4	Uncus with serrate crest	.	.	.	.	.	.	5
	Uncus without serrate crest	.	.	.	.	.	6

5 Serrate crest complete . . . . *Pandoriana*
Serrate crest only at base of uncus . . . . . *Argynnis*

6 Uncus curved upwards . . . . *Argyronome*
Uncus curved downwards **7**

7 Hw outer margin rounded . . . . . . *Fabriciana*
Hw outer margin angled at v1b and at v8 . . . . *Issoria*

8 Hw outer margin angled at v8 . . . . . *Boloria*
Hw outer margin not angled at v8 . . . . . **9**

9 Uncus slightly downturned . . . . . . *Proclossiana*
Uncus sharply downturned . . . . . . *Clossiana**

*In the aberrant species *Clossiana dia* L. outer margin of hw is angled at v8 but valve structure confirms *Clossiana* as the correct genus. This Key relates to European species. It is not valid for Asiatic, American or African species.

Genus **ARGYNNIS** F. 1807   TS: *Papilio paphia* L.
Male with sex-brands upf along v1-4.
Genitalia. See *A. paphia.*

ARGYNNIS PAPHIA L.   CN 29   FG p. 90; Pl. 18
Three subspecies with similar genitalia.
Genitalia. Uncus crested, base of crest deeply serrated; valve wide, costal process bears spine pad, harpe elongate, slender; vanni extensive and well defined but lightly chitinised; penis very short with large cornuti

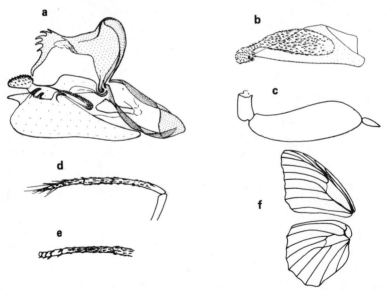

235. *Argynnis paphia,* Switzerland: **a,** genitalia, penis removed; **b,** penis; **c,** palpus; **d,** ♂ fore-leg; **e,** ♀ fore-tarsus; **f,** wing venation.

A. p. paphia L. 1758.
Range. N Spain and across temperate Europe and Asia to Japan. Absent from Mediterranean islands, except Sicily.

A. p. immaculata Bellier 1862.
Slightly different external characters.
Range. Corsica, Sardinia and Giglio. Occasional intermediate specimens on Sicily and S Italy.

A. p. dives Oberthur 1908.
Slightly different external characters.
Range. Algeria.

Genus **PANDORIANA** Warren 1942   TS: *Papilio pandora* D. & S.
Male with sex-brands along v2 and v3.
Genitalia. Serrate crest of uncus complete; apex of valve rounded, costal process long, slender, harpe short and blunt, oblique dentate crest prominent, vanni present; penis lacks cornuti.

PANDORIANA PANDORA   D. & S. 1775   CN 29 FG p. 89; Pl. 19
Genitalia. Described above.
Range. From Canary Islands, N Africa and W Europe eastwards to Iran and Chitral.

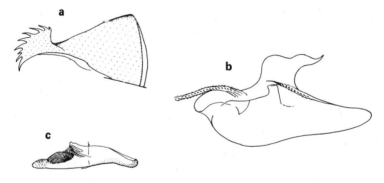

236. *Pandoriana pandora,* Spain: **a,** uncus and tegumen; **b,** valve; **c.** penis.

Genus **ARGYRONOME** Hübner 1818   TS: *Papilio laodice* Pallas
Male upf with sex-brands along v1 and v2.
Genitalia. Uncus short, upturned; valve short, apex blunt and heavily spined, costal process with two strong teeth, lacking oblique dentate crest; penis large, cornuti prominent.

ARGYRONOME LAODICE   Pallas 1771   CN 31

FG p. 91; Pl. 19

Genitalia. See previous page.
Range. From Baltic countries, Poland and E Hungary across Asia to Japan.

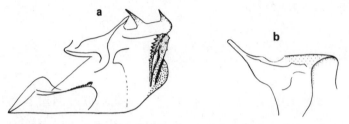

237. *Argyronome laodice*, Lithuania: **a,** valve; **b,** tegumen and uncus.

Genus **MESOACIDALIA** Reuss 1926   TS: *Papilio aglaja* L.
Male upf with sex-brands along VI–4; uph black pd spots lacking.
Genitalia. See *M. aglaja.*

MESOACIDALIA AGLAJA   L.   CN 29   FG p. 91; Pl. 19

Two subspecies with slightly different genitalia.

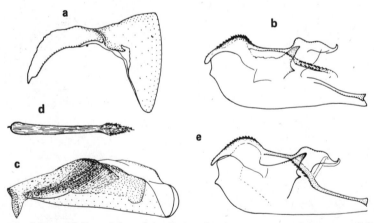

238. *Mesoacidalia aglaja aglaja*, Switzerland: **a,** uncus and tegumen; **b,** valve;
c, penis; **d,** androconial scale. *M. a. lyauteyi*, Middle Atlas, Morocco: **e,** valve.

M. a. aglaja L. 1758.
Genitalia. In side view uncus wide, apex downturned, dorsum slightly serrate; valve wide, costal process tapering, dorsum serrated, oblique

dentate crest prominent; vanni well defined and chitinised; penis short with small spiculate cornuti.

Range. All Europe excepting boreal regions and eastwards across Asia to Japan.

M. a. lyauteyi Oberthur 1920.
Genitalia. Valve slightly shorter, base of costal process wider.
Range. Morocco.

Genus **FABRICIANA** Reuss 1920   TS: *Papilio niobe* L.
Uph pd black spots present; unh with or without silver spots. Male sex-brands upf on vi–4 weak, sometimes absent.
Genitalia. Uncus with short basal crest, apex downturned; vanni fully developed; valve short, costal process slender, almost straight; penis short, cornuti very small, spiculate.

FABRICIANA NIOBE L.   CN 29   FG p. 93; Pl. 19
Sex-brands upf reduced or absent in Spanish and Asiatic specimens.
Androconial scales long, slender, with apical fibrils.
Two subspecies with similar genitalia.

F. n. niobe L. 1758.
Genitalia. Valve short, dentate crest not prominent, arms of furca divergent.
Range. C France, C Italy, rare further east.

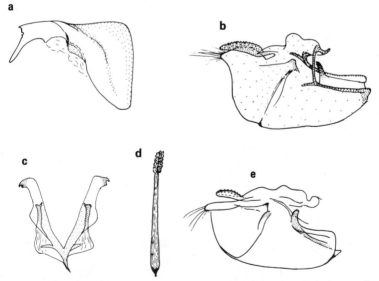

239. *Fabriciana niobe niobe*, N Italy: **a,** uncus and tegumen; **b,** valve; **c,** furca; **d,** androconial scale. *F. n. auresiana*, Middle Atlas, Morocco: **e,** valve.

F. n. eris Meigen 1829.
Unh without silver markings.
Range. Fennoscandia and most of C and E Europe, extending eastwards across W Asia to Iran, often with occasional *F. n. niobe.*

Note. Taxonomic status of these two subspecies uncertain. As in *F. adippe* D. & S., eastern and western subspecies are quite well defined, and completely integrated over a wide frontier area.

F. n. auresiana Fruhstorfer 1908.
Like *F. adippe chlorodippe,* unh silver markings reduced in number and size. *Androconial scales* shorter and wider.
Genitalia. Valve wider, posterior margin evenly rounded, costal process shorter.
Range. Morocco, Algeria.

FABRICIANA ELISA   Godart 1824   CN unknown
FG p. 94; Pl. 19
Sex-brands upf along v3 and v4 only. *Androconial scales* long and slender.
Genitalia. Like *F. niobe,* arms of furca almost parallel.
Range. Restricted to Corsica and Sardinia.
F. elisa is closely related to *F. niobe,* and possibly represents that species in Corsica and Sardinia.

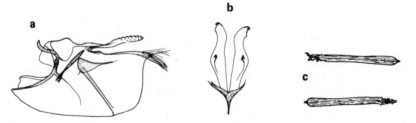

240. *Fabriciana elisa,* Corsica: **a,** valve; **b,** furca; **c,** androconial scales.

FABRICIANA ADIPPE   D. & S.   CN 29   FG p. 92, 93; Pl. 18
Androconial scales slightly longer and more slender than those of *F. niobe.*
Three subspecies, one with slightly different genitalia.

F. a. adippe D. & S. 1775.
Sex-brands on v2+v3. Unh silver markings fully developed.
Genitalia. Like *F. niobe;* valve slightly longer, posteriorly truncate, distal section of costal process toothed, free above costal border, apex of valve hairy, projecting beyond cuillier; arms of furca almost parallel; penis as in *F. niobe.*
Range. NW Europe esp. C France, Britain, Scandinavia; Pyrenees, N Switzerland, Germany and Austria, often associated with *F. a. cleodoxa,* following subspecies, rare in eastern Europe and Asia.

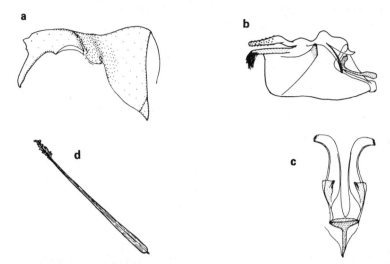

241. *Fabriciana a. adippe,* Bavaria: **a,** uncus and tegumen; **b,** valve; **c,** furca; **d,** androconial scale.

F. a. cleodoxa Ochsenheimer 1816.
Unh silver markings absent except pupils of pd spots.
Genitalia. Like *F. a. adippe.*
Range. From Hungary, Yugoslavia and Italy across E Europe and W Asia. In C Europe completely integrated with *F. a. adippe* and often flying with this, e.g. Pyrenees, Bavaria etc., occurring as a rarity in NW Europe (Britain etc.), constant in Sicily and Greece, in Asia *F. a. adippe* extremely rare.

F. a. chlorodippe Herrich-Schäffer 1851.
Like *F. a. adippe,* unh silver markings fully developed. Upf sex-brands often thin, partially obsolete. Differs from *F. a. adippe* in green unh gc.
Genitalia. Like *F. a. adippe.*
Range. Spain, Portugal. In N Spain, including Pyrenees, sometimes with characters of *F. a. cleodoxa* not fully developed (*F. a. cleodippe* Staudinger 1871 intermediate).

Genus **ISSORIA**   Hübner 1819   TS: *Papilio lathonia* L.
Hw outer margin angled at v1b and v8; unh silver spots very large.
Genitalia. Uncus not crested, narrow, apex downturned; below uncus the diaphragm elaborately chitinised, transtilla lacking; valve elongate, tapering to narrow apex crested with two large teeth, costal process stout, gently curved; penis slender, lacking cornuti, proximal opening partly dorsal.

187

ISSORIA LATHONIA L. 1758   CN 30   FG p. 94; Pl. 19
Genitalia. Described above.
Range. Canary Islands, N Africa and across S and C Europe and temperate Asia to W China.

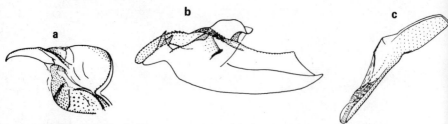

242. *Issoria lathonia,* Pyrenees: **a,** uncus, tegumen and scaphial plates; **b,** valve; **c,** penis.

Genus **BRENTHIS** Hübner 1818   TS: *Papilio hecate* D & S.
Markings and venation as in *Fabriciana* but unh lacking silver spots.
Genitalia. Uncus narrow, apex cleft with small bilobed tubercle at base of cleft, suture between uncus and tegumen membranous; valve like *I. lathonia,* costal process more slender and lacking apical teeth, harpe small but firmly chitinised, oblique dentate crest prominent; proximal opening of penis partly dorsal, vesical membrane spiculate. The genitalia scarcely differ in the three European species.

BRENTHIS HECATE D. & S. 1775   CN 34   FG p. 95; Pl. 20
Genitalia. Described above.
Range. SW Europe and eastwards to Iran, flying in scattered colonies. Absent from Mediterranean islands and S Italy.

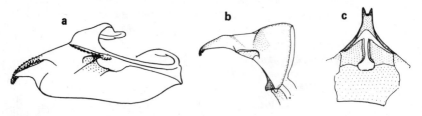

243. *Brenthis hecate,* N Italy: **a,** valve; **b,** uncus and tegumen; **c,** uncus and tegumen, dorsal view.

BRENTHIS DAPHNE D. & S. 1775   CN 13   FG p. 95; Pl. 20
Genitalia. Like *B. hecate*; apex of valve slightly more slender.
Range. SW Europe and eastwards across temperate Asia to Japan. Absent from S Spain, Portugal and Mediterranean islands except Sicily.

244. *Brenthis daphne,* Yugoslavia: **a,** valve; **b,** uncus and tegumen.

BRENTHIS INO Rottemburg 1775   CN 12–13 FG p. 98; Pl. 22
Genitalia. Like *B. hecate*; costal process of valve slightly more slender, tubercles at base of uncal cleft very small.
Range. N Spain and across temperate Europe and Asia to Japan. Absent from Mediterranean islands.

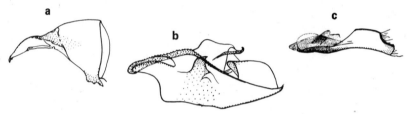

245. *Brenthis ino,* Switzerland · **a,** uncus and tegumen; **b,** valve; **c,** penis.

In the following genera, *Boloria, Proclossiana* and *Clossiana,* v10 of fw arises from stalk of v7–9 some distance beyond cell-apex; proximal opening of penis is dorsal behind a small caecum.

Genus **BOLORIA** Moore 1900   TS: *Papilio pales* D. & S.
Rather small butterflies, fw narrow, pointed; hw outer margin angled at v8, unh often with silver spots. Hw dc vein well defined.
Genitalia. See *B. pales* D. & S. described below. Structure similar in all species, specific characters poorly defined.

BOLORIA PALES D. & S.   CN 30   FG p. 98; Pl. 21
Three subspecies with similar genitalia.

B. p. pales D. & S. 1775.
Genitalia. In dorsal view uncus conical, elongate, hairy, with membranous central hiatus, apex shortly cleft and downturned; valve elongate, apex with two dorsal teeth, costal process rather short, dorsal hump at base; penis very short, vesicular folds elaborate.

Range. Eastern Alps and Carpathians, Austria, Bavaria, Julian Alps, Monte Baldo. Pontic Mts.

References. du Cormier & Guérin 1947. de Toulgouet 1952.

B. p. palustris Fruhstorfer 1909.
Smaller, black markings ups more delicate.
Range. W Alps, eastwards to Engadin (Pontresina) and Brenner Alps.

B. p. pyrenesmiscens Verity 1932.
Unh markings subdued.
Range. Pyrenees and Cantabrian Mts. (Picos de Europa).

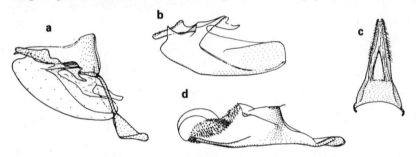

246. *Boloria pales,* Austria: **a,** genitalia, penis removed; **b,** valve; **c,** uncus dorsal view; **d,** penis.

BOLORIA NAPAEA Hoffmannsegg 1804   CN 31   FG p. 99; Pl. 21
Larval food plants *Viola* spp.
Genitalia. Like *B. pales* but slightly larger.
Range. Common on mountains in Fennoscandia, the Alps and Tatra Mts., very local in E Pyrenees. Further in C Asia and known in N America. Absent from peninsular Italy and Balkans.

247. *Boloria napaea,* Norway: valve.

BOLORIA AQUILONARIS Stichel 1908   CN 30   FG p. 102; Pl. 21
Larval food plant *Vaccinium oxycoccus.*
Genitalia. Like *B. pales,* valve costal process sometimes with downwards curve but this is inconstant.

248. *Boloria aquilonaris,* Switzerland: valve.

Range. Fennoscandia and locally in France, Switzerland and eastwards to Austria and Baltic countries. C Asia, sometimes referred to *B. sifanicus* Groum-Grshimaïlo. NE Siberia.

References. Crosson de Cormier, Guérin & Toulgouet 1953. de Lesse 1953(C).

BOLORIA GRAECA Staudinger 1870   CN 31 FG p. 103; Pl. 21
Unh round pd spots better defined. Two subspecies with similar genitalia.

B. g. graeca Staudinger 1870.
Genitalia. Like *B. pales*, valve dorsal teeth more widely separated, costal process shorter, wider, downward curve constant.
Range. Macedonia, Greece.

B. g. balcanica Rebel 1903.
Smaller, ups black markings less prominent.
Range. Albania, Bulgaria, Yugoslavia in Montenegro, Serbia etc., Rumania (?) and rather local in SW Alps.

249. *Boloria graeca balcanica,* Alpes Maritimes: valve.

Genus **PROCLOSSIANA** Reuss 1921   TS: *Papilio eunomia* Esper
Like *Boloria* but fw apex more rounded; hw outer margin not angled at v8.
Genitalia. Like *B. pales*; uncus very slender, almost straight, apex slightly hooked and deeply cleft; dorsal teeth of valve widely separated, costal process massive; penis slender, caecum long.

PROCLOSSIANA EUNOMIA Esper   CN 30 FG p. 103; Pl. 22
Two subspecies with similar genitalia.

191

250. *Proclossiana eunomia,* E Pyrenees: **a,** genitalia; **b,** penis.

P. e. eunomia Esper 1799.
Range. Widely scattered colonies in E Pyrenees, France, Belgium, Germany, Austria, Bulgaria and C Russia.

P. e. ossianus Herbst 1800.   CN 28
Like *P. e. eunomia,* smaller, unh more brightly marked.
Range. Boreal regions of Fennoscandia, Estland, distribution in Asia not recorded. Also in N America in boreal regions and in Rocky Mts. southwards to Colorado.

Genus **CLOSSIANA** Reuss 1920   TS: *Papilio selene* D. & S.
Description. Small or medium-sized butterflies, ups markings often like *Brenthis*; outer margin of hw rounded, very rarely angled at v8, unh with or without silver spots.
Genitalia. Uncus usually rather short, curved sharply downwards, with central membranous hiatus and apex cleft; valve narrow, tapering, with apical and costal processes of various shapes; penis with long caecum and elaborate vesicular structure in some species.

CLOSSIANA SELENE D. & S. 1775   CN 30 FG p. 104; Pl. 20
Genitalia. Valve tapered abruptly to narrow apex folded downwards, costal process narrow with bulbous spiny apex.
Range. Widely distributed across Europe, temperate Asia and in N

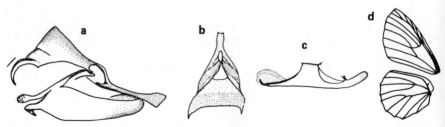

251. *Clossiana selene,* S England: **a,** genitalia, penis removed; **b,** uncus and tegumen, dorsal view; **c,** penis; **d,** wing venation.

America. Absent from S Spain, Portugal, peninsular Italy, Balkans and Mediterranean islands.

CLOSSIANA FREIJA Thunberg 1791 CN 31 FG p. 106; Pl. 22
Genitalia. Like *C. selene*; valve tapers to hooked apical process, costal process narrow, downturned, bearing long, slender terminal spines.
Range. Fennoscandia and N Europe and eastwards to Japan. N America in boreal regions and at high altitudes in Rocky Mts., south to Colorado.

252. *Clossiana freija*, Norway: valve.

In the following five species uncus, tegumen and penis resemble *C. selene* rather closely. Well marked specific characters are present in the valves, and usually only these parts are shown in figures.

CLOSSIANA DIA L. 1767 CN unknown FG p. 107; Pl. 22
Outer margin of hw angled at v8.
Genitalia. Valve small, tapering, apical process blunt, costal process slender, straight, extending beyond apex of valve.
Range. N Spain, France and eastwards across Europe and Asia to W China.

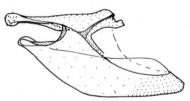

253. *Clossiana dia*, N Spain: valve.

CLOSSIANA POLARIS Boisduval 1828 CN unknown
FG p. 107; Pl. 22
Genitalia. Terminal process of valve straight, costal process short, robust, with spiny rounded apex.
Range. Circumpolar, in far north of Europe, Asia and America.

254. *Clossiana polaris*, Norway: valve.

CLOSSIANA THORE   Hübner   CN 30   FG p. 107; Pl. 22
Two subspecies with similar genitalia.

C. t. thore Hübner 1803.
Genitalia. Uncus rather long; valve terminal process short, apex turned inwards, costal process straight, robust, apex rounded.
Range. N and E Alps including Dolomites. E Finland.

255. *Clossiana thore thore,* Bavaria: valve.

C. t. borealis Staudinger 1861.
Ups black pattern reduced.
Range. Boreal regions of Fennoscandia, not south of 62°N. Altai Mts.

CLOSSIANA FRIGGA   Thunberg 1791   CN 31 FG p. 110; Pl. 22
Genitalia. Apex of valve narrow, upturned, slightly expanded and armed with teeth, costal process slender, longer than terminal process, apex slightly bulbous and armed with small teeth.
Range. N Europe and eastwards across Asia to the Amur. N America; W Canada and locally in the Rocky Mts. to Colorado.

256. *Clossiana frigga,* Norway: valve.

CLOSSIANA IMPROBA   Butler 1877
CN unknown FG p. 111; Pl. 22
Genitalia. Terminal process of valve slightly expanded and hooked, pointing upwards, costal process slender with small apical teeth.
Range. Circumpolar, confined to far north of Europe, Asia and America.

257. *Clossiana improba,* N Sweden: valve.

In the three species following the penis is larger, the caecum long and narrow, the apex expanded to form two wide lateral plates.

194

CLOSSIANA TITANIA Esper   CN 31   FG p. 105; Pl. 20
Two subspecies with similar genitalia.

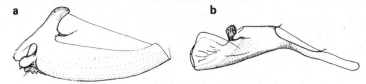

258. *Clossiana titania cypris,* Switzerland: **a,** valve; **b,** penis.

C. t. titania Esper 1793.
Genitalia. Valve wide, terminal process expanded and toothed, costal margin oblique, costal process robust; penis apex with wide lateral plates and small erect globular cornutus.
Range. Mountains of C France, Dauphiné (?), Cottian Alps, Hautes Alpes (?). S. Finland.

C. t. cypris Meigen 1828.
Gc bright fulvous with heavier black markings.
Range. C and S Alps to Bavaria and Austria; Balkans on Trebević, Durmitor etc., Poland, Hungary.

CLOSSIANA EUPHROSYNE L. 1758   CN 31 FG p. 105; Pl. 20
Genitalia. Valve narrow, terminal process expanded and toothed, costal margin slightly oblique, terminating in an oval spiny swelling; penis as in *C. titania.*
Range. Widely distributed across Europe, including boreal regions, and through N and C Asia to Kamschatka.

259. *Clossiana euphrosyne,* S England: **a,** valve; **b,** penis.

CLOSSIANA CHARICLEA Schneider 1794   CN unknown
FG p. 106; Pl. 22
Genitalia. Valve narrow, apical process expanded and turned inwards; costal process stout, apex bulbous, lacking teeth; penis as in *C. titania.*
Range. Boreal regions of Europe not south of 66°N, Greenland, NE Asia, N America, probably circumpolar.

260. *Clossiana chariclea,* Norway: valve.

195

Subfamily MELITAEINAE Reuter 1896

Description. Small or medium-sized butterflies resembling the smaller Argynninae. *Palpi* variable, semi-porrect or ascending, second segment clothed with hair but without bristles. *Antennae* slender, club oval, abrupt. *Eyes* smooth. *Androconial scales* absent. *Venation.* Fw v10 arising before or after cell-end, cell closed; hw cell open, rarely partly closed.

Genitalia. Uncus absent or (rarely) vestigial, sub-unci present in many species; apex angularis lacking; valve without costal process but harpe prominent, usually densely chitinised; saccus wide, centrally notched in *Melitaea* and *Mellicta*, continuous with furca, forming a massive plate supporting the penis, but in *Euphydryas* saccus absent and basal plate formed by furca alone; penis of moderate length, usually almost straight, vesica expanding below apex; cornuti if present, very small (spicules).

Early stages. Ovum barrel-shaped, ribbed and reticulate. Larvae with seven rows of hairy tubercles or unbranched spines, living gregariously when young. Larval food plants *Plantago, Veronica, Centaurea* etc. Represented in the region by three genera of which *Melitaea* and *Mellicta* are closely related, with wide Palearctic distributions. *Euphydryas* is very distinct anatomically, with relatively few species and Holarctic distribution, perhaps better graded with tribal rank.

Key to genera of Melitaeinae

1 Saccus absent . . . . *Euphydryas*
  Saccus present **2**

2 Penis apex with ostium-keel . . . . . . *Mellicta*
  Penis apex pointed without ostium-keel . . . . *Melitaea*

Genus **MELITAEA** F. 1807   TS: *Papilio cinxia* L.

Markings ups macular or (rarely) linear; unh base usually with three black spots above cell. *Antennal* club abrupt, pyriform. *Venation.* fw v10 arises from stalk of v7–9.

Genitalia. Variable, generic characters not well defined; sub-unci very small if present; valve in side view oval, rarely truncate posteriorly, apex of penis upturned, ostium-keel not defined (see *Mellicta*).

Early stages. Ovum with ribs extending half way from crown to base. Larval spines short. Pupa short with dorsal tubercles.

Note. Melitaea is a composite genus with about twenty-two species of which seven occur in Europe and N Africa. It has been suggested that the European species are best separated into smaller genera.

Reference. Higgins 1941. 1944. Verity 1950.

MELITAEA DIDYMA   Esper 1779   CN 28   FG p. 116; Pl. 23

Palpi ascending, terminal segment short, porrect.

Genitalia. Elongate; tegumen narrow, conical; valve oval, terminal process slender, posterior margin finely toothed, irregular, often with sharp prominence at angle with costa, lower border of harpe toothed, but teeth not visible from above, penis robust, terminal part sharply upturned and proximal limb ascending, almost semicircular.

Range. Morocco, Algeria, Tunisia, Tripolitania and Fezzan, S and C Europe, and eastwards to C Asia.

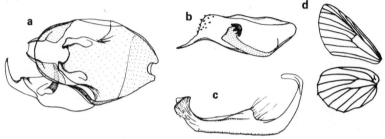

261. *Melitaea didyma*, Switzerland: **a,** genitalia, penis removed; **b,** valve; **c,** penis; **d,** wing venation.

MELITAEA DESERTICOLA   Oberthur 1876   CN 28
FG p. 117; Pl. 23

Palpi as in *M. didyma.*

Genitalia. As in *M. didyma*, the following slight differences appear to be constant: tegumen has small sub-unci; costal angle of valve rounded, smooth, posterior process more sharply curved, harpe more slender, lacking teeth along lower border; apex of penis less sharply upturned. The species is more easily identified by wing-markings.

Range. N Africa, extending far into the desert and eastwards across Tripolitania, Fezzan and Egypt to Jordan and Lebanon.

262. *Militaea deserticola*, Algeria: **a,** valve; **b,** tegumen with sub-unci.

MELITAEA TRIVIA   D. & S.   CN 31   FG p. 118; Pl. 23

Two subspecies with slightly different genitalia.

M. t. trivia D. & S. 1775.

Genitalia. Small, compact, tegumen narrow, conical; valve wide, posteriorly

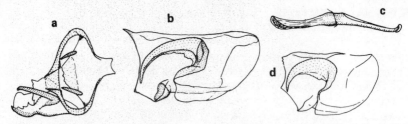

263. *Melitaea trivia trivia*, Hungary: **a,** genitalia, penis removed; **b,** valve; **c,** penis. *M. t. ignasiti*, Portugal; **d,** valve.

truncate, costal angle very prominent, harpe long, sickle-shaped, lower border slightly toothed; penis slender, short, apex slightly upturned.
Range. From C Italy eastwards across Austria, Hungary, Yugoslavia, Greece, Bulgaria and Rumania. Small colonies exist near Lake Garda etc.

M. t. ignasiti Sagarra 1926.
Smaller, gc paler, less heavily marked.
Genitalia. Valve shorter, costal angle less pronounced, harpe shorter and wider.
Range. Piedmont (Susa) and across N Spain and Portugal.

MELITAEA ARDUINNA Esper 1784   CN unknown
FG p. 114; Pl. 24
Widely distributed in S Russia and W Asia, a single subspecies occurs in SE Europe.

M. a. rhodopensis Freyer 1836.
Genitalia. Like *M. cinxia* but valve more elongate, terminal section almost straight in dorsal view with a few small teeth along inner border, apex curved downwards, harpe slender without teeth; penis like *M. cinxia* but more robust, apex upturned.
Range. Very local in E Macedonia and Rumania.

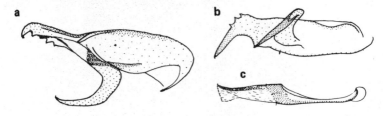

264. *Melitaea arduinna* subspecies, Iraq: **a,** valve, dorsal view; **b,** valve, side view; **c,** penis.

MELITAEA PHOEBE D. & S. 1775 CN 31 FG p. 114; Pl. 14, 23
Genitalia. Rather massive; like *M. cinxia*; valve in side view short, posteriorly truncate with three pointed posterior processes, harpe strong, massive in dorsal view, penis stout, apex pointed, ostium-folds prominent.
Range. From N Africa across S and C Europe to China.

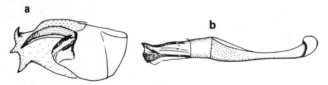

265. *Melitaea phoebe,* Switzerland: **a,** valve; **b,** penis.

MELITAEA AETHERIE Hübner 1826 CN unknown
FG p. 115; Pl. 23
Genitalia. Like *M. phoebe,* rather massive, valve in side view short, apex truncate with sharply pointed dorsal tooth and smaller tooth from posterior inferior angle, harpe less massive than that of *M. phoebe* and in side view more strongly curved; penis straight, apex slightly upturned.
Range. N Africa, Sicily and extreme south of Spain and Portugal.

266. *Melitaea aetherie,* Morocco: valve.

MELITAEA CINXIA L. 1758 CN 31 FG p. 111; Pl. 24
Palpi slender, porrect or nearly so.
Genitalia. Tegumen wide but shallow; valve elongate, terminal process slender, curved downwards and bearing two small dorsal teeth, harpe sickle-shaped and without teeth; penis straight, slender, apex slightly upturned, ostium-folds prominent.
Range. N Africa, S and C Europe northwards to S Scandinavia and Isle of Wight and eastwards across temperate Asia to Mongolia.

267. *Melitaea cinxia,* Bavaria: **a,** genitalia, right valve and penis removed; **b,** valve; **c,** penis.

199

MELITAEA DIAMINA Lang   CN 31   FG p. 118; Pl. 25
Unh black basal spots absent. Two subspecies with similar genitalia.

M. d. diamina Lang 1789.
Genitalia. Like *M. cinxia*; terminal process of valve with two large dorsal teeth, harpe massive; penis as in *M. cinxia*, small cornutus in ostium-folds.
Range. From C France across temperate Europe and Asia to Japan.

268. *Melitaea d. diamina,* N Italy: **a,** valve; **b,** penis.

M. d. vernetensis Rondou 1902.
Ups less heavily marked.
Range. E Pyrenees, and NE Spain (Catalonia), Cantabrian Mts.
Note. In this species wing-markings are those of the following genus *Mellicta*, with which it is associated by many authors. The genitalia differ and their anatomy points to closer relationship with *Melitaea*, and especially with *M. cinxia*. The butterfly has intermediate features and in the author's opinion the genitalia characters are of greater taxonomic significance. The species is placed therefore in the genus *Melitaea*.

Genus **MELLICTA** Billberg 1820   TS: *Papilio athalia* Rottemburg
Description. Small or rather small butterflies resembling *Melitaea* but ups black markings mostly reticulate and linear; uph never with black postdiscal spots; unh without black basal spots. *Antennae* slender, club abrupt, oval or pyriform, spatulate in dried specimens. *Palpi* slightly ascending, terminal segment exposed, almost half as long as middle segment, depressed. *Venation.* In fw v10 arises from stalk of v7–9.
Genitalia. Tegumen with or without sub-uncal points or sub-unci fully developed; valve short, wide, with process at posterior inferior angle; ostium-keel and vesical folds of penis show important specific characters.
Early stages. Ovum subconical and truncate, with about 20 ribs descending half way from crown to base. Larva black or dark brown with minute white spots over sides and back. Pupa not distinctive.

Note. Specific identification may be difficult in this group, but characters in the genitalia are well defined. Important features include the formation of the tegumen and shape of the posterior process of the valve.
Reference. Higgins 1955.

MELLICTA ATHALIA Rottemburg CN 31 FG p. 120; Pl. 25
Three subspecies, one with different genitalia. The species is extremely
variable.

M. a. athalia Rottemburg 1775.
Genitalia. Sub-unci well developed; valve wide, posterior process rather
short, apex usually forked and with small dorsal teeth; harpe curved with
teeth along lower border; penis straight, ostium-keel large.
Range. N and C Europe including Balkans, Asia Minor and across
temperate Russia to Lake Baical.

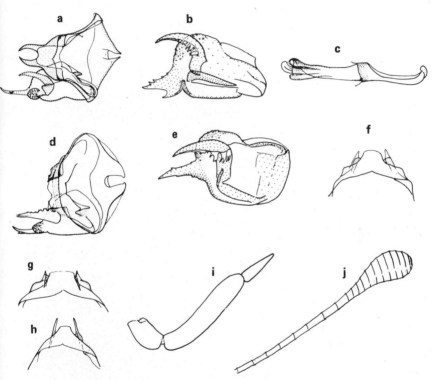

269. *Mellicta athalia athalia*, Hungary: **a,** genitalia, right valve and penis
removed; **b,** valve; **c,** penis. *M. a. celadussa,* Pyrenees: **d,** genitalia, right valve
and penis removed; **e,** valve. Éclepens, W Switzerland: **f,** tegumen. Lozère:
g, tegumen. Glarus, N Switzerland: **h,** tegumen; **i,** palpus; **j,** antennal apex.

M. a. norvegica Aurivillius 1888.
Small, ups markings fine and regular.
Genitalia. As in *M. athalia*.
Range. Fennoscandia, from western mountains northwards to Lapland.
See Note 1 next page.

201

M. a. celadussa Fruhstorfer 1910.
Genitalia differ; sub-unci vestigial or absent, posterior process of valve longer, apex rarely forked, harpe longer, straight, teeth along lower border larger.
Range. SW Europe, including peninsular Italy, Spain and Portugal and S Switzerland (see map).

Note 1. The small *M. a. norvegica* with its special habitats on mountains and boreal bogs, is distinct in appearance from *M. a. athalia* which flies in S Sweden. It represents a major subspecies although no constant difference in genitalia has been found.
Note 2. The distribution areas of *M. a. athalia* and of *M. a. celadussa* meet in France, Switzerland and Italy. At these frontiers genitalia with intermediate characters occur over a belt of country from 20–100 miles wide. Incomplete development of the sub-unci is a noticeable feature of these intermediate forms, of which three examples are illustrated here.

References. Higgins 1932. Bourgogne 1953.

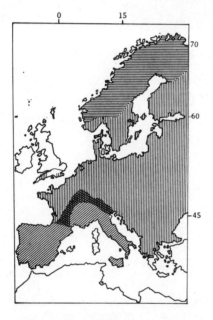

Map showing approximate frontier between the subspecies *M. athalia athalia*, *M. athalia celadussa*, and *M. a. norvegica*.

MELLICTA DEIONE Geyer   CN unknown   FG p. 121; Pl. 24
Three subspecies all with similar genitalia.

M. d. deione Geyer 1832.
Genitalia. Like *M. a. celadussa* Fruhstorfer, but valve usually differs, posterior process more irregular in shape; penis ostium-keel short, apex of penis abruptly upturned (specific character).
Range. Spain, Portugal and S France, esp. mountains of SE.

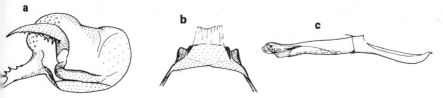

270. *Mellicta deione deione,* C Spain: **a,** valve; **b,** tegumen; **c,** penis.

M. d. berisalii Rühl 1891.
Ups gc darker.
Range. Very local in Switzerland (Rhône valley), N Italy, near Ulzio in Cottian Alps.

M. d. nitida Oberthur 1909.
Lightly marked, uph pd spots reduced or absent.
Range. N Africa, Algeria and Morocco (El Rif).

MELLICTA PARTHENOIDES Keferstein 1851   CN unknown
FG p. 123; Pl. 24
Genitalia. Sub-unci well developed and firmly chitinised; posterior process of valve short, curving down to pointed apex, lower border slightly dentate; penis ostium-keel very small.
Range. Spain, Portugal, France, northwards to Paris, Switzerland, S Belgium and W Germany.

271. *Mellicta parthenoides,* C Spain: **a,** valve; **b,** tegumen.

MELLICTA BRITOMARTIS Assmann 1847   CN unknown
FG p. 124; Pl. 24
Genitalia. Tegumen long with short, firmly chitinised sub-unci; valve short, almost quadrilateral, costal angle prominent, posterior process small with variable number of teeth; ostium-keel very short.

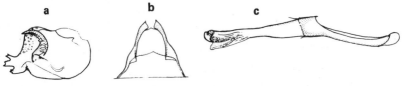

272. *Mellicta britomartis,* N Italy: **a,** valve; **b,** tegumen; **c,** penis.

Range. E Europe from Bulgaria northwards to Bavaria; Italy, a few isolated colonies near Turin; further in Russia (Dniepopetrovsk) and C Asia to Transbaikal and Korea.

References. Rocci 1930; Urbahn 1952.

MELLICTA AURELIA Nickerl 1850   CN 32   FG p. 123; Pl. 24
Genitalia. Sub-unci small or absent; posterior process of valve wide, apex downturned and slightly hooked; ostium-keel elongate, apex upturned with a small bunch of cornuti present on each side.
Range. From Basses Alpes and Ligurian Apennines northwards to Belgian Ardennes and thence across Europe to Balkans, sometimes flying with *M. britomartis.* Italy, rare south of river Po.

273. *Mellicta aurelia,* Switzerland: **a,** valve; **b,** tegumen; **c,** penis.

MELLICTA VARIA Meyer-Dür 1851   CN 31   FG p. 122; Pl. 25
Genitalia. Tegumen narrow, conical, without sub-unci; valve oval, terminating in two strong divergent teeth; penis short, without distinctive characters.
Range. From Basses Alpes and Savoie eastwards to Oetztal Alps; very local in C Apennines.

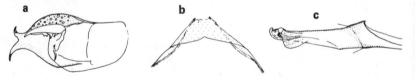

274. *Mellicta varia,* Switzerland: **a,** valve; **b,** tegumen; **c,** penis.

MELLICTA ASTERIA Freyer 1828
                      CN unknown FG p. 125; Pl. 24
Genitalia. Tegumen with small sub-uncal processes; terminal process of valve curved strongly inwards (medially) with a small tooth on the upper border.
Range. Confined to Alps at high altitudes, from Chur to Gross-Glockner.

275. *Mellicta asteria,* Switzerland: valve.

Genus **EUPHYDRYAS** Scudder 1872   TS: *Papilio phaeton* Drury
Description. Hw often with black submarginal spots. *Palpi* ascending, bushy, hair red or orange, terminal segment short. *Antennae* slender, club pyriform. Sexes similar (except *E. cynthia*). *Venation.* Variable, fw v10 from near apex of cell or from stalk of v7–9.
Genitalia. Tegumen wide but shallow, labides broad; basal plate of furca with pointed central process (except *E. desfontainii*); valve short, truncate, teeth at inferior posterior angle prominent, shape of harpe variable; saccus absent; penis slender, sinuous, apical segment downturned.
Early stages. Ovum strongly ribbed. Larval spines usually long, but short (tubercles) in *E. aurinia* and *E. desfontainii*, larva black, dorsum scattered with white dots. All species single-brooded.
Note. The European species fall into two groups each with distinct genitalia. In *E. maturna* and three following species the specific characters are not well marked in the genitalia. In fw origin of v10 is variable. The genitalia characters also seem slightly inconstant, especially in *E. intermedia* and close relatives. In *E. aurinia* and *E. desfontainii* the genitalia have strongly marked specific characters; valve more elongate and harpe semicircular.

Reference. Higgins 1950.

EUPHYDRYAS INTERMEDIA   Ménétriès   CN unknown
FG p. 125; Pl. 26
Range. Widely distributed on mountains from the Alps across temperate Asia to Sutschan and Korea. A single subspecies occurs in Europe.

E. i. wolfensbergeri Frey 1880.
Genitalia. Pointed apex of furcal plate narrow (distinction from *E. maturna*); in side view harpe with three processes, central process longest, pointed and curved, armed with teeth along lower concave border; apex of penis tapered to a slender point.
Range. At subalpine levels in the southern Alps, from Savoie Alps to Julian Alps.

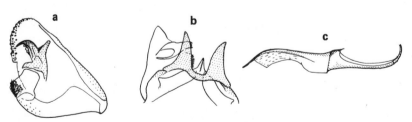

276. *Euphydryas intermedia wolfensbergeri,* Switzerland: **a,** valve; **b,** tegumen; **c,** penis.

EUPHYDRYAS MATURNA L. 1758 CN 31 FG p. 125; Pl. 26

Genitalia. Like *E. intermedia*; in dorsal view labides longer and narrower; apex of furcal plate slightly wider, harpe with two processes, longer process curved, apex bifid, teeth along lower border small if present; penis as in *E. intermedia*.

Range. From N France and S Sweden in local colonies eastwards north of the Alps to N Yugoslavia, N Greece and Rumania, Altai Mts. and Sajan Mts. Colonies often widely separated, at valley levels or moderate altitudes.

277. *Euphydryas maturna*, NE France: **a,** valve; **b,** tegumen.

EUPHYDRYAS CYNTHIA D. & S. 1775 CN unknown
FG p. 126; Pl. 26

Sexes dissimilar.

Genitalia. Like *E. intermedia*; furca slightly wider posteriorly, but specific characters scarcely perceptible.

Range. W Alps, from Basses Alpes across Switzerland to Bavaria and Austria; very local in Rhodope Mts., Bulgaria.

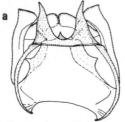 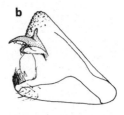

278. *Euphydryas cynthia,* Switzerland: **a,** genitalia, penis removed; **b,** valve.

EUPHYDRYAS IDUNA Dalman 1816 CN 31 FG p. 127: Pl. 26

Genitalia. Like *E. maturna*; labides shorter; harpe with two processes, dorsal process small; penis as in *E. intermedia*.

Range. Boreal regions of Fennoscandia, Altai Mts., Sajan Mts., Caucasus.

279. *Euphydryas iduna,* N Sweden: valve.

EUPHYDRYAS AURINIA Rottemburg CN 30

FG p. 127; Pl. 26

Range very extensive, from N Africa, Portugal and France across Europe and Asia to Mongolia and Ussuri, with several subspecies. Two subspecies with similar genitalia.

E. a. aurinia Rottemburg 1775.
Flies at valley levels or moderate altitudes, but occasionally at high levels, e.g. up to 2,000m. in C Pyrenees.
Genitalia. Labides short, triangular, a vestigial tegumen sometimes visible; valve almost quadrilateral with an area of strong spines at posterior angle, harpe curved, convexity downwards; penis as in *E. intermedia* but less curved.
Range. Algeria, Morocco, S and C Europe to 62°N, very variable, local populations forming clinal series, large in N Africa, Spain and Portugal; *E. a. beckeri* Herrich-Schäffer 1851.

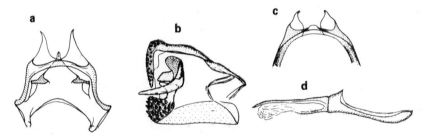

280. *Euphydryas aurinia aurinia,* C Spain; **a,** genitalia, valves and penis removed; **b,** valve; **c,** dorsal structures, view slightly oblique to show vestigial uncus. *E. a. debilis,* Switzerland: **d,** penis.

E. a. debilis Oberthur 1909.
Small, flying at alpine levels on high mountains.
Genitalia. Small, otherwise indistinguishable from *E. a. aurinia.*
Range. E Pyrenees, Alps, Caucasus and C Asia.

Note. These two subspecies are graded species by some authors, and their taxonomic status is uncertain. Their colonies may occur in close proximity, with *aurinia* still flying in the valley when *debilis* begins to appear in an alpine biotope on the neighbouring mountain. The small size and extended black markings of the latter are common ecological modifications in high alpine forms of other species. No precise character has been found to support specific separation. A similar situation exists in C Asia.

EUPHYDRYAS DESFONTAINII Godart 1819   CN unknown
FG p. 131; Pl. 22, 26
Genitalia. Like *E. aurinia* but more elongate; sub-unci more slender; valve massive with four or five strong teeth at posterior inferior angle, harpe strongly curved.
Range. N Africa, S and E Spain northwards and recorded from France in E Pyrenees.

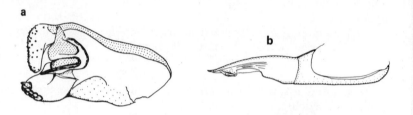

281. *Euphydryas desfontainii*, C Spain: **a,** valve; **b,** penis.

Subfamily CHARAXINAE Guénée 1865

Description. Large, very robust butterflies, abdomen short, hw almost always with short tails on v2 and v4; sexes rarely similar. *Eyes* smooth. *Palpi* ascending, smoothly scaled, set close together. *Antennae* strong, rigid, with long cylindrical club. *Venation*. Fw v7 and v8 longer than their common stalk, cell closed; hw cell closed by vestigial vein, precostal vein rising far beyond origin of v8.
Genitalia. See below (*C. jasius*).
Early stages. Ovum large, domed, with flat base, ribbed and reticulate. Larval cuticle shagreened, two or four cephalic spines and cervical shield. Pupa suspended.

Genus **CHARAXES**   Guénée 1865   TS: *Papilio jasius* L.
Androconial scales absent. Characters as for *C. jasius*.

CHARAXES JASIUS L. 1766   CN unknown   FG p. 75; Pl. 15
Genitalia. Uncus lacking, tegumen wide ending in two divergent points; valve wide, without secondary processes; furca greatly developed to support the long penis; sacculus elongate; penis massive, straight, about three times the length of valve.
Range. Mediterranean region, especially coastal districts, eastwards to Greece, with subspecies in Ethiopian Africa.

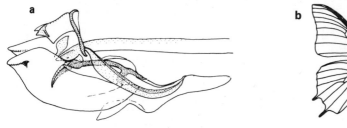

282. *Charaxes jasius*, Elba: **a,** genitalia, proximal section of penis omitted; **b,** wing venation.

Subfamily APATURINAE Boisduval 1840

Description. Butterflies of medium or large size, thorax massive, body of normal length, wings strong and rigid; sexes dissimilar. *Androconial scales* absent. *Eyes* smooth. *Palpi* porrect, smoothly scaled, pointed and pressed together. *Antennae* over half the length of fw, rigid, with long cylindrical club. *Venation*. Fw with v10 and v11 from subcostal vein before apex of cell; in hw precostal vein very long, curving outwards, cell open in both wings.

Genitalia. Remarkable for the great length of saccus and penis; gnathos present as slender arms meeting below to form a floor to the anal compartment; valve broad, without a definite condyle.

Early stages. Ovum sub-conical with slender ribs (12 ribs in *A. iris*). Larva slightly spindle-shaped, head with twin horns, tail with two small flaps. Pupa suspended, short, thorax massive, tapering at each extremity and with two small cephalic prominences (*A. iris*). Hibernation as larva.

Genus **APATURA** F. 1807   TS: *Papilio iris* L.

Description. Male ups with iridescent blue flush. *Palpi*: middle segment long. *Legs*: ♂ fore-leg well formed, three tarsal segments; ♀ fore-leg larger with five tarsal segments, without claws in both sexes. *Venation*. As for subfamily.

Genitalia. Apices angulares absent; valve large, oval, lacking secondary processes; furca small, each plate quadrilateral. In European species specific characters are present in valve-shapes but are not prominent.

APATURA METIS Freyer 1829   CN unknown

FG p. 79; Pl. 15

Genitalia. Small, costal margin of valve slightly concave posteriorly, apex pointed, prominent, placed centrally; penis more than twice as long as valve.

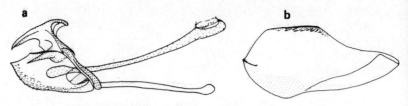

283. *Apatura metis,* Bulgaria: **a,** genitalia; **b,** valve.

Range. Austria, Hungary, Rumania, Bulgaria and Greece? Further across S Russia and Siberia to China, Japan and Korea.

Reference. Nguen thi Hong 1970.

APATURA ILIA   D. & S. 1775   CN 31   FG p. 78; Pl. 15
Genitalia. Slightly larger than *A. metis,* costal margin of valve rounded to meet the small centrally placed apex; penis more than twice as long as valve.
Range. N Portugal. N Spain (Catalonia). S and C Europe and eastwards across Russia and Siberia to China and Korea.

284. *Apatura ilia,* Austria: valve.

APATURA IRIS   L. 1758   CN unknown   FG p. 75; Pl. 15
Genitalia. Larger than *A. ilia*; costal border of valve straight, to meet the

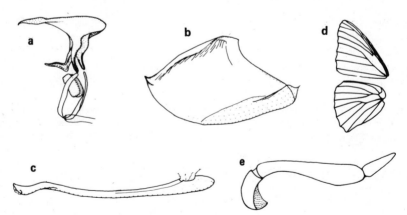

285. *Apatura iris,* Switzerland: **a,** genitalia, valves and penis removed to display gnathos; **b,** valve; **c,** penis; **d,** wing venation; **e,** palpus.

apex which is placed almost in line with the costa; penis shorter than that of *A. ilia*.

Range. From Spain (Cantabrian Mts.) and Pyrenees across temperate Europe and Asia eastwards to China; absent from Mediterranean countries including peninsular Italy and Balkans.

Subfamily LIMENITININAE Butler 1869

Description. Butterflies of medium or rather large size, wing-margins slightly scalloped; ups usually black marked with white spots and bands. Sexes similar. *Eyes* smooth or hairy. *Palpi* variable, usually slender, porrect, often with white lateral stripe. *Antennae* often over half the length of fw. *Androconial scales* absent. *Venation*. Fw cell open or closed by vestigial vein.

Genitalia. Sometimes very small, subfamily characters marked; uncus well developed, usually slender; gnathos present descending vertically, the arms meeting below to define the floor of the anal compartment; apices angulares present; valve longer than wide, with condyle; penis short.

Early stages. Ovum variable. Larva with paired dorsal lobes or fleshy club-shaped processes on several segments, vertex of head bifid. Pupa with twin cephalic pointed projections and characteristic dorsal lobe on second abdominal segment.

Key to genera of Limenitininae

1 Palpi with apical segment short, valve with spiny ampullary process . . . . *Limenitis*

2 Palpi with apical segment long; valve without ampullary process *Neptis*

Genus **LIMENITIS** F. 1807   TS: *Papilio populi* L.

Description. Robust butterflies, fw pointed, outer margin concave; sexes similar or nearly so. *Palpi* terminal segment short. *Antennae* strong, rigid, with slender gradual clubs. *Venation*. Fw cell closed; hw cell open in European species.

Genitalia. Valve with characteristic spiny pyramidal process arising from ampullary region.

Early stages. Ovum taller than wide, sculptured with hexagonal pits. Larva with paired dorsal processes or hairy tubercles, usually largest on segments 2, 3, 5, 10, 11. It hibernates at an early larval stage (after emergence?) and is thought to feed only after hibernation. Larval food plants honeysuckle and foliage of trees. Pupa suspended, with twin cephalic prominences and large dorsal hump.

LIMENITIS POPULI L. 1758   CN 30   FG p. 79; Pl. 15

Eyes smooth. *Palpi* ascending, terminal segment depressed.
Genitalia. Valve slightly longer than uncus+tegumen, terminating in downturned, hooked tooth, conical ampullary process prominent.
Range. Widely distributed in C Europe excepting NW but generally absent from Mediterranean region, further across Russia and Siberia to Japan.

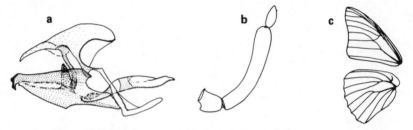

286. *Limenitis populi,* N Italy: **a,** genitalia; **b,** palpus; **c,** wing venation.

LIMENITIS REDUCTA   Staudinger 1901   CN 30 FG p. 79; Pl. 16

Eyes smooth. *Palpi* porrect or slightly ascending.
Genitalia. Relatively large; valve slender, tapering, about one and a half times as long as tegumen+uncus, ampullary process short, not rising above costal margin.
Range. S Europe to about 50° N, extending widely into W Asia.

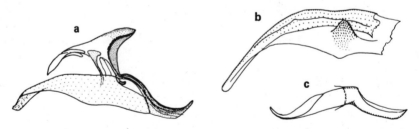

287. *Limenitis reducta,* C Spain: **a,** genitalia; **b,** valve, medial aspect; **c,** penis.

LIMENITIS CAMILLA L. 1763   CN 31   FG p. 82; Pl. 16

Eyes hairy. *Palpi* slender, porrect.
Genitalia. Like *L. populi* but small; valve short, apex rounded.
Range. C Europe including S England, across Russia and Siberia to Japan.

Note. Placed by some authors in the genus *Ladoga* Moore 1898 on account of its hairy eyes. The genitalia suggest close relationship with *L. populi* L.

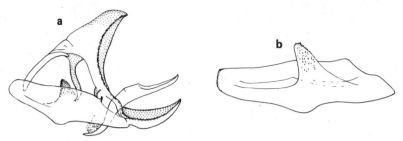

288. *Limenitis camilla*, Switzerland: **a,** genitalia; **b,** valve, medial aspect.

Genus **NEPTIS** F. 1807   TS: *Papilio sappho* Pallas
Description. Butterflies of medium size, fw outer margin evenly curved or (rarely) concave; ups generally black with white markings, a pale stripe upf in cell and wide discal band uph are particularly constant. *Eyes* smooth. *Palpi* slender, porrect, terminal segment half the length of middle segment. *Antennae* filiform, half the length of fw, club very slender. *Venation.* Slightly variable; in European species in fw v8 arises from cell; in hw v8 reaches costa before apex of wing; cell open in both wings.
Genitalia. With slender brachia like *Limenitis*; apex angularis well developed, valve with terminal costal process often hooked, but without the pyramidal ampullary process; saccus short.
Early stages. Larva hibernates in late larval stage. Food plants Leguminosae, Malvaceae and other herbaceous plants.

Reference. Eliot 1969.

NEPTIS SAPPHO   Pallas 1771   CN 30   FG p. 82; Pl. 16
Genitalia. Small, valve elongate, costal process distinctive, hooked and turned cephalad through almost a full circle; apex of penis with complicated structure.
Range. From Austria and Slovenia eastwards across Asia to Japan.

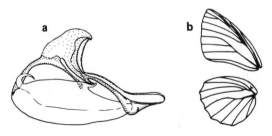

289. *Neptis sappho*, N Yugoslavia: **a,** genitalia; **b,** wing venation.

NEPTIS RIVULARIS   Scopoli 1763   CN unknown

FG p. 83; Pl. 16

Genitalia. Costal border of valve terminates in a short, downturned process; apex of penis with complicated structure.

Range. From C Europe (Turin and Val Maggia) eastwards across Russia to Ural Mts. and Caucasus.

290. *Neptis rivularis,* N Italy: **a,** genitalia; **b,** penis; **c,** palpus.

Family **SATYRIDAE** Boisduval 1833

Description. This very large cosmopolitan family is well represented in Europe especially in the Alps and in Mediterranean countries. All species show a strong family likeness, coloured usually some shade of brown or buff. On ups the characteristic postdiscal ocelli are rarely absent; sexes almost always differ. Modern classification is based upon the characters of the male genitalia. Many species do not segregate well into groups and a large number of monotypic genera have been introduced. *Eyes* smooth or hairy. *Palpi* variable, often ascending with terminal segment depressed. *Antennae* variable, club short, abrupt, or more often gradual, sometimes scarcely developed. *Androconial scales* upf very common, characteristically very slender, tapering to small apical bunch of fibrils, fig. 5, p. 23. *Legs and feet*: fore-legs extremely reduced, especially in ♂, useless for walking, middle and hind-legs with five tarsal segments, simple claws with paronychia and pulvilli; tibiae with paired terminal spurs, tarsi often heavily spined. *Venation.* Fw with 12 veins, one or more almost always swollen at the base; cell closed in both wings.

Genitalia. Characteristic; uncus well developed, with prominent brachia in all European species; peduncle usually well formed; valve elongate and condyle articulating with apex angularis, valve base attached also in the region of the saccus, often with terminal teeth but lacking accessory processes (distinction from Nymphalidae); furca variable; penis rarely with cornuti. In many species the genitalia are relatively unstable. The minor characters often differ individually and regional (subspecific) variation may be very marked, e.g. *Maniola jurtina* etc.

Early stages. Ovum taller than wide, surface ribbed and pitted, closely resembling Nymphalid ovum. Larva slightly fusiform, often pubescent, with short forked tail, similar to that of the Nymphalid *Apatura.* Pupa smooth, abdominal segments rigid, suspended or lying free among grass. Hibernation usually as small larva.

Key to subfamilies of Satyridae

1 Eyes hairy .   .   .   .   Pararginae
   Eyes smooth **2**

2 Wings chequered black and white .   .   .   .   Melanargiinae
   Wings not so coloured **3**

3 Fw vi, median v. and v12 bases greatly swollen .   .   Coenonymphinae
   Fw base of vi not greatly swollen **4**

4 Antennal club well defined .   .   .   .   .   .   Satyrinae
   Apex of antenna slightly thickened, no true club   .   Maniolinae

Subfamily SATYRINAE Boisduval 1833

Description. Butterflies of medium or large size, ♂ upf usually with sex-brands oblique below cell and single ocelli in s2 and s5, the former sometimes inconstant or absent in ♂; uph with single very small ocellus near anal angle in s2, often absent in ♂; unh markings cryptic. *Eyes* smooth. *Palpi* generally ascending with terminal segment depressed, but porrect in genera *Satyrus* and *Minois*. *Antennal* shaft slender, club variable, usually well developed. *Legs* anterior terminal spine of middle tibia sometimes conspicuous. *Venation.* Fw v12 and median vein dilated at base, base of v1 thickened (except in *Minois*); hw precostal vein small or vestigial. *Genitalia.* Uncus long, slender; tegumen with slender upturned brachia, apices angulares well developed; valve elongate, narrow, often with prominent costal shoulder before apex, terminal section sometimes armed with teeth; vesica penis expands below ostium.

This extensive subfamily is most characteristic of the mountainous districts of southern Europe and of western and central Asia.

References. de Lesse 1951A, 1951B.

Key to tribes of Satyrinae

1 Fw with ocelli or black spots in s4,5 . . . . Erebiini
  Fw with ocellus or black spot in s5 but not in s4 . . 2

2 Antennal club short, spatulate . . . . . . Hipparchiini
  Antennal club elongate, narrow, not spatulate . . . Satyrini

Tribe SATYRINI Boisduval 1833

Rather large butterflies, outer margin of hw scalloped, ocellar pupils sometimes blue. *Antennal* club slender, three to four times as long as wide. *Venation.* Fw v12 greatly dilated, median vein somewhat dilated in *Arethusana* but not in other European species, hw precostal vein variable; upf sex-brand perpendicular to v1 when present.

Key to genera of Satyrini

1 Fw median vein somewhat dilated at base . . . *Arethusana*
  Fw median vein not dilated 2

2 Apex of valve without teeth 3
  Apex of valve with teeth 4

3 Apex of valve rounded . . . . *Berberia*
  Apex of valve upturned, pointed . . . . . *Satyrus*

4 Apex of valve slender with large teeth . . . . *Minois*
  Valve very elongate with small apical teeth . . . *Brintesia*

Genus **SATYRUS** Latreille 1810   TS: *Papilio actaea* Esper

Ups ♂ ground-colour very dark. *Antennal* club slender. *Palpi* porrect. *Genitalia.* Valve simple, tapering to pointed apex; penis straight or nearly so.

Reference. de Lesse 1951C.

SATYRUS ACTAEA Esper 1780 CN 27 FG p. 152; Pl. 34
Male upf with sex-brand.
Genitalia. Apex of penis upturned; vesica with small cornuti.
Range. Portugal, Spain and S France. Italy, only in Maritime Alps and
northwards locally to Cottian Alps (Susa). Closely allied species or sub-
species occur in W Asia.

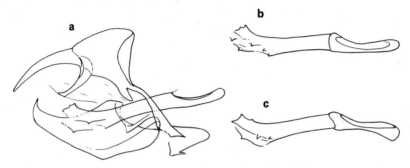

291. *Satyrus actaea,* S Spain: **a,** genitalia; **b,** penis. S France: **c,** penis.

SATYRUS FERULA F. CN 27 FG p. 152; Pl. 34
Male upf without sex-brand. Two subspecies with similar genitalia.

S. f. ferula F. 1793.
♂ and ♀ upf with ocellus in s2.
Genitalia. Like *S. actaea* but apex of penis almost straight in side view,
usually with small dorsal projection; vesica as in *S. actaea.*
Range. From France across S Europe to Greece, common in mountainous
areas but local, with subspecies or closely related species in W Asia.
Absent from Portugal and Spain, rare in Pyrenees.

S. f. atlanteus Verity 1927.
♀ usually with ocellus upf in s2, absent in ♂.
Range. Confined to Morocco.

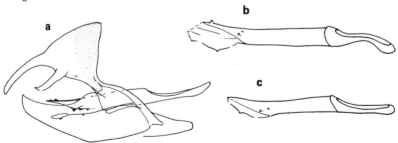

292. *Satyrus ferula atlanteus,* Morocco: **a,** genitalia; **b,** penis. *S. f. ferula,*
C Italy: **c,** penis.

217

Genus **MINOIS** Hübner 1819   TS: *Papilio dryas* Scopoli
Description. Hw outer margin scalloped, slightly in ♂, more deeply in ♀.
Antennal club slender. *Palpi* porrect. *Venation.* Fw v12 dilated, median
vein slightly thickened, vein 1 normal; hw precostal vein absent or
vestigial.
Genitalia. Uncus shorter than tegumen, peduncle elongate, curved;
vinculum slender, strongly curved; valve tapering to pointed apex, with
five large apical teeth, costal tubercle prominent; penis slender, longer
than valve.

MINOIS DRYAS Scopoli 1763   CN 28   FG p. 153; Pl. 34
Male sex-brand present upf.
Genitalia described above.
Range. In local colonies from N Spain and France eastwards to Balkans
(Serbia), C Asia and Japan. Absent from Mediterranean region.

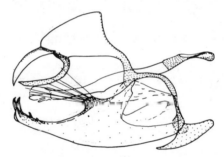

293. *Minois dryas*, Vienna: genitalia.

Genus **BRINTESIA** Fruhstorfer 1911   TS: *Papilio circe* D. & S.
Description. Male often small but sexes otherwise almost similar. *Palpi*
ascending, apical segment depressed. *Antennal* club slender. *Venation.*
Hw precostal vein present.
Genitalia. Tegumen longer than uncus, peduncles elongate, curved to
right-angle; vinculum slender, strongly curved; valve about twice the
length of uncus+tegumen, slender, tapering gradually to a small bunch
of apical spines; penis slender, slightly shorter than valve.

BRINTESIA CIRCE F. 1775   CN 29   FG p. 154; Pl. 33
Male sex-brand present upf.
Genitalia. Described above.
Range. From S and C Europe across W Asia to Iran and Himalaya Mts.

294. *Brintesia circe*, Czechoslovakia: **a,** genitalia; **b,** androconial scale.

Genus **ARETHUSANA** de Lesse 1951   TS: *Papilio arethusa* D. & S.
Upf single blind ocellus in s5; male sex-brand present. *Palpi* ascending, terminal segment depressed. *Antennal* club slender.
Genitalia. Tegumen longer than uncus, peduncles elongate; vinculum strongly curved; valve about one and a half times the length of uncus + tegumen, with slender costal shoulder prominent, long slender posterior process curving upwards; penis longer than valve, slender.

ARETHUSANA ARETHUSA   D. & S. 1775   CN unknown
                                                             FG p. 155; Pl. 33
Genitalia. Described above.
Range. Morocco, local and rare in High Atlas. S and C Europe and across S Russia and Asia Minor to C Asia. Absent from C Alps.

Reference. Varin 1953.

295. *Arethusana arethusa*, Vienna: genitalia.

Genus **BERBERIA** de Lesse 1951   TS: *Satyrus abdelkader* Pierret
Description. *Palpi* ascending, terminal segment depressed. *Antennal club* gradual, pyriform. *Venation.* Fw bases of v12 and median vein dilated, vein 1 thickened; hw precostal vein present.
Genitalia. Uncus and brachia short, robust; peduncles not developed; valve rather narrow, as long as uncus + tegumen, hairy, apex rounded; penis long, slender, slightly sinuous.

BERBERIA ABDELKADER   Pierret 1837   CN unknown

FG p. 154; Pl. 33, 34

Hw with small ocelli in s2 and s5.
Genitalia. Described above.
Range. N Africa including Tripolitania.

Reference. Le Cerf 1914.

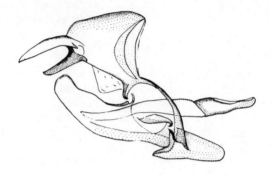

296. *Berberia abdelkader*, Morocco: genitalia.

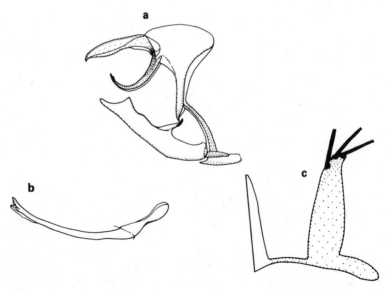

297. *Hipparchia fagi,* S France: **a,** genitalia, penis removed; **b,** penis; **c,** Jullien organ, left lamella partially omitted.

Tribe HIPPARCHIINI

Butterflies of medium or large size, outer margin on hw wavy or slightly scalloped; ocelli never with blue pupils. *Antennal club* short, abrupt. *Venation.* Fw v12 and median vein greatly swollen, vi less swollen; precostal vein present in hw; upf male sex-brand usually oblique along median vein.

Reference. de Lesse 1951c.

Key to genera of Hipparchiini

1 Tegumen with uncus anticus . . . . *Pseudotergumia*
  Tegumen without uncus anticus **2**

2 Jullien organ well developed . . . . . . *Hipparchia*
  Jullien organ not present. **3**

3 Valve narrow, costal shoulder prominent . . . . . *Neohipparchia*
  Valve without costal shoulder **4**

4 Penis rather stout, shorter than valve . . . *Pseudochazara*
  Penis very slender, longer than valve . . . . *Chazara*

Genus **HIPPARCHIA** F. 1807   TS: *Papilio fagi* Scopoli
Description. Palpi ascending, terminal segment depressed. *Antennal club* abrupt, oval, spatulate in dried specimens. *Legs* tibial spines greatly developed on mid- and hind-legs. *Venation.* Fw vi thickened.
Genitalia. Uncus usually as long as or longer than the tegumen; vinculum smoothly curved; valve narrow with small angular costal shoulder followed by a short terminal process; penis very slender, gently curved in side view. Jullien organ present in many species. The last abdominal tergite is divided into two lateral lamellae on the posterior margins of which hair scales are modified to form stiff black or brown rods (batons) varying in number and in size in different species and subspecies.

HIPPARCHIA FAGI   Scopoli 1763   CN 29   FG p. 137; Pl. 29
Genitalia. Uncus with slight central bulge; brachia long, strongly and evenly curved; saccus small. Jullien organ: lateral lamellae narrow, each bearing three or four long slender batons.
Range. C and S Europe to 52°N, extending to Bulgaria and Greece, but frontiers in SE uncertain. Absent from C and S Spain, Portugal, Germany and Fennoscandia.

Reference. Jullien 1909.

HIPPARCHIA ALCYONE D. & S.   CN 29–30 FG p. 138 Pl. 29

Genitalia. Like *H. fagi* but brachia not so long nor so strongly curved. Four subspecies are recognised in N Africa and in Europe, indistinguishable by wing-markings but each with small anatomical distinctions especially in the organ of Jullien. Three occurring in Europe appear to be strictly allopatric, but the distributions are not well known. There is not any record of cohabitation or overlap. Each subspecies is described independently. The species is absent from NW Europe, Alto Adige and Venezia Giulia, Sicily, Corsica, Sardinia, Elba and Crete.

H. a. alcyone D. & S. 1775

Genitalia. Uncus slender, tapering gradually to obtusely pointed apex. Jullien organ: lamellae well separated, broad, each with 18–24 rather short and heavily pigmented batons, crowded.
Range. Seen from Vienna and from Czechoslovakia. Also similar, *H. a. vandalusica* Oberthur 1894. *Range.* Spain and Pyrenees figured FG Pl. 29 2a, Cuenca, Arragon.

H. a. genava Fruhstorfer 1908

Genitalia. Like *H. a. alcyone.* Jullien organ: lamellae well separated, wide, each with 8–10 batons, well spaced and densely pigmented (not crowded). FG Pl. 22 from C Italy.
Range. S France (Lozère), Alps from Alpes Maritimes to Valais, C Italy.

H. a. caroli Rothschild 1933   CN unknown   FG. No figure

Genitalia. Like *H. a. alcyone*; uncus moderately dilated near apex. Jullien organ: like *H. a. alcyone* but lamellae less widely separated, batons 15–18 on each side, longer and more slender.
Range. Morocco, confined to Middle Atlas.

H. a. syriaca Staudinger 1871   CN 29   FG p. 138; Pl. 29

Genitalia. Like *H. a. alcyone*, uncus in side view relatively shorter, more massive, prominently dilated before apex. Jullien organ: lamellae close together, each bearing eight large batons, well separated.
Range. Balkan countries from Slovenia (Mt. Nanos) and Velebit Mts. to Greece and eastwards to Asia Minor, Lebanon, S Russia (Kieff) and Caucasus (Borjom). There is no overlap with the most easterly colony of *H. a. alcyone* in the main alpine chain. *H. a. syriaca* is ranked a distinct species by many authors. FG fig 2c from Macedonia

References. Hemming 1943. de Lesse 1951B.

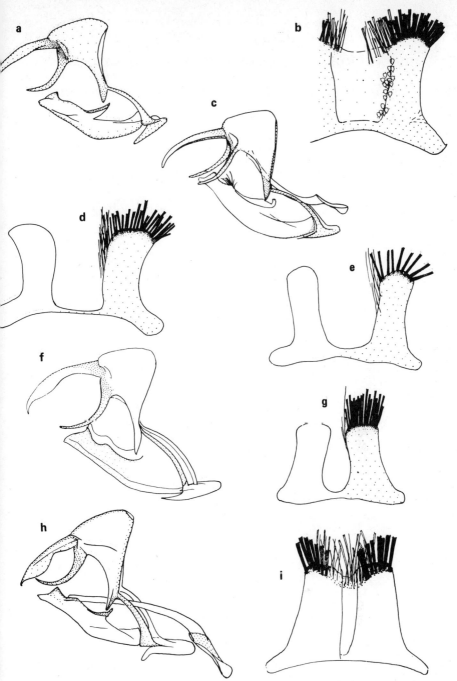

298. *Hipparchia alcyone alcyone,* Vienna: **a,** genitalia, **b,** Jullien organ. *H. a. vandalusica,* S Spain: **c,** genitalia; **d,** Jullien organ. *H. a. genava,* S France: **e,** Jullien organ. *H. a. caroli,* Morocco: **f,** genitalia; **g,** Jullien organ. *H. a. syriaca.* Macedonia: **h,** genitalia; **i,** Jullien organ.

HIPPARCHIA ELLENA   Oberthur 1894   CN unknown

FG p. 139; Pl. 29

Genitalia. Uncus strong, brachia slender, slightly sinuous but less curved than those of *H. alcyone*; apical process of valve very short, almost truncate. Jullien organ: lamellae wide, 10-12 batons on each.
Range. Confined to E Algeria and Tunisia.

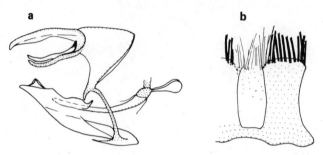

299. *Hipparchia ellena,* E Algeria: **a,** genitalia; **b,** Jullien organ.

HIPPARCHIA NEOMIRIS   Godart 1824   CN unknown

FG p. 139; Pl. 48

Genitalia. Like *H. alcyone*; small, uncus strong, brachia slender, almost straight; costal shoulder of valve prominent, finely spined; penis as in *H. alcyone.* Jullien organ: lateral lamellae elongate, narrow, with many long narrow batons mostly coloured pale brown.
Range. Confined to Sardinia, Corsica and Elba.

300. *Hipparchia neomiris,* Corsica: genitalia.

HIPPARCHIA SEMELE   L.   CN 29   FG p. 139; Pl. 30

Two subspecies with different genitalia.

H. s. semele L. 1758.

Variable in size and markings, many subspecies named.
Genitalia. Uncus almost one and a half times as long as tegumen, brachia long, strongly divergent, evenly curved; peduncle narrow, very long,

slightly curved, apex angularis prominent; vinculum short, not longer than peduncle, strongly curved; valve apex elongate; penis as in *H. alcyone*. Jullien organ narrow, margin bordered with coarse brown hairs, many with apical notch.

Range. Widely distributed throughout Europe, extending to N Turkey. Northern specimens usually small, but alpine and southern specimens larger and darker, *H. s. cadmus* Fruhstorfer 1908, more correctly an extreme clinal form. Absent from Sardinia, Corsica, Malta and Balearic islands.

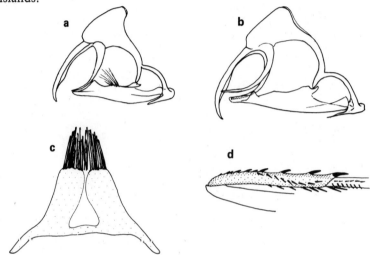

301. *Hipparchia semele semele,* Scotland: **a,** genitalia. S Spain: **b,** genitalia; **c,** Jullien organ; **d,** middle-leg tibia with spines.

H. s. cretica Rebel 1916.

Like *H. s. semele*, external markings not distinctive.

Genitalia. Very large, uncus more than twice as long as tegumen, very slender, brachia also very long. Jullien organ as in *H. s. semele*.

Range. Crete.

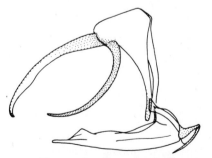

H. s. cretica, Crete: genitalia.

HIPPARCHIA ARISTAEUS Bonelli CN 29 FG p. 140; Pl. 30

Widely distributed across W Mediterranean region. Five subspecies, mostly very localised with restricted distributions, genitalia slightly variable in one.

H. a. aristaeus Bonelli 1826.
♂ ups brightly marked, ocellus upf in s2 small.
Genitalia. Like *H. semele* but relatively small; uncus more robust, slightly longer than tegumen, brachia shorter, less strongly curved; peduncle shorter, wider, tapering; vinculum about twice as long, less curved; valve costal shoulder more prominent.
Range. Sardinia, Corsica, Elba, Giglio and Lipari Islands.

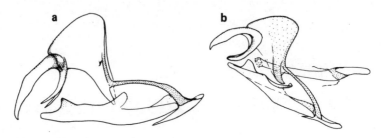

302. *Hipparchia aristaeus aristaeus,* Corsica: **a,** genitalia. *H. a. azorinus,* Azores Islands: **b,** genitalia.

H. a. siciliana Oberthur 1914.
♂ like *H. a. aristaeus,* upf pd ocellus in s2 large.
Genitalia. Like *H. a. aristaeus.*
Range. Sicily, (S Italy ?).

H. a. algirica Oberthur 1876.
♂ like *H. a. siciliana,* ups markings paler.
Genitalia. Like *H. a. aristaeus.*
Range. N Africa, Greece (Peloponnesus) dark markings slightly more extensive.

H. a. maderensis B. Baker 1891.
♂ and ♀ ups very dark.
Genitalia. Like *H. a. aristaeus.*
Range. Madeira.

H. a. azorina Strecker 1899.
Ups markings distinctive.
Genitalia. Like *H. a. aristaeus* but small, brachia more massive.
Range. Azores.

Genus **NEOHIPPARCHIA** de Lesse 1951
 TS: *Papilio statilinus* Hufnagel 1766
External characters as in *Hipparchia* Fabricius.
Genitalia. Uncus shorter than tegumen, curved, brachia short, almost straight arising from base of uncus; peduncle not developed; valve like *H. fagi*, truncate posteriorly with prominent costal shoulder and posterior margin finely toothed, posterior process small; proximal ostium of penis more expanded than that of *H. fagi*. Jullien organ: lateral lamellae broad with borders parallel, posterior margins bordered with coarse hair.
Reference. de Lesse 1952(B).

NEOHIPPARCHIA STATILINUS   Hufnagel 1766   CN 29
 FG p. 142; Pl. 31
Genitalia. Described above; apex angularis short.
Range. N Africa, Portugal, Spain and across S and C Europe to Asia Minor, northwards to Baltic coast but rare and local in the north. Absent from NW Europe, Sardinia and Corsica.

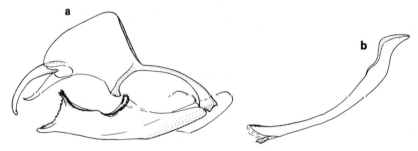

303. *Neohipparchia statilinus,* S Spain: **a,** genitalia; **b,** penis.

NEOHIPPARCHIA FATUA   Freyer 1844   CN 29 FG p. 143; Pl. 31
Genitalia. Like *N. statilinus*; brachia small, about half the length of uncus; apex angularis slightly longer; costal angle of valve less prominent but terminal process slightly longer.
Range. S Balkans, Asia Minor, Syria, Lebanon.

304. *Neohipparchia fatua,* Macedonia: genitalia.

227

NEOHIPPARCHIA HANSII Austaut   CN unknown

FG p. 143; Pl. 31, 32

Two subspecies with similar genitalia.

N. h. hansii Austaut 1879.

Genitalia. Like *N. statilinus*; uncus shorter, apex angularis well developed; valve posteriorly truncate at prominent costal shoulder, terminal process very small.
Range. Morocco, Algeria, and Tunisia in Middle Atlas Mts. Locally and individually variable.

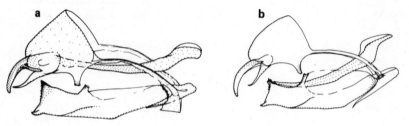

305. *Neohipparchia hansii hansii*, Morocco: **a**, genitalia. *N. h. powelli*, Algeria: **b**, genitalia.

N. h. powelli Oberthur 1910.

Unh veins lined pale grey.
Range. Southern districts of E Algeria and Tunisia. Taxonomic status uncertain.

Genus PSEUDOTERGUMIA Agenjo 1947   TS: *Papilio fidia* L.

Genitalia. Like *Neohipparchia*, a small uncus anticus is present; costal shoulder of valve rounded, posterior process longer.

PSEUDOTERGUMIA FIDIA L. 1767   CN 29–31

FG p. 146; Pl. 32

Genitalia. Uncus anticus single, slender; apex angularis robust; penis as in *N. statilinus*.

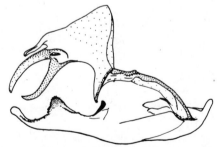

306. *Pseudotergumia fidia*, S France: genitalia.

Range. N Africa, Spain and Portugal, SE France and Italy in the Basses Alpes and Alpes Maritimes.

PSEUDOTERGUMIA WYSSII Christ
CN unknown FG p. 146; Pl. 31

Two subspecies, genitalia differ slightly.

P. w. wyssii Christ 1889.
Genitalia. Like *P. fidia* L.; uncus and brachia slightly more massive, uncus anticus shorter, wider, bilobed; penis as in *N. statilinus.*
Range. Confined to Tenerife, Canary Islands.

P. w. bacchus Higgins 1967.
Genitalia. Similar but costal shoulder of valve wider, posterior margin dentate.
Range. Gomera and Hierro, Canary Islands.

References. de Lesse 1951E. Higgins 1967.

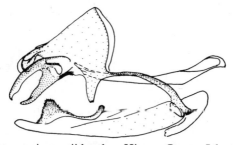

307. *Pseudotergumia wyssii bacchus,* Hierro, Canary Islands: genitalia.

Genus **CHAZARA** Moore 1893   TS: *Papilio briseis* L.
Large butterflies, ups dark brown with white or orange markings; sexes almost similar; male sex-brand inconspicuous.
Genitalia. Uncus slightly shorter than tegumen, brachia long and very slender, peduncle short; valve wide, terminal process slender, short; penis elongate and very slender.

CHAZARA BRISEIS L. 1764   CN 28   FG p. 147; Pl. 32
Genitalia. Uncus and slender brachia almost straight; valve lacks a costal shoulder.

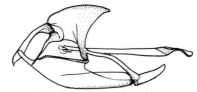

308. *Chazara briseis* S Spain: genitalia.

Range. S and C Europe and eastwards across W Asia to Iran and Turkestan. Absent from NW Europe, Corsica, Sardinia and Elba.

CHAZARA PRIEURI   Pierret 1837   CN unknown   FG p. 147; Pl. 32
Genitalia. Like *C. briseis*; apex angularis slightly longer; uncus gently curved.
Range. Morocco and Algeria, local in Middle Atlas. C Spain, local in Montes Universales and near Saragossa.

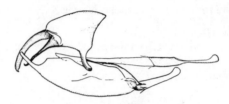

309. *Chazara prieuri,* C Spain: genitalia.

Genus **PSEUDOCHAZARA**   de Lesse 1951
   TS: *Hipparchia pelopea* Klug
Butterflies of medium size, markings variable, hw outer margin slightly wavy. Antennal club short, abrupt.
Genitalia. Uncus robust, gently curved, brachia slender, short, tapering to pointed apex; valve narrow, without teeth or abrupt angles, tapered gently to upturned apex, costal prominence often indicated by a few bristles; penis short, straight, lacking marked features.

Reference. de Lesse 1951A.

PSEUDOCHAZARA ATLANTIS   Austaut 1905.   CN unknown
FG p. 148; Pl. 48
Genitalia. Valve apex rounded, costal prominence bearing a few bristles.
Range. Morocco, in Atlas Mts., at high altitudes.

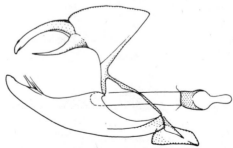

310. *Pseudochazara atlantis,* Morocco: genitalia.

PSEUDOCHAZARA HIPPOLYTE   Esper 1784   CN 28

FG p. 148; Pl. 48

Range. Widely distributed from S Russia eastwards to C Asia and Mongolia. A single subspecies occurs in W Europe.

P. h. williamsi Romei 1927.
Genitalia. Like *P. atlantis,* valve apex more pointed.
Range. S Spain, in Sierra Nevada at high altitudes.

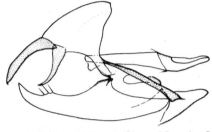

311. *Pseudochazara hippolyte williamsi,* Sierra Nevada, S Spain: genitalia.

PSEUDOCHAZARA MAMURRA   Herrich-Schäffer 1846

FG p. 149; Pl. 48

Range. Mountains of Asia Minor and eastwards to Iran. A single subspecies occurs in SE Europe.

P. m. graeca Staudinger 1870.
Genitalia. Like *P. hippolyte.*
Range. Greece, Mt. Chelmos, Mt. Parnassus etc.

312. *Pseudochazara mamurra graeca,* S Greece: genitalia.

PSEUDOCHAZARA ANTHELEA   Hübner 1824   CN 28

FG p. 149; Pl. 35

Range. Widely distributed in Asia Minor and eastwards to C Asia. A single well defined subspecies occurs in SE Europe.

P. a. amalthea   Frivaldsky 1845.

Genitalia. Like *P. atlantis*, uncus longer and more slender, peduncle well defined; valve longer, a row of small teeth at extreme apex.
Range. Greece, Yugoslav Macedonia, Albania, Crete (differs slightly).

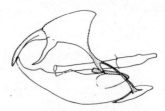

313. *Pseudochazara anthelea amalthea,* Greece: genitalia.

PSEUDOCHAZARA GEYERI   Herrich-Schäffer 1846   CN 27

FG p. 149; Pl. 48

Genitalia. Like *P. atlantis,* uncus slightly longer, tegumen less domed, brachia gently sinuous; apex of valve blunt.
Range. Widely distributed from Asia Minor to Transcaucasus and S Asia. A single subspecies occurs in SE Europe.

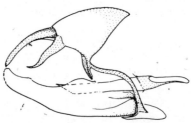

314. *Pseudochazara geyeri,* N Turkey: genitalia. No European specimens available.

P. g. occidentalis   Rebel & Zerny 1931.

Genitalia not available for examination.
Range. Albania, a few isolated colonies known near Lake Ochrid.

Tribe EREBIINI Tutt 1896

Closely related to the Satyrini but differ in markings, on upf usually with a fulvous pd band enclosing black spots or white-pupilled ocelli in s4 and s5.

The species of this tribe usually live in arctic or alpine biotopes, some at great altitudes, forming a characteristic feature of the Alpine butterfly fauna. All fly in a single annual brood. The high mountain habitats imply isolation of populations and some species with wide distribution are extremely variable. Several are adapted on the one hand to an alpine climate, several on the other hand to less severe conditions, the former being small and dark, the latter larger and brighter. In some cases true geographical subspecies have evolved, but intermediate phenotypes are common, forming clines. In the genitalia minor characters in the valves are sometimes so variable that it is impossible to illustrate the situation properly with two or three figures, but the dorsal characters are less variable. For most species only the valves are figured unless some feature of special interest is present. The group shows unusual features. The forty-five different species recognised in this book are placed in a single genus; all are so closely related that attempts at generic division have not been successful, and *Erebia* remains by far the largest genus of European butterflies. Over 75% of species are endemic, including several narrowly restricted to a few alpine valleys or mountain groups, and we may suppose that these are relict forms surviving from preglacial times.

Genus **EREBIA** Dalman 1816   TS: *Papilio ligea* L.

Description. Butterflies of small or medium size, gc dark brown or black, ups with fulvous pd bands or ocelli ringed fulvous; unh with cryptic markings. *Eyes* smooth. *Palpi* porrect or nearly so, hairy beneath. *Antennae* variable, club often slender and elongate but more abrupt in *E. gorge* and in the *E. epiphron* group. *Legs:* ♂ fore-leg very small with single tarsal segment; ♀ fore-leg slightly larger with four tarsal segments, hair scanty, middle and hind-legs not heavily spined (cf. *Hipparchia* p. 225.) *Venation.* Fw base of v12 greatly dilated, median vein less dilated, v1 usually thickened; hw precostal vein vestigial or absent.

Genitalia. Uncus rather short, brachia slender, usually tapering, apex angularis prominent; valve often with costal teeth and well defined specific characters; penis short, variable; furca extensive, often embracing the penis and a prominent character in side view, p. 248.

Early stages. Ovum barrel-shaped with up to 30 longitudinal ribs. Larva densely pubescent with dark longitudinal stripes. Pupa short, smooth, abdominal segments rigid. So far as known hibernation occurs as small larva, and this stage is thought to last for two years or longer in some cases.

References. de Lesse 1960A. Warren 1936. Lorković 1960.

EREBIA LIGEA L. 1758   CN 29   FG p. 156; Pl. 36
Male sex-brand present upf.
Genitalia. Peduncles well developed; valve narrow, tapering with single series of slightly irregular costal teeth; penis slightly sinuous.
Range. Widely distributed in mountainous areas, extending across Asia to Japan; absent from Britain and SW Europe including the Pyrenees.

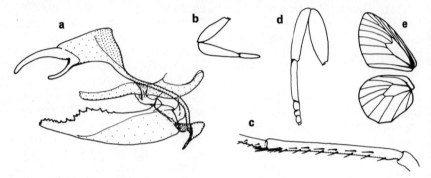

315. *Erebia ligea,* Bavaria: **a,** genitalia; **b,** ♂ fore-leg; **c,** ♂ middle-leg tibia; **d,** ♀ fore-leg; **e,** wing venation.

EREBIA EURYALE Esper   CN unknown   FG p. 156; Pl. 36
Upf male sex-brand absent. Widely distributed on mountains of C Europe and eastwards to Ural Mts. and C Asia. Three subspecies defined by wing-markings, with similar genitalia.
Genitalia. Like *E. ligea;* valve slightly more slender, costal teeth series partially double.

316. *Erebia euryale,* Yugoslavia: valve.

E. e. euryale Esper 1805.
Upf ocelli small, blind.
Range. Cantabrian Mts., Pyrenees, C France, Jura, Bavaria, Austria part, Czechoslovakia, Carpathians, Balkans. Absent from Fennoscandia.

E. e. ocellaris Staudinger 1861.
Upf fulvous pd fascia greatly reduced, broken, sometimes absent.
Range. Carinthia, Alto Adige and Venezia Giulia.

E. e. adyte Hübner 1822.
Upf ocelli larger, white pupilled.
Range. Alps of SE France, S Switzerland, NW Italy eastwards to Engadine, Abruzzi.

EREBIA ERIPHYLE Freyer 1839   CN 29   FG p. 158; Pl. 38, 28
Genitalia. Uncus short, straight; valve with rounded shoulder before slender terminal process, with numerous marginal teeth.
Range. Central and eastern Alps.

317. *Erebia eriphyle,* Austria: valve.

EREBIA MANTO D. & S.   CN 29   FG p. 158; Pl. 39
Two subspecies with similar genitalia.
Genitalia. Like *E. eriphyle*, costal shoulder of valve less wide, teeth much larger but variable; penis almost straight.

318. *Erebia manto manto,* Austria: valve.

E. m. manto D. & S. 1775.
♂ upf fulvous pd markings present.
Range. Alps and Carpathians, a small colony also in Serbia.

E. m. constans Eiffinger 1908.
♂ upf fulvous markings absent.
Range. Pyrenees, Central France. At very high altitudes small, *pyrrhula* Frey 1880 with or without fulvous markings ♂ upf.

EREBIA CLAUDINA Borkhausen 1789   CN 18   FG p. 159; Pl. 37
Genitalia. Costal margin of valve gently curved, tapering to rounded apex with teeth, rather large at base but terminal teeth very small; penis almost as long as valve, slender, gently curved.
Range. Restricted to a few high mountains in eastern Alps.

319. *Erebia claudina,* Carinthia, Austria: valve.

235

EREBIA FLAVOFASCIATA Heyne 1895   CN unknown

FG p. 162; Pl. 37

Genitalia. Valve almost straight, slender, gradually tapered to rounded apex with small, rather irregular teeth along distal third of costal margin, penis gently sinuous.

Range. Restricted to a few high mountains in southern Alps.

320. *Erebia flavofasciata,* Switzerland: valve.

EREBIA EPIPHRON Knoch   CN 17   FG p. 162; Pl. 38

Very variable, many local races or minor subspecies on various mountains. Two major subspecies rather vaguely differentiated in C Europe, a third with well defined characters in Bulgaria; genitalia similar in all.

Genitalia. Like *E. flavofasciata,* valve straight, tapered, small regular teeth along distal two-thirds of costal margin; penis short, stout.

E. e. epiphron Knoch 1783.

♂ upf fulvous band of even width, enclosing four small blind ocelli.

Range. Characters well defined in Bohemia (Altvater Mt.), Tatra and Carpathians, E Pyrenees, less striking, ups markings subdued, three or four ocelli, C France, Britain, Bavaria etc.

E. e. aetheria Esper 1805.

♂ upf red pd band reduced or broken in s3 with absence of black spot.

Range. W and C Alps, best defined in Switzerland, N Italy, Abruzzi and Austria, specimens from Htes. Pyrénées and Cantabrian Mts. somewhat intermediate.

321. *Erebia epiphron aetheria,* Switzerland: valve.

E. e. orientalis Elwes 1900.

♂ fw pointed, red pd band narrow, regular, twin white-pupilled sub-apical ocelli.

Range. Rilo, Rhodope and Perim Mts., Bulgaria. Characters quite constant, perhaps better graded as distinct species.

EREBIA SEROTINA   Descimon & de Lesse 1953   CN unknown
FG p. 166; Pl. 44

Genitalia. Like *E. christi*; for figure see reference below.

Range. First seen near Cauterets, C Pyrenees, in September 1953. Between 20 and 30 specimens known, all males. Not seen again in recent years.

Reference. Descimon & de Lesse 1953 (genitalia figure).

EREBIA CHRISTI   Rätzer 1890   CN unknown FG p. 166; Pl. 38

Genitalia. Like *E. pharte*, valve more slender, almost straight, teeth along costal margin larger.

Range. Very local in southern Alps of Switzerland.

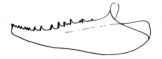

323. *Erebia christi,* Switzerland: valve.

EREBIA PHARTE   Hübner 1804   CN 19–22   FG p. 166; Pl. 38

Genitalia. Like *E. christi*; valve generally wider, tapering rather abruptly near apex, costal teeth larger and more regular but scanty in basal area; penis slender, almost straight.

Range. Restricted to Europe; widely distributed in the Alps and N Carpathians.

324. *Erebia pharte,* Slovenia: valve.

EREBIA MELAMPUS   Fuessli 1775   CN 19 ? FG p. 167; Pl. 37

Genitalia. Valve very slender, curved gently upwards and tapered to rounded apex, costal margin crested with small regular teeth, these slightly larger near base.

Range. Restricted to Europe; widely distributed in the Alps.

325. *Erebia melampus,* Switzerland: valve.

EREBIA SUDETICA Staudinger 1861

CN unknown FG p. 168; Pl. 37

Genitalia. Like *E. melampus*; valve even more slender with gentle upwards curve, costal teeth slightly larger.

Range. Sudeten and Carpathian Mts., France in Lozère and a small colony known in C Switzerland near Grindelwald.

Reference. Warren 1949.

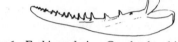

326. *Erebia sudetica,* Czechoslovakia: valve.

EREBIA AETHIOPS Esper 1777   CN 21 FG p. 168; Pl. 39, 44

Genitalia. Brachia truncate; valve slender, bowed and tapering, a small costal shoulder and narrow apex both crested with small teeth and larger teeth may be present on shaft; penis straight, stout.

Range. Widely distributed, especially in hilly districts, across C Europe northwards to the Baltic, including Britain. Absent from Fennoscandia, Pyrenees, peninsular Italy and Mediterranean region.

327. *Erebia aethiops,* Yugoslavia: valve.

EREBIA TRIARIA de Prunner 1798   CN 16? FG p. 169; Pl. 39

Genitalia. Brachia short, pointed, curved upwards; valve elongate, slender, lacking teeth, tapered to downturned, rounded apex; penis straight, robust.

Range. Restricted to Europe, from C Spain and SE France along southern slopes of the Alps to the Balkans.

328. *Erebia triaria,* C Spain: valve.

EREBIA MEDUSA D. & S.   CN 11   FG p. 171; Pl. 40

Widely distributed in W Europe to Asia Minor. Variable on a cline with larger, brightly marked forms at valley levels. Small races, markings greatly reduced, at high altitudes in some areas. Two subspecies occur in Europe united by intermediate forms of every grade, genitalia similar.

Genitalia. Brachia short, pointed; apex angularis very large; valve tapering to slightly bulbous apex with small costal teeth.

E. m. medusa D. & S. 1775.

Ups fulvous markings well defined.

Range. At valley levels and moderate altitudes, northwards to Paris, W Germany (Brocken etc.) and Lithuania, and eastwards to Balkans, Greece and Asia Minor. Italy, only in Alps and Etruscan Apennines. Absent from Pyrenees, Mediterranean area and Fennoscandia.

E. m. hippomedusa Ochsenheimer 1820.

Small, ups fulvous markings greatly reduced.

Range. SE Alps, Styria, Carinthia, Dolomites, Monte Baldo etc.

329. *Erebia medusa,* Yugoslavia: genitalia.

EREBIA POLARIS Staudinger 1871   CN 11   FG p. 174; Pl. 40

Genitalia. Like *E. medusa* D. & S.

Range. Restricted to small area in arctic Lapland, not south of 68°N., N. Siberia (Yakutsen), probably widely distributed there.

330. *Erebia polaris,* Lapland, Norway: valve.

Note. By external markings distinct from *E. medusa*; especially in ♀, with distinctive pattern unh.

EREBIA DISA   Thunberg 1791   CN 29   FG p. 170; Pl. 38
Genitalia. Uncus short, brachia straight, directed obliquely downwards, apices bulbous; base of valve wide, tapering abruptly to narrow distal section about one-third total length, small costal teeth present from mid-point of costa, slightly larger near apex; penis short, stout.
Range. Circumpolar; from Arctic Fennoscandia eastwards to Siberia and arctic America.

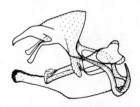

331. *Erebia disa,* arctic Norway: genitalia.

EREBIA EMBLA   Thunberg 1791   CN unknown   FG p. 170; Pl. 38
Genitalia. Like *E. disa;* costal teeth of valve very small, present only near and at apex.
Range. Fennoscandia, especially in arctic regions, and eastwards to the Amur.

332. *Erebia embla,* S Norway: valve.

EREBIA ALBERGANUS   de Prunner 1798   CN 17–18 ?
                                             FG p. 174; Pl. 42
Genitalia. Uncus almost straight, longer than tegumen; apex angularis large; valve bowed, upturned, finely toothed with small costal shoulder, apex narrow; penis slightly sinuous.
Range. In local colonies from Alpes Maritimes to Hohe Tauern with an isolated colony in Bulgaria.

333. *Erebia alberganus,* SE France: valve.

EREBIA PLUTO de Prunner   CN 19   FG p. 175; Pl. 41
Confined to European Alps. Four subspecies, phases of clinal series and all connected by intermediate specimens. Genitalia similar, variable and probably showing minor racial characters.

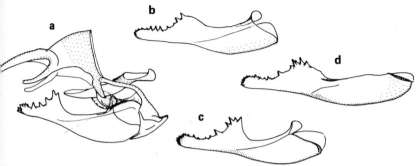

334. *Erebia pluto pluto,* C Italy: **a,** genitalia. Julian Alps: **b,** valve. *E. p. oreas,* Switzerland; **c,** valve. *E. p. nicholli,* N Italy: **d,** valve.

E. p. pluto de Prunner 1798.
Ups black, unmarked.
Range. Abruzzi, Alpes Maritimes and north to Savoie, Bernese Oberland, Dolomites and Carinthia (part), Julian Alps (Triglav).

E. p. alecto Hübner 1804.
Ups black, upf twin subapical white-pupilled ocelli.
Range. Central Alps, Bavarian Alps, Oetztal, Ortler etc.

E. p. nicholli Oberthur 1896.
Ups black, pd ocelli with intensely white pupils, fw with four, hw with three.
Range. Monte Baldo and Brenta Group of Alps.

E. p. oreas Warren 1933.
Ups black less intense, wide reddish pd bands, ocelli absent.
Range. Haute Savoie and east across S Switzerland to Albula. Commonly intergrades with *E. p. alecto.*

EREBIA GORGE Hübner   CN 21   FG p. 178; Pl. 37
Widely distributed through Pyrenees, Alps and Balkans to Bulgaria. Four subspecies well defined, genitalia similar but variable, perhaps with minor racial characters.

335. *Erebia gorge erynis,* Maritime Alps: **a,** valve. *E. g. triopes,* N Italy: **b,** valve.

Genitalia. Uncus stout; apex angularis large; valve slender, prominent shoulder near centre of costal margin, crowned with large teeth, continued to slender apex; penis strong, almost straight.

E. g. gorge Hübner 1804.
Fw with twin apical ocelli in both sexes.
Range. E Pyrenees, Savoie, Bavaria, S Switzerland, Austria, Balkans to Albania and Bulgaria. Also Cantabrian Mts., large specimens.

E. g. ramondi Oberthur 1909.
Uph large pd ocelli.
Range. Pyrenees, west of Andorra; distribution sharply defined.

E. g. erynis Esper 1805.
Upf lacking apical ocelli.
Range. Constant form in Alpes Maritimes, becoming less common northwards. Abruzzi, Gran Sasso etc.

E. g. triopes Speyer 1865.
Upf three apical ocelli, uph pd ocelli large.
Range. Switzerland (S Engadine) and Ortler Mts, a constant form over a wide area, Brenta and Monte Baldo.

EREBIA AETHIOPELLA Hoffmannsegg CN 7 FG p. 180; Pl. 37
Distribution centres in Maritime Alps and in S Balkans. Two subspecies with similar genitalia.
Genitalia. Like *E. gorge*, costal shoulder of valve placed more distally, posterior process shorter. Valves slightly variable.

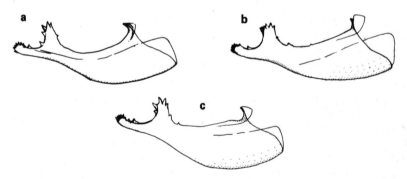

336. *Erebia aethiopella*, Cottian Alps, NW Italy: **a,** valve. *E. a. rhodopensis,* Bulgaria: **b,** valve. *E. a. sharsta,* Macedonia: **c,** valve.

E. a. aethiopella Hoffmannsegg 1806.
♂ upf sub-apical ocelli small.
Range. Maritime Alps and north to Mont Genèvre and Sestrières.

E. a. rhodopensis Nicholl 1900.
♂ upf sub-apical ocelli larger.
Range. Rilo and Rhodope Mts., Pirin Mts. Bulgaria. *E. a. sharsta* Higgins 1965, intermediate, Schar Planina, Yugoslav Macedonia.

EREBIA GORGONE Boisduval 1833   CN 12 FG p. 181; Pl. 40
Genitalia. Like *E. aethiopella* but with a few small teeth along costal margin of valve, shoulder less prominent, apical process slightly more robust, development of teeth variable.
Range. Only in the Pyrenees.

337. *Erebia gorgone,* C Pyrenees: valve.

EREBIA MNESTRA Hübner 1804   CN 12   FG p. 181; Pl. 37
Genitalia. Like *E. gorgone,* distal half of costal margin of valve with a few small teeth, costal shoulder and terminal process stout but short; individual variation may be marked.
Range. From Hautes Alpes and Hte. Savoie eastwards to Salzburg Alps and Monte Ademello; recorded from Tatra Mts.

Reference. de Lesse 1959A.

338. *Erebia mnestra,* Ortler Alps, N Italy: **a,** valve. Pontresina, E Switzerland: **b,** valve.

EREBIA EPISTYGNE Hübner 1824   CN 28–29 FG p. 182; Pl. 40
Genitalia. Uncus short, brachia very short, tapering rapidly; apex angularis large; valve massive with single large costal tooth and three or four large apical teeth; penis slender, longer than valve.
Range. Only in S France and C Spain, in local colonies.

339. *Erebia epistygne,* SE France: valve.

The six species following form a well defined group in which the male genitalia are small, compact, and details of valve structure variable, with poorly defined specific characters. Figures given below have been drawn from specimens considered to show average anatomy, but it is not possible to illustrate here the full extent of individual variation. For further information the reader is referred to the paper by de Lesse with many figures and with distribution maps. Important specific characters are present in the chromosome numbers which have been investigated especially by de Lesse and Lorković. These show constant differences between the species.

References. de Lesse 1960A, Lorković 1957. Lorković & de Lesse 1965.

EREBIA TYNDARUS Esper 1781   CN 10   FG p. 183; Pl. 42
Genitalia. Uncus slightly shorter than tegumen, brachia curved, apex angularis short and strong; valve most variable, usually with large costal tooth followed by four or five smaller teeth decreasing in size to a rounded apex; penis short, stout, slightly curved.
Range. Restricted to central Alps from Hte. Savoie (Val Ferret) eastwards to the Oetztal and northwards to the Allgäuer Alps.

340. *Erebia tyndarus,* Bavaria: **a,** genitalia. Pontresina, E Switzerland: **b,** valve.

EREBIA CASSIOIDES   Hohenwarth 1793
CN 10   FG p. 183; Pl. 42
Genitalia. Like *E. tyndarus,* variable; first spine of valve usually large and prominent; sometimes less prominent in specimens from E Alps; penis slightly curved.
Range. Cantabrian Mts., Pyrenees, France in Massif Central, W Switzerland and eastwards to Gross-Glockner, but absent over a wide area in

341. *Erebia cassioides,* Gross-Glockner, Austria: **a,** valve; **b,** penis. Cantabrian Mts., N Spain: **c,** valve.

Switzerland occupied by *E. tyndarus*; local in the Apennines and very local on a few high mountains in Yugoslavia.

EREBIA HISPANIA Butler   CN 25   FG p. 184; Pl. 42
Two subspecies with similar genitalia.
Genitalia. Like *E. cassioides*; valve tapered rather gradually to rounded apex, costal teeth relatively small.

342. *Erebia hispana hispana,* Sierra Nevada, S Spain: **a,** valve. Luchon, C Pyrenees: **b,** valve.

E. h. hispania Butler 1868.
Large, ♂ fw 19–21mm, upf sub-apical ocelli large.
Range. Confined to Sierra Nevada, S Spain.

E. h. rondoui Oberthur 1908.
Smaller, ♂ fw 15–18mm, upf ocelli smaller.
Range. E Pyrenees, flying at high altitudes, and westwards to Luchon and Col d'Aubisque.

EREBIA NIVALIS Lorković and de Lesse 1954   CN 11
                                                FG p. 185; Pl. 42
Genitalia. Like *E. tyndarus*; valve slightly shorter and wider, costal spine arises about mid-costa, followed by some small teeth and slender terminal process. In most specimens these characters are distinctive.
Range. E Alps, from Oetztal through Niederer and Hohe Tauern. A single colony has been found in the Bernese Alps (Faulhorn).

Reference. Lorković & de Lesse 1954B.

343. *Erebia nivalis,* Gross-Glockner, Austria: valve.

EREBIA CALCARIA Lorković 1949   CN 8   FG p. 185; Pl. 42
Genitalia. Like *E. cassioides*; valve usually tapering with large costal and

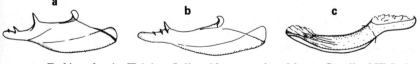

344. *Erebia calcaria,* Triglav, Julian Alps: **a,** valve. Monte Cavallo, NE Italy; **b,** valve; **c,** penis.

one to five small terminal spines, not specifically distinctive; penis more strongly curved than that of *E. cassioides*.
Range. Karawanken and Julian Alps and E Italy on Monte Cavallo and Monte Santo.

EREBIA OTTOMANA Herrich-Schäffer

CN 40 FG p. 185; Pl. 42

Isolated colonies in W Turkey, Balkans, N Italy and C France. Several poorly differentiated subspecies.
Genitalia. Uncus long, distinctive; valve usually with prominent costal spine arising near apex.

345. *Erebia ottomana balcanica,* Macedonia: **a,** genitalia, penis removed. Monte Baldo, NE Italy; **b,** valve.

E. o. ottomana Herrich-Schäffer 1851
Large, upf sub-apical ocelli large.
Range. S Yugoslav Macedonia, Greece, Bulgaria.

E. o. balcanica Rebel 1913.
Smaller, upf sub-apical ocelli smaller.
Range. Yuvoslavia, from Schar Planina northwards to Sarajevo; Monte Baldo (very dark); C France.

EREBIA PRONOE Esper CN 19 FG p. 186; Pl. 43
Two subspecies with similar genitalia.
Genitalia. Brachia long, valve slender, with small teeth at mid-costa, with or without smaller basal teeth, variable, distal section elongate, tapering, with small apical teeth; penis straight, stout.

346. *Erebia pronoe pronoe,* Austria: **a,** valve. *E. p. vergy,* Switzerland: **b,** valve.

E. p. pronoe Esper 1780
Upf fulvous pd band.
Range. E Alps, Styria etc., Carpathians, Balkans.

E. p. vergy Ochsenheimer 1807.
Upf dark, pd band vestigial or absent.
Range. NW Alps, in Vaud, Valais, Grisons, Jura etc.

EREBIA SCIPIO Boisduval 1832   CN 22   FG p. 189; Pl. 39
Genitalia. Like *E. pronoe*; valve elongate with costal spine before slender
distal section, apex bulbous, minutely toothed.
Range. At high altitudes in SW Alps, Basses Alpes and northwards.

347. *Erebia scipio,* Basses Alpes, SE France: valve.

EREBIA MELAS Herbst 1796   CN 21   FG p. 187; Pl. 40
Variable with several weakly differentiated named subspecies.
Genitalia. Base of valve wide tapering posteriorly, apex slightly expanded
with small teeth, usually a small tooth at base of distal section, or with
variable costal teeth.
Range. S Carpathians and Balkans, westwards to Mt. Nanos in Slovenia.

Reference. König 1965.

348. *Erebia melas,* Herzegowina, Yugoslavia: valve.

EREBIA LEFEBVREI Boisduval   CN 22   FG p. 188; Pl. 36
Genitalia. Valve elongate, costa strongly toothed usually with prominent
shoulder before slender distal section, apex slightly expanded and with
small teeth. Three named subspecies are phases of a single cline.

349. *Erebia lefebvrei lefebvrei,* Luchon, C Pyrenees: **a,** valve. Mt. Canigou,
E Pyrenees: **b,** valve.

247

E. l. lefebvrei Boisduval 1828.
♂ upf red pd band more or less defined in all specimens.
Range. Hautes Pyrénées, Basses Pyrénées.

E. l. astur Oberthur 1884.
♂ ups red pd band absent.
Range. Cantabrian Mts. (Picos de Europa). *E. l. pyrenaea* Oberthur 1884, intermediate, ♀ usually has traces of red pd band, transitional to *E. l. lefebvrei* (E Pyrenees).

EREBIA STYRIA   Godart 1824   CN 21–22   FG p. 189; Pl. 43
Genitalia. Valve elongate, tapering gradually to blunt apex crowned with very small teeth, a series of small teeth about mid-point of costal border; penis in dorsal view base expanded, shaft constricted at zone.
Range. E Alps from Monte Baldo and Seiser Alp to Karawanken, Julian Alps and Carnic Alps.

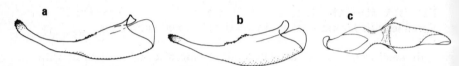

350. *Erebia styria,* Trenta Valley, NW Yugoslavia: **a,** valve. Monte Baldo, NE Italy: **b,** valve; **c,** penis.

EREBIA STYX   Freyer   CN 23   FG p. 190; Pl. 43
Three subspecies with similar genitalia.
Genitalia. Variable; like *E. styria* but costal border of valve usually smooth or with one or two small irregular teeth near base; penis as in *E. styria.*

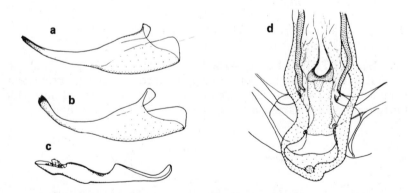

351. *Erebia styx trentae,* Trenta Valley, Slovenia: **a,** valve. *E. s. triglites,* Monte Generoso, N Italy: **b,** valve; **c,** penis, side view; **d,** A-P view of vinculum with valve bases, enclosing furca.

E. s. styx   Freyer 1834.
♂ ups ocelli often small.
Range. Dolomites and northern Alps of Austria and Switzerland, e.g.
Cortina, Brenner, Allgäuer Alps.

E. s. triglites Fruhstorfer 1918.
♂ ups more brightly marked, ocelli larger.
Range. Bergamasker Alps. Distinction from *E. s. styx* sometimes difficult.

E. s. trentae Lorković 1952.
♂ larger, ups markings dark, red pd band reduced.
Range. Slovenia, Trenta Valley etc.

References. Lorković 1952, 1955.

EREBIA MONTANA   de Prunner 1798   CN 24   FG p. 191; Pl. 40
Genitalia. Like *E. styria* and *E. styx*; valve often with small teeth or even
a larger spine near mid-costal area; compared with *E. styx* penis probably
narrower, in dorsal view less constricted at zone. Organs indistinguishable
in many cases.
Range. Widely distributed in W Alps, Ligurian and Etruscan Apennines,
more local in E Alps to Brenner area. Tatra Mts. (?).

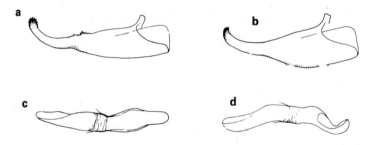

352. *Erebia montana,* Maritime Alps: **a,** valve. Pontresina, E Switzerland:
b, valve; **c,** penis, A-P view; **d,** penis, side view.

EREBIA ZAPATERI   Oberthur 1875
                            CN unknown   FG p. 194; Pl. 41
Genitalia. Apex angularis slender; valve as in *E. montana* but prominent
shoulder before slender posterior process; penis in side view slender.
Range. Confined to mountains of C Spain.

353. *Erebia zapateri,* C Spain: **a,** valve; **b,** penis, side view.

EREBIA NEORIDAS Boisduval 1828   CN 23 FG p. 195; Pl. 41
Genitalia. Like *E. zapateri*; valve usually with single group of low teeth near mid-costa; penis as in *E. zapateri*.
Range. Restricted to S Europe; S France, NE Spain (Catalonia); Italy, only in Cottian Alps and C Apennines.

354. *Erebia neoridas,* NW Italy: valve.

EREBIA OEME Hübner   CN 14   FG p. 195; Pl. 40
Restricted to Europe. Variable on a cline with three subspecies.
Genitalia. Valve fusiform with short, slender terminal process; apex angularis large; penis slender, slightly longer than valve. Genitalia similar in all subspecies.

E. o. oeme Hübner 1804.
♂ upf with two subapical ocelli clearly white-pupilled in small fulvous macule.
Range. C Pyrenees, C France (Mont Dore), Bavaria, Julian Alps, Bosnia etc. Without precise geographical significance.

E. o. lugens Staudinger 1901.
♂ upf almost unmarked, upf ocelli very small, sometimes blind, with or without traces of fulvous macule.
Range. NW Alps, N Switzerland, Allgäuer Alps, Glarus etc.

E. o. spodia Staudinger 1871.
Ups ♂ ocelli and fulvous macule enlarged, ♀ additional ocelli often present, uph often five to six ocelli, large, white pupils brilliant.
Range. Especially in eastern range, Velebit, Styria, E Pyrenees. Form in any colony constant, often with intermediate features and difficult to place.

a   b

355. *Erebia oeme oeme,* C Pyrenees: **a,** valve; **b,** penis.

EREBIA MEOLANS de Prunner   CN 14   FG p. 198; Pl. 39, 44
Widely distributed in mountains of W Europe including N and C Spain.
Variable on a cline with three subspecies, genitalia similar in all.
Genitalia. Uncus and brachia long, almost straight; apex angularis large;
valve elongate, tapering to slender posterior process, apex crowned with
teeth; penis as long as valve, slightly sinuous.

E. m. meolans de Prunner 1798.
Beyond middle size, ♂ ups markings fully developed.
Range. Basses Alpes to Valais, Pyrenees, Jura (often with additional
ocelli) etc. C France (usually small).

E. m. valesiaca Elwes 1898.
Smaller, ♂ ups markings greatly reduced.
Range. Switzerland, in SE, extending to Unterengadin, N Tirol and
Allgäuer Alps (slightly larger).

E. m. bejarensis Chapman 1902.
Large, brightly marked, ♂ upf red pd band wide, extending to s1b.
Range. C Spain.

356. *Erebia meolans meolans,* Piedmont, NW Italy: valve.

EREBIA PALARICA   Chapman 1905
                                          CN unknown FG p. 199; Pl. 41
Genitalia. Like *E meolans*, posterior process of valve slightly shorter.
Range. Confined to NW Spain, mountains of Oviedo and Leon.

357. *Erebia palarica,* NW Spain: valve.

EREBIA PANDROSE Borkhausen   CN 28–29 FG p. 200; Pl. 39, 44
Two subspecies with slightly different genitalia.

358. *Erebia pandrose pandrose,* E Pyrenees: **a,** valve. *E. p. sthennyo,* C Pyrenees:
b, valve.

E. p. pandrose Borkhausen 1788.
Genitalia. Valve cylindrical, posterior process upturned with small apical teeth, costal border smooth, rarely with small central tooth.
Range. Fennoscandia, mountains of C Europe and C Asia (Altai Mts. etc.). E Pyrenees, Alps, general on high mountains, Carpathians, Balkans (local). Abruzzi, single record by de Lesse (Monte della Largo).

E. p. sthennyo Graslin 1850.
Genitalia. Like *E. p. pandrose*, valve costal border usually humped with two or three teeth (variable).
Range. Hautes and Basses Pyrénées.

Reference. de Lesse 1951D.
Note. de Lesse found the subspecific frontier slightly east of Salau, subspecies strictly segregated, separated by a belt of 15–20 miles in width. No evidence of overlap or cohabitation.

EREBIA PHEGEA   Borkhausen 1788

CN unknown   FG p. 201; Pl. 44
In hw precostal vein well developed.
Genitalia. Uncus long; vinculum long, erect; valve shorter than tegumen +uncus, tapering rapidly to a short, upturned apical process; costal border smooth; penis short with double curve in side view.
Range. S Russia, C Asia and Transcaucasus to N Iran. An isolated colony occurs on the Dalmatian coast near Zadar, but the species there is reputedly very rare.

Note. With well-developed precostal vein in hw and unusual structure of the genitalia, this butterfly is not well placed in *Erebia*.

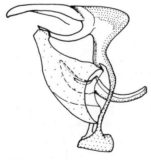

359. *Erebia phegea,* S Russia: genitalia. No European specimen available.

Tribe OENEINI Wheeler 1903
The characters are those of the genus *Oeneis*.

Genus **OENEIS** Hübner 1819   TS: *Papilio norna* Thunberg
Description. Butterflies of medium or rather large size, flying usually in boreal regions or at high altitudes, and widely distributed around the northern Hemisphere. A sex-brand below the median vein upf is present in many species. *Antennae* short, thickened gradually to form a slender club. *Tongue* short. *Palpi* longer than the length of the head, porrect, sparsely hairy. *Legs* fore-legs minute in both sexes, middle and hind-legs normal, tibiae and tarsi heavily spined. *Venation*. Male fw narrow, pointed, bases of costal and median veins slightly thickened but not truly swollen; hw precostal vein present.
Genitalia. Uncus and brachia short, often massive; apex angularis well formed; valve tapering to pointed or rounded apex, sometimes with small costal or apical teeth; saccus developed; penis straight, slender. Specific characters well marked.
Early stages. Not well known. Ovum barrel-shaped, rugose but not ribbed (Frionnet). Larva pubescent, light brown with darker longitudinal stripes. Pupa short, stout, rigid, in soil among grass roots. Hibernation probably as larva, perhaps in some species repeated for two seasons before pupation.

OENEIS GLACIALIS Móll 1783   CN unknown FG p. 151; Pl. 35
Genitalia. Brachia about quarter the length of uncus; in side view tegumen undulate, peduncles short and wide; base of valve wide, tapering evenly to a pointed apex minutely toothed.
Range. From Maritime Alps and Savoie through Switzerland and Bavaria to the Tirol and Carnic Alps.

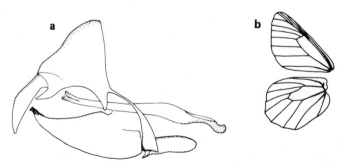

360. *Oeneis glacialis*, Switzerland: **a,** genitalia; **b,** wing venation.

253

OENEIS NORNA   Thunberg 1791   CN unknown FG p. 150; Pl. 35
Genitalia. Like *O. glacialis*; brachia slightly longer and more massive; valve narrower, apex oblique.
Range. Arctic and mountainous districts in Fennoscandia, N Asia, Altai Mts. and probably further into NE Asia.

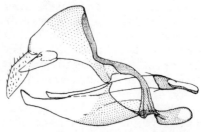

361. *Oeneis norna,* Norway: genitalia.

OENEIS BORE   Schneider 1792   CN unknown FG p. 150; Pl. 35
Genitalia. Like *O. glacialis*; uncus longer, less massive, brachia more slender; valve short, slightly tapered, with short costal process near base, apex rounded.
Range. Fennoscandia, not south of 67°N; N America; probably also in N Siberia.

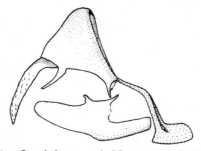

362. *Oeneis bore,* arctic Norway: genitalia.

OENEIS JUTTA   Hübner 1806   CN 32   FG p. 151; Pl. 35
Genitalia. Brachia rather slender, almost as long as uncus; peduncle well developed; valve only slightly tapered, costal margin toothed in distal third.
Range. Fennoscandia and Baltic countries eastwards to Siberia and N America.

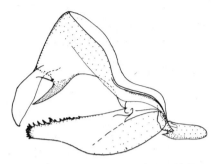

363. *Oeneis jutta,* S Sweden: genitalia.

Subfamily MELANARGIINAE Wheeler 1903

Butterflies of medium size, gc white with bold black pattern on both surfaces, varying only slightly between species; unh ocellus always absent in s4; sexes alike, males without androconial scales. The subfamily is restricted to the Palearctic Region, well represented in the Mediterranean area and again with fewer species in E Asia.

Genus **MELANARGIA**   Meigen 1838   TS: *Papilio galathea* L.
Description. Eyes smooth. *Palpi* hairy beneath, slender, porrect. *Antennae* half the length of fw, very slender, slightly thickened to apex but lacking a true club. *Legs* fore-legs minute in both sexes; tibiae of mid- and hind-legs moderately spined. *Venation.* Fw base of v12 dilated; hw pre-costal vein present.
Genitalia. Similar in all species; uncus and brachia arise together, apex angularis not prominent; valve short with apical teeth; penis slightly longer than valve, straight with few features; valve shapes and arrangement of apical teeth slightly variable. Specific characters in shapes of tegumen, brachia and valve are not really well defined except in *M. arge* and *M. ines. Early stages.* Ovum barrel-shaped, slightly taller than wide, finely reticulate but not ribbed. Larva sandy or greenish with darker longitudinal lines. Pupa lies free upon the ground among litter. Larval food plants especially *Phleum pratense, Holcus* etc. Hibernation as small larvae.

MELANARGIA GALATHEA L.   CN 24   FG p. 132; Pl. 27
Range. N Africa, Europe, northwards to Baltic coast, S Russia, Asia Minor, Caucasus and N Iran with several subspecies. Absent from Mediterranean islands except Sicily. Three subspecies, genitalia differ slightly, graded species by many authors.

255

M. g. galathea L. 1758.

Genitalia. Uncus shorter than tegumen, base wide, tapering abruptly to narrow pointed apex; distal part of brachia narrow, sharply pointed; peduncle short, not well developed; valve as long as tegumen, tapering to blunt apex with small bunch (variable) of crowded teeth; penis straight, robust.

Range. S and C Europe, excepting Portugal and Spain. In SE France partially replaced by *M. g. lachesis*; present in Cantabrian Mts. and in Hautes Pyrénées and Basses Pyrénées.

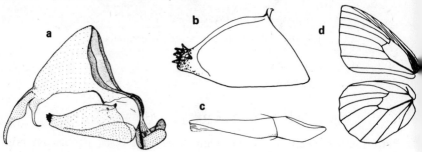

364. *Melanargia galathea galathea*, C France: **a,** genitalia; **b,** valve; **c,** penis; **d,** wing venation.

M. g. lachesis Hübner 1790   CN 24

Like *M. g. galathea*, but dark markings reduced, upf cell white.

Genitalia. As in *M. g. galathea*, valve usually slightly longer but indistinguishable in some specimens.

Range. SE France, Spain and Portugal south of Pyrenees.

M. g. lachesis, S Spain: **a,** valve. Bronchales, C Spain: **b,** valve.

M. g. lucasi Rambur 1858.

Genitalia. Like *M. g. galathea*, valve shorter, apical teeth fewer, arranged more regularly.

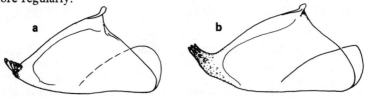

M. g. lucasi, Morocco: **a,** valve. Algeria: **b,** valve.

Note. It has proved difficult to define in *M. galathea* the correct relation-ship between its subspecies *M. g. galathea, M. g. lachesis* and *M. g. lucasi.* This situation needs further clarification. It is known that, broadly speaking, *M. g. lachesis* replaces *M. g. galathea* in SE France west of the Rhône, and its distribution continues southwards through the E Pyrenees into C and S Spain, where *M. g. galathea* does not occur, but the exact distribution of the two forms has not been mapped and the relationships of their colonies is not well understood. An attempt was made by the writer to examine the relationship between *M. g. lachesis* and *M. g. galathea* in the area of Aiguilles Mortes in S France, where the subspecific frontier is well defined. The colonies appeared to be completely segregated, *M. g. lachesis* did not encroach upon *M. g. galathea* areas on either side of the Rhône, and the frontier was well defined without any true overlap. In a few areas where the subspecies approached one another closely, within a mile or less, rather worn specimens of both might fly together, but these appeared to be wanderers from their original colonies. Several specimens with intermediate characters were found, suggesting occasional hybridisation. It is recorded (Frionnet) that the principal food plant of *M. g. galathea* is *Phleum pratense*; but for *M. g. lachesis* it is *Lamarkia aurea.*

M. g. galathea, M. g. lachesis and *M. g. lucasi* are clearly closely related. In these forms alone among European *Melanargia* the white cell on upf is not crossed by a black bar, the markings vary only in the extent of a common black pattern, the genitalia of *M. g. galathea* and *M. g. lachesis* are not easily separable and the general similarity of all three forms is extremely close. In the writer's opinion this relationship should be indicated in terminology, and this is done most conveniently by grading all these forms as subspecies of a single taxon.

Reference. Higgins 1969.

MELANARGIA RUSSIAE   Esper 1784

CN 24–26   FG p. 133; Pl. 27

Occurs in widely spaced colonies from Spain across S Europe and C Asia to W Siberia. In Europe two subspecies with minor variation in different colonies, genitalia similar.

Genitalia. Like *M. galathea*; brachia shorter, bases wider, apices more

365. *Melanargia russiae cleanthe,* N Spain: genitalia.

sharply downturned; valve elongate, apical teeth numerous, set in oval pad; apex angularis well defined; penis as in *M. galathea.*

M. r. japygia Cyrillo 1787.
Ups heavily marked.
Range. Peninsular Italy, Sicily, Macedonia, colonies very local.

M. r. cleanthe Boisduval 1833.   CN 24–26
Often larger, ups paler, less heavily marked.
Range. Portugal, Spain (common), S France.

MELANARGIA LARISSA   Geyer 1828   CN unknown
FG p. 134; Pl. 28
Widely distributed in W Asia to Iran with numerous localised subspecies or species. A single subspecies occurs in SE Europe.

M. l. larissa Geyer 1828.
♂ ups black markings heavy, variable, often lighter in very dry areas.
Genitalia. Like *M. r. cleanthe*; valve elongate, costal margin convex, apical teeth set in oval pad; vinculum slightly angled at junction with peduncle; penis as in *M. galathea.*
Range. S Balkan countries, northwards to Dalmatia. Black markings greatly reduced in Karst region (*herta* Geyer 1828).

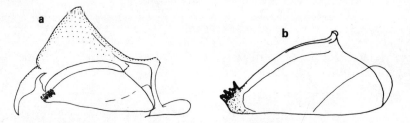

366. *Melanargia larissa,* Corfu: **a,** genitalia. Greece: **b,** valve.

MELANARGIA OCCITANICA   Esper   CN unknown
FG p. 135; Pl. 28
Two subspecies with slightly variable genitalia.
Genitalià. Like *M. galathea,* brachia shorter, lacking narrow terminal part; valve shorter with several terminal teeth; penis as in *M. galathea* but apical third curved slightly upwards and vinculum often somewhat angled at junction with peduncle. Valve shapes slightly variable.
Range. Restricted to W Mediterranean.

M. o. occitanica Esper 1793.
Uph rather heavily marked, upf blue spot beyond cell very small or vestigial.
Range. Algeria, Morocco, Spain, Portugal, S France.

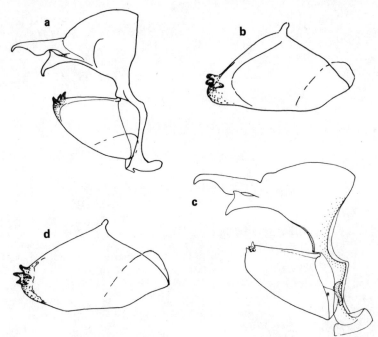

367. *Melanargia occitanica occitanica,* C Spain: **a,** genitalia, penis removed. *M. o. pelagia,* Morocco: **b,** valve. *M. o. pherusa,* Sicily: **c,** genitalia, penis removed: **d,** valve.

M. o. pherusa Boisduval 1833.
Uph less heavily marked, upf blue spot beyond cell larger.
Range. Sicily.

MELANARGIA ARGE Sulzer 1776

CN unknown FG p. 136; Pl. 27
Genitalia. Brachia short, blunt, apex angularis well defined; valve short, triangular, one to three apical teeth; penis small, slightly curved.
Range. Restricted to peninsular Italy from Lazio southwards.

368. *Melanargia arge,* C Italy: valve.

MELANARGIA INES Hoffmannsegg 1804   CN unknown

FG p. 136; Pl. 27

Genitalia. Like *M. galathea*, uncus shorter, brachia apex longer, down-turned; valve elongate, apex oblique with two large and several smaller costal teeth; penis slightly curved.

Range. N Africa, Cyrenaica, Tripolitania, Spain, Portugal.

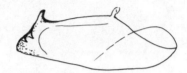

369. *Melanargia ines*, S Spain: valve.

Subfamily MANIOLINAE Grote 1897

Description. Butterflies of small or medium size, ups brown, fw with single sub-apical ocellus; unh markings cryptic; ♂ upf with sex-brand; ♀ discal area fulvous. *Eyes* smooth. *Palpi* hairy, porrect or slightly ascending, variable. *Antennae* slender, half the length of fw or less, terminal third thickened but no true club. *Legs* fore-legs minute in both sexes with single tarsal segment; middle and hind-legs normal, tibial spines scanty. *Venation.* Fw bases of v12 and median vein greatly swollen, base of submedian vein slightly dilated; hw precostal vein vestigial, outer margin more or less scalloped.

Genitalia. Variable, see generic descriptions.

Early stages. Ovum barrel-shaped, ribbed and reticulate. Larva and pupa with usual Satyrid characters. So far as known all species hibernate as small larvae and fly in a single annual brood.

Key to genera of Maniolinae

1 Upf conspicuous ocellus in s4–5 with twin white pupils . *Pyronia*
Upf not so marked **2**

2 Unh pd ocelli prominent. . . . . . *Aphantopus*
Unh ocelli, if present, inconspicuous and small . . . **3**

3 Valve wide . . . . *Maniola*
Valve narrow. . . . . *Hyponephele*

Genus MANIOLA Schrank 1801   TS: *Papilio jurtina* L.

Upf sub-apical ocellus white-pupilled, fulvous discal markings usually absent in ♂; uph without ocelli; unh ocelli minute if present; at lateral angles of eighth tergite scales forming rods fig. 370c.

Genitalia. Uncus and tegumen of almost equal lengths, bases of brachia wide, tapering rapidly to acicular apices; apex angularis present; valve wide, flexible, structure simple.

MANIOLA JURTINA L.   CN 29   FG p. 201; Pl. 45

Range. Canary Islands, N Africa, Europe to 62°N and eastwards to Ural Mts., Caucasus and N Iran, generally common in suitable localities. Two (possibly three) European subspecies, genitalia differ.

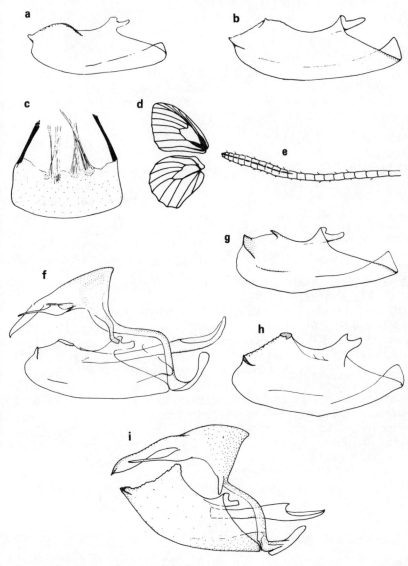

370. *Maniola jurtina jurtina,* Sweden: **a,** valve. S Italy: **b,** valve; **c,** 8th tergite spread; **d,** wing venation; **e,** antennal apex. *M. j. hispulla,* Ireland: **f,** genitalia. Portugal: **g,** valve. Orkney Islands: **h,** valve. *M. j. telmessia,* Lesbos, Aegean: **i,** genitalia.

M. j. jurtina L. 1758.
Genitalia. Uncus slender, apex slightly depressed, brachial bases wide, apices acicular; vinculum angled; valve wide, distal extremity rounded with pointed apical process; penis slender; hair-pencils on eighth tergite rather short.
Range. C Europe from Germany, Switzerland and Italy eastwards, including Crete.

M. j. hispulla Esper ante 1805.
Genitalia. Like *M. j. jurtina*, valve apex a rounded bulge with sharply pointed process above; a more proximal process marks the end of costa.
Range. Canary islands, N Africa and W Europe including Britain and Ireland, Corsica, Sardinia and Malta.

M. j. telmessia Zeller 1847.
Genitalia. Like *M. j. jurtina*, uncus slightly sinuous, expanded near apex; valve wide, apex truncate; penis shorter; hair-pencils on eighth tergite longer, very slender.
Range. Widely distributed in S Turkey and W Asia including Lebanon and Cyprus. It occurs on Greek island of Lesbos, but records from European Greece need confirmation.
Note. Distribution imperfectly understood. Included here as subspecies with *M. jurtina*, but probably better graded with specific rank.

Note on *M. j. jurtina* = *M. j. hispulla*. These two subspecies are clearly defined by their genitalia. The frontier between them extends in a wide belt from Scandinavia across Holland, Belgium and NE France to the Rhine and W Alps. Along this belt the subspecies appear to be completely integrated, with intermediate and abnormal forms of genitalia. These disappear further west where the *M. j. hispulla* type alone is present from the Canary Islands, N Africa, Spain, Portugal, C and W France, and across Britain and Ireland to the Orkney Isles, extending in the Mediterranean to Sicily and Malta. In the east, the Baltic countries, C and E Germany, Switzerland, Italy and eastwards to Iran, the *M. j. jurtina* valve type occurs, with various small, local, perhaps subspecific modifications. In general *hispulla* forms are more brightly marked, but similar specimens occur in S Europe east of Sicily, in which genitalia examined have been of the *jurtina* type.
Reference. de Lattin 1950.

MANIOLA NURAG Ghiliani 1852

CN unknown FG p. 203; Pl. 46
Genitalia. Like *M. jurtina* but smaller; uncus slightly more robust, brachia curved slightly upwards; valve pointed apex prominent, resembling closely some specimens of *M. j. jurtina*.
Range. Confined to Sardinia.

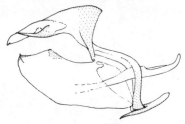

371. *Maniola nurag,* Sardinia: genitalia.

Genus **HYPONEPHELE** Muschamp 1915   TS: *Papilio lycaon* Kühn
Butterflies of medium size or rather less, resembling *Maniola*; upf sub-
apical ocellus usually blind. *Legs:* ♂ fore-leg slender with single tarsal
segment.
Genitalia. Uncus variable, apparently continuous at its base with the short
brachia; valve flexible, narrow, hairy, structure very simple; apex angularis
well developed; penis slender, straight, lacking marked features.

HYPONEPHELE LYCAON   Kühn 1774   CN 29 FG p. 206; Pl. 45
Genitalia. Uncus long, slender, curved gently downwards, brachia short,
upturned, less than half the length of uncus; valve very slender, straight,
tapering and flexible.
Range. All Europe except NW areas and boreal regions, Asia Minor,
Caucasus and eastwards to Iran and C Asia, where identification may be
difficult.

372. *Hyponephele lycaon,* N Italy: genitalia, penis removed.

HYPONEPHELE LUPINA   Costa   CN 29 FG p. 206; Pl. 45
Three subspecies with similar genitalia.
Genitalia. Like *H. lycaon,* uncus shorter, curved sharply downwards;
valve more robust, distal part slightly angled towards uncus.
Range. S Europe and, W Asia and N Africa.

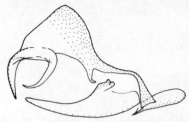

373. *Hyponephele lupina mauretanica,* C Spain: genitalia, penis removed.

H. l. lupina Costa 1836.
Ups with golden reflection marked; size moderately large, ♂ fw 20–22mm.
Range. C Italy, S Yugoslavia (local, slightly larger).

H. l. rhamnusia Freyer 1845.
Ups golden reflection more extensive, larger ♂ fw 26–27mm.
Range. Sicily; transitional but smaller in S Greece.

H. l. mauretanica Oberthur 1881.
Ups gc grey-brown, golden reflection not prominent, size ♂ fw 20–23mm.
Range. N Africa, Spain, SE France (rare), Asia Minor, Lebanon.

HYPONEPHELE MAROCCANA Blachier   CN unknown
                                               FG p. 203; Pl. 45
Two subspecies with similar genitalia.
Genitalia. Like *H. lycaon*; uncus slightly shorter, brachia very short,
pointed; valve base wider, distally upturned.

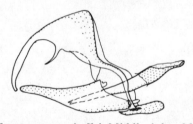

374. *Hyponephele maroccana nivellei,* Middle Atlas, Morocco: genitalia.

O. m. maroccana Blachier 1908.
♂ fw 20–21mm.
Range. Morocco, High Atlas.

O. m. nivellei Oberthur 1920.
♂ fw 17–18 mm.
Range. Morocco, Middle Atlas.

Genus **APHANTOPUS** Wallengren 1853   TS: *Papilio hyperantus* L.
Uns with white-pupilled black pd ocelli on both wings, often present on
ups in ♀. Male sex-brand upf below cell. Legs ♂ fore-leg minute but
relatively stout. *Venation*. As for *Maniola*.
Genitalia. Small, uncus straight, joined to short, straight brachia; valve
with slender upturned apex armed with four or five strong spines; penis
straight, slightly shorter than valve.

APHANTOPUS HYPERANTUS   L. 1758

CN 29 FG p. 207; Pl. 33

Genitalia. Described above.
Range. Widely distributed in C Europe and eastwards across Siberia to
the Ussuri. Absent from boreal regions and from C and S Spain, Portugal
and Peninsular Italy.
Early stages. Ovum domed, finely reticulate, without ribs. Larva densely
pubescent. Abdominal segments of pupa sharply tapered and very short.

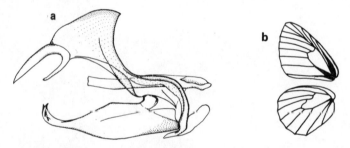

375. *Aphantopus hyperantus,* S England: **a,** genitalia: **b,** wing venation.

Genus **PYRONIA** Hübner 1818   TS: *Papilio tithonus* L.
Butterflies of middle size or rather less; ups orange-fulvous with wide
dark marginal borders and upf a single prominent apical ocellus with twin
white pupils. Upf sex-brand prominent in ♂. Legs ♂ fore-legs minute
but relatively stout.
Genitalia. Variable, uncus slightly curved or straight, valves with or
without teeth.

Reference. de Lesse 1952D.

PYRONIA TITHONUS   L. 1771   CN 29   FG p. 210; Pl. 46
Genitalia. Valve narrow, tapering gradually to upturned apex and with
six or seven small costal teeth; penis straight.
Range. S and C Europe to about 52°N, and eastwards to Asia Minor and
the Caucasus Mts.; also on many Mediterranean islands. Absent from the
Alps, much of Germany and the Carpathian Mts.

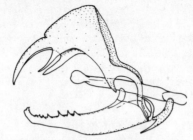

376. *Pyronia tithonus,* N Italy: genitalia.

PYRONIA BATHSEBA F. 1793   CN 33   FG p. 211; Pl. 46
Genitalia. Uncus long, straight, tapered to a point; valve narrow, curving upwards, tapered to a blunt apex, lacking teeth.
Range. N Africa and S Europe and eastwards to Asia Minor, but local.

377. *Pyronia bathseba,* S Spain: genitalia.

PYRONIA JANIROIDES Herrich-Schäffer 1851   CN unknown
FG p. 211; Pl. 46
Genitalia. Uncus stout, slightly curved; valve narrow curving upwards and tapered to a blunt apex without costal teeth.
Range. Restricted to E Algeria and Tunisia.

378. *Pyronia janiroides,* E Algeria: genitalia.

PYRONIA CECILIA Vallantin 1894   CN 28   FG p. 210; Pl. 46
Genitalia. Uncus stout with double dorsal curve; tegumen domed; valve elongate, of even width with nine or ten small teeth along costal border. *Range*. N Africa and S Europe to western Asia Minor.

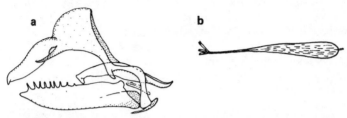

379. *Pyronia cecilia*, C Spain: **a,** genitalia; **b,** androconial scale.

Note. de Lesse 1952 has proposed a new genus *Idata* for this species. This action seems unnecessary to the writer, and unfortunate as it separates *P. cecilia* in a monotypic genus from its nearest relatives.

Subfamily COENONYMPHINAE Tutt 1896

The characters are those of the genus *Coenonympha* Hübner.

Genus **COENONYMPHA** Hübner 1818   TS: *Papilio oedippus* F.
Description. Small butterflies, ups sandy yellow to dark brown, upf generally with single apical ocellus and unh with submarginal ocelli. *Eyes* smooth. *Palpi* slender, porrect, rather long, middle segment hairy beneath, apical segment half as long as middle segment. *Antennae* short, slightly thickened in apical third. *Legs* ♂ fore-leg very small with single tarsal segment; ♀ fore-leg, four tarsal segments and terminal spine; middle and hind-legs normal. *Androconial scales* upf present in some species, often scattered over the wing. *Venation*. Fw bases of v12, median and submedian veins all greatly swollen; hw precostal vein absent, origin indicated by a small bulge near median vein.
Genitalia. Uncus longer than tegumen, brachia slender, pointed, attached to a process from base of uncus ('uncal process'); apex angularis well developed; valves hairy, tapering, slender and flexible, longer than tegumen+uncus, penis short, slightly sinuous in side view.
Early stages. Ovum ribbed and reticulate. So far as known all species hibernate as larvae.

Note 1. C. oedippus alone of European species has well marked specific characters in the genitalia, which otherwise are almost similar throughout the genus and of little value in specific identification. In order to complete the series of illustrations, drawings have been made of the genitalia of every European species and of some important subspecies. The very long slender valves of *C. corinna* and *C. elbana* are noteworthy, also the long brachia of the latter.

The taxonomic arrangement in the Field Guide is not entirely satisfactory. *C. darwiniana* is here treated as a species distinct from *C. arcania*, occurring locally from Chamonix eastwards through the Alps of Valais and Sudschweiz. *C. elbana* also looks well placed as an independent species. *C. iphioides* is better ranked as a subspecies of *C. glycerion*. The correct rank for a few forms is uncertain and chromosome counts have not been helpful, since these may be variable, perhaps due to fragmentation of chromosomes. For example de Lesse (1960A) found the CN 29–36 in *C. arcania* and CN 29–43 in *C. gardetta*. Hybrids between these two species have been obtained without difficulty. *C. darwiniana* appeared to be exceptionally variable with CN 31–52. The results of these laborious investigations were too inconstant to be helpful in establishing the taxonomic status of these difficult forms.

Note 2. By some authors *C. oedippus* alone is retained in *Coenonympha* and all other European species are placed in the genus *Chortobius* Dunning & Packhard 1858. This seems unnecessary to the writer and unfortunate as it separates *C. oedippus* from its nearest relatives.

COENONYMPHA OEDIPPUS F. 1787   CN 29   FG p. 223; Pl. 47
Genitalia. Uncus slightly hairy with central expansion; brachia sinuous, tapered gradually; tegumen short, uncal processes well developed; penis slightly sinuous.

Range. In scattered colonies from W Europe across Russia and Siberia to China and Japan.

380. *Coenonympha oedippus,* SE France: **a,** genitalia; **b,** wing venation.

COENONYMPHA PAMPHILUS L.

CN 28–29   FG p. 214; Pl. 48

Four subspecies with similar genitalia, subspecific characters in unh markings.

Genitalia. Uncus gently bowed, scarcely tapering, apex blunt; brachia very slender, tapering to upturned apices; penis slightly sinuous.

Range. N Africa and all Europe except boreal regions, eastwards to Caucasus and N Iran.

C. p. pamphilus L. 1758.
Unf pd stripe vestigial or absent; unh grey.
Range. N and C Europe, and also S Europe in gen. 1.

C. p. lyllus Esper 1805.
Unf pd stripe well marked; unh yellowish, faintly marked.
Range. Summer brood form in N Africa, S Spain and S Portugal. Subspecific characters develop in summer brood.

C. p. sicula Zeller 1847.
Unh complete pattern well developed.
Range. Summer brood form in Sicily. Subspecific characters develop in summer brood.

C. p. thyrsis Freyer 1845.
Unh pattern well developed, almost similar to *C. p. sicula,* reported in all broods.
Range. Crete.

Note. The taxonomic status of *C. p. lyllus* is uncertain. It appears as a seasonal form with geographical distribution.

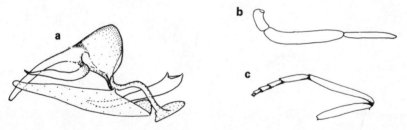

381. *Coenonympha pamphilus,* S England: **a,** genitalia: **b,** palpus: **c,** ♀ fore-leg

COENONYMPHA TULLIA Müller   CN 29   FG p. 212; Pl. 47
Genitalia. Like *C. pamphilus,* uncus slender, smoothly curved with tegumen, brachia slightly more robust, apices very slender.

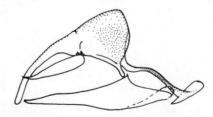

382. *Coenonympha tullia,* Bavaria: genitalia.

Range. N and C Europe to Balkans, Baltic countries and eastwards across Russia and Siberia to the Pacific; also N America from Alaska to California. A series of clinal forms of which three are described below as subspecies. Genitalia similar in all.

C. t. tullia Müller 1764.
Uns markings distinct; unh usually six pd ocelli; ups colour variable, locally dark, *rothliebii* Herrich-Schäffer.
Range. C Europe, esp. Germany, Switzerland and Austria.

C. t. demophile Freyer 1844.
Uns markings incomplete, ocelli vestigial or absent.
Range. Fennoscandia, small, Scotland, larger, flying on moorland.

C. t. rhodopensis Elwes 1900.
Small, unf pd band vestigial or absent.
Range. C Italy (very local), Balkans, from Dalmatia southwards, absent from Greece. Flies at about 1,500m in woodlands.

COENONYMPHA ARCANIOIDES Pierret 1837   CN unknown
FG p. 220; Pl. 47
Genitalia. Like *C. tullia*; valve slender, scarcely tapered, apex blunt.
Range. Restricted to N Africa.

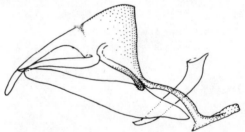

383. *Coenonympha arcanioides*, Morocco: genitalia.

COENONYMPHA DORUS Esper   CN 29   FG p. 216; Pl. 48
Genitalia. Tegumen steeply domed, brachia almost straight; uncal curve quite marked.

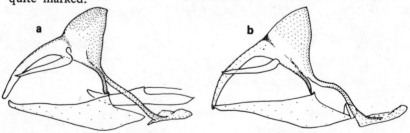

384. *Coenonympha dorus dorus*, Maritime Alps: **a,** genitalia. *C. d. fettigii*, High Atlas, Morocco: **b,** genitalia.

Range. Confined to N Africa and SW Europe. Three subspecies with similar genitalia.

C. d. dorus Esper 1782.
Uph fulvous, markings well developed.
Range. C and S Spain, S France, N and C Italy.

C. d. fettigii Oberthur 1874.
Uph fulvous, markings not well developed, often vestigial.
Range. N Africa with local variation in different colonies.

C. d. bieli Staudinger 1901.
Uph brown, fulvous discal area small or absent.
Range. NE Spain and N Portugal.

COENONYMPHA AUSTAUTI Oberthur 1881   CN unknown
FG p. 218; Pl. 46
Genitalia. Like *C. dorus,* tegumen slightly domed, brachia almost straight, uncal process not distinct.
Range. Algeria, near Bone etc., common near coast.
Status of this species slightly uncertain; it probably flies with *C. d. fettigii.*

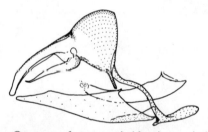

385. *Coenonympha austauti,* Algeria: genitalia.

COENONYMPHA CORINNA Hübner 1804   CN unknown
FG p. 216; Pl. 48
Genitalia. Tegumen domed; uncus relatively long, with distinct curve, uncal process prominent and brachia ascending.
Range. Corsica and Sardinia.

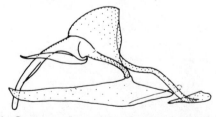

386. *Coenonympha corinna,* Corsica: genitalia.

COENONYMPHA ELBANA Staudinger 1901 CN unknown
FG p. 216; Pl. 48

Genitalia. Tegumen scarcely domed; brachia appear relatively longer than those of *C. corinna.*
Range. Elba and Italian mainland near Orbitello.

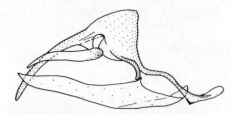

387. *Coenonympha elbana,* Elba: genitalia.

COENONYMPHA HERO L. 1761

CN unknown FG p. 222; Pl. 46

Genitalia. Tegumen scarcely domed, uncal process well defined, brachia rather wide, ascending.
Range. S Fennoscandia and NE France eastwards across Siberia to Japan.

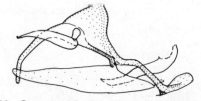

388. *Coenonympha hero,* Bavaria: genitalia.

COENONYMPHA DARWINIANA Staudinger 1871 CN 31–52
FG p. 219; Pl. 47

Genitalia. Tegumen slightly domed, uncal process well defined, brachia straight, evenly tapered to pointed apex.
Range. Restricted to W Alps and eastwards to Sudschweiz.

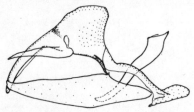

389. *Coenonympha darwiniana,* Switzerland: genitalia.

COENONYMPHA LEANDER   Esper 1784   CN unknown
FG p. 221; Pl. 47
Genitalia. Like *C. darwiniana,* tegumen slightly domed, uncal process less well defined, valve apex tapered rather abruptly.
Range. S Balkans including Greece (Pindus Mts.), Rumania, Hungary and eastwards across Russia and Asia Minor to N Iran.

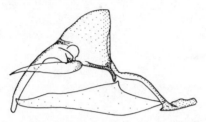

390. *Coenonympha leander,* Bulgaria: genitalia.

COENONYMPHA VAUCHERI   Blachier 1905   CN unknown
FG p. 218; Pl. 46
Genitalia. Tegumen not domed, uncal process prominent, brachia slightly sinuous, slender and long.
Range. Morocco, in Atlas Mts.

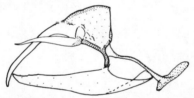

391. *Coenonympha vaucheri,* Morocco: genitalia.

COENONYMPHA GARDETTA   de Prunner 1798   CN variable,
usually about 29   FG p. 220; Pl. 47
Genitalia. Tegumen slightly domed, uncal suture marked but uncal process not well defined, brachia ascending.

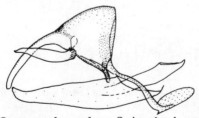

392. *Coenonympha gardetta,* Switzerland: genitalia.

Range. Monts du Forez and throughout the Alps to Dolomites and Gr. Glockner.
There is clinal variation with several named forms.

COENONYMPHA ARCANIA L. 1761　　CN 29–35

FG p. 219; Pl. 47

Genitalia. Tegumen slightly domed and uncal process defined, brachia ascending.
Range. Widely distributed in C Spain and Portugal northwards to S Sweden, eastwards across Europe to Asia Minor and the Ural Mts.

Reference. de Lesse 1949A.

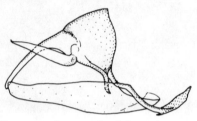

393. *Coenonympha arcania,* C Pyrenees: genitalia.

COENONYMPHA GLYCERION Borkhausen　　CN 29

FG p. 221; Pl. 47

Genitalia. Tegumen slightly domed, uncus curved, uncal process not well defined (absent ?). Two subspecies; genitalia differ slightly.

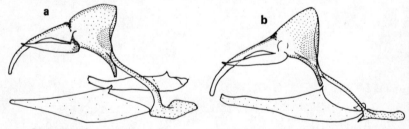

394. *Coenonympha glycerion glycerion,* C Italy: **a,** genitalia. *C. g. iphioides,* C Spain: **b,** genitalia.

C. g. glycerion Borkhausen 1788.
Small, ♂ fw 16–18mm, unh ocelli not prominent, often vestigial.
Range. C France across C Europe to C Asia (Altai Mts.) and Far East.

C. g. iphioides Staudinger 1870.
Larger, ♂ fw 17–19mm, unh six prominent submarginal ocelli.
Range. C Spain. Colonies with transitional characters occur in E Pyrenees, Cantabrian Mts. etc.

Subfamily PARARGINAE Tutt 1896

Description. Butterflies of medium size, markings very varied. Most species are widely distributed in Europe and in W Asia. Sex-brand present upf in ♂. *Eyes* hairy. *Palpi* ascending, terminal segment porrect. *Antennae* variable, club usually slender, pyriform. *Legs* ♂ fore-leg very small with one or two tarsal segments; ♀ fore-leg larger, tarsus clubbed with four or five compressed segments. Middle and hind-legs normal, tibiae and tarsi heavily spined. *Venation.* Fw base of v12 dilated, median vein less dilated or only thickened; in hw precostal vein usually short or vestigial, but well developed in *Kirinia*, lower dc vein runs to v3.
Genitalia. Uncus hairy, with narrow neck; tegumen domed, brachia short, straight; valve long and narrow, lacking special features.
Early stages. Ovum oval, reticulate but not ribbed. *Larva* and *pupa* without special features.

Reference. de Lesse 1952D.

Key to genera of Pararginae

1	Ups dark grey-brown without fulvous markings	. .	*Lopinga*
	Ups with fulvous markings		**2**
2	Hw precostal vein well developed		*Kirinia*
	Hw precostal vein absent or vestigial		**3**
3	Antennal club very slender, slightly arcuate . . .		*Pararge*
	Antennal club pyriform		*Lasiommata*

Genus **PARARGE** Hübner 1819   TS: *Papilio aegeria* L.
Antennae gradually thickened to form a slender club. *Venation.* Fw base of median vein slightly dilated; hw outer margin scalloped.
Genitalia. Valve with angled costal shoulder before apex; penis variable.

PARARGE AEGERIA L.   CN 28   FG p. 226; Pl. 49
Range. From Madeira, Canary Islands, N Africa and W Europe across S Russia and W Asia to Ural Mts. and Caucasus. Four subspecies, three with differing genitalia.

P. a. aegeria L. 1758.
Ups gc bright fulvous.
Genitalia. Valve with wide costal tooth.

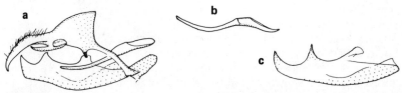

395. *Pararge aegeria tircis,* S England: **a,** genitalia: **b,** penis. *P. a. xiphioides,* Canary Islands: **c,** valve.

Range. N Africa, Spain, Portugal, S and C France and Italy, Mediterranean islands east to Malta.

P. a. tircis Butler 1867.
Ups gc yellow-grey.
Genitalia. As for *P. a. aegeria*.
Range. N Europe, Switzerland, Balkans, S Russia, absent from boreal regions.

P. a. xiphioides Staudinger 1871.
Ups gc tawny-fulvous.
Genitalia. Like *P. a. aegeria*, valve costal tooth narrower, more pointed.
Range. Canary Islands.

P. a. xiphia F. 1775.
Fw outer margin gently convex, apex pointed; ups gc tawny-fulvous.
Genitalia. Valve wider, terminal process short, penis straight.
Range. Madeira.

References. de Lesse 1952C. Bernardi 1964.

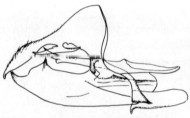

P. a. xiphia, Madeira: genitalia.

Pararge aegeria provides an excellent example of a polytypic species in which the extremes are widely different yet are obviously closely related to the nominate subspecies and derived from the same common stem, i.e. monophyletic. The butterfly occurs on the mainland of Europe in well-marked northern and southern subspecies which satisfy the criteria of the definition. In the Canary Islands there flies *xiphioides* Staudinger, which shows slight differences in markings and genitalia which might be assessed as valid for subspecific or for specific rank. In Madeira modification goes further, and the local *xiphia* Fabricius is altogether larger and a more handsome insect, although still unmistakably related to *aegeria*. Modification on this scale in related species would merit specific rank, but the evidence of close relationship with *xiphioides* and *aegeria* introduces a factor which is usually absent between species simply united generically. The special relationships of such a group of phenotypes is sometimes indicated by calling the whole group a superspecies; to other authors such a group will have all the qualities of a genus. Neither device helps to decide at what point in time or place the step from subspecies to species has taken place, whether indeed it has taken place, or whether there should be two species or three. The whole question is largely subjective. When evolutionary stages are so clearly indicated, it is best, in the author's opinion, to regard *P. aegeria* simply as a polytypic species with very marked subspecies.

Genus **LASIOMMATA** Westwood 1841   TS: *Papilio maera* L.
Butterflies of medium size; sex-brand present ♂ upf. *Antenna club* pyriform. *Venation*. Fw base of v12 greatly swollen, median vein less swollen, sub-median vein thickened.
Genitalia. Tegumen domed, uncus and brachia slender, pointed; valve flexible, elongate, borders almost parallel, apex pointed; penis slender, base with dorsal teeth.

LASIOMMATA MEGERA L.   CN 29   FG p. 227; Pl. 49
Two subspecies with similar genitalia.
Genitalia. Described above.
Range. N Africa, Europe to about 60°N, including Mediterranean islands, eastwards to W Asia and N Iran.

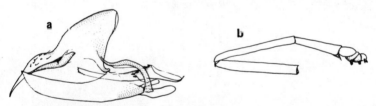

396. *Lasiommata megera*, S England: **a,** genitalia: **b,** ♀ fore-leg.

L. m. megera L. 1767.
Uph dark pattern fully developed.
Range. As above but absent from Sardinia and Corsica.

L. m. paramegaera Hübner 1824.
Uph dark pd band absent, rarely vestigial.
Range. Sardinia and Corsica.

LASIOMMATA MAERA L. 1758   CN 28–29
                                FG p. 228; Pl. 49
Genitalia. Like *L. megera* but tegumen more steeply domed; valve slightly angled, posterior section inclined upwards; base of penis wider with two ventral teeth beyond zone.

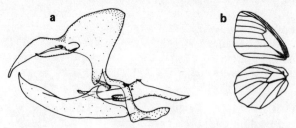

397. *Lasiommata maera,* Switzerland: **a,** genitalia: **b,** wing venation.

Range. Morocco. Europe, widely distributed to 68°N, absent from NW including Britain, absent also from Corsica, Sardinia, Crete and other Mediterranean islands; widely distributed in W Asia to Iran and Himalaya Mts.

LASIOMMATA PETROPOLITANA F. 1787
CN 29 FG p. 229; Pl. 49

Genitalia. Uncus sinuous; penis with two large dorsal teeth at zonal region and ventral teeth as in *L. maera.*
Range. Fennoscandia to 68°N, Ardennes and Bavarian Mts., Alps and Pyrenees, Balkans and eastwards in suitable localities to the Amur.

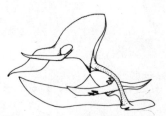

398. *Lasiommata petropolitana,* Switzerland: genitalia.

Genus **LOPINGA** Moore 1895   TS: *Pararge dumetorum* Oberthur
Antennal apex slightly swollen but lacking a true club. *Palpi* porrect, smoothly scaled above, hairy beneath. *Androconial scales* present uph.
Venation. Fw base of v2 greatly swollen, median vein slightly thickened, sub-median vein normal; hw precostal vein present.
Genitalia. Tegumen slightly domed, uncus dilated, brachia slender, short; valve elongate, extending cephalad beyond vinculum; penis as long as valve, very slender, tapering.

LOPINGA ACHINE Scopoli 1763   CN unknown

FG p. 229; Pl. 33

Genitalia. Described on p. 278.

Range. France and N Spain northwards to S Sweden and across C Europe and Asia to Japan.

399. *Lopinga achine,* N Italy: genitalia.

Genus **KIRINIA** Moore 1893   TS: *Lasiommata epimenides* Ménétriés
Description. The species are widely distributed from Asia Minor to the Pamir Mts. and China. A single species just enters SE Europe. *Palpi* slightly ascending. *Antennal club* slender but well defined. *Venation.* Fw base of v12 greatly dilated, median vein less dilated, v1 thickened; hw outer margin scalloped, precostal vein present.
Genitalia. Tegumen slightly domed, uncus and brachia variable; peduncle very short; valve slender, elongate; penis shorter than valve.

KIRINIA ROXELANA Cramer 1777   CN. 25   FG p. 230; Pl. 14
Male with prominent sex-brand which distorts venation in fw.
Genitalia. Uncus with central expansion, apical section slender, brachia short, slender; valve narrow, tapering gradually to pointed apex; saccus large.
Range. SE Europe in Balkans and northwards to E Hungary. Widely distributed in W Asia.

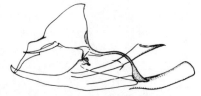

400. *Kirinia roxelana,* Bulgaria: genitalia.

Family **DANAIDAE** Bates 1861

Description. Large butterflies characteristically marked with small white spots on the black head, thorax and wing-margins. The species are usually confined to the tropics but two species occur in the Canary Islands. *Eyes* smooth. *Palpi* small, ascending, hairy, terminal segment depressed. *Antennae* slender, club slender, slightly arcuate. *Legs and feet*: fore-legs greatly reduced, useless for walking, male with single tarsal segment, female with three tarsal segments, wide but compressed, middle and hind-legs normal, tarsi strongly spined; foot with a lobe on each side identified by Urquhart as a pulvillus, paronychia absent; claws long, set on the foot at an acute angle. Males of all species have sex-brands, usually on the hind-wing, and often other scent organs. *Venation*; fw with 12 veins; hw precostal vein straight, arising from origin of costal vein; cell closed in both wings.

Genitalia. Anatomy atypical and most variable between species. There are remarkable hair-pencils which can be extruded from the abdomen at mating.

Early stages. Ovum taller than wide, reticulate. Larva conspicuously coloured, with fleshy processes arising from the second thoracic and eighth abdominal segments. Pupa suspended, short, abdominal segments compressed, often with metallic reflections.

All species have tough integuments, are extraordinarily tenacious of life and have an unpleasant smell, distasteful to birds.

The small degenerate fore-legs, larvae with paired dorsal processes and suspended pupa show relationship with the true Nymphalid butterflies.

Reference. Urquhart 1960.

Genus **DANAUS** Kluk 1802   TS: *Papilio plexippus* L.
Wings ample, apex of fw produced; the small sex-brand is present on hw on v2.

DANAUS PLEXIPPUS L. 1758   CN unknown FG p. 72; Pl. 14
Genitalia. Structure most unusual with incomplete chitinisation; uncus probably represented by lightly chitinised lobes from the largely membranous tegumen; hair-pencil about half the length of the genitalia, attached to a prominence at base of tegumen; vinculum not chitinised, perhaps fused with posterior border of valve which is wide, with two narrow posterior processes, and firmly chitinised; basal furca present and a long saccus; penis long and very slender. Abdominal segment eight modified into a strong horseshoe-shaped unit which embraces the lateral walls and floor of the true genitalia.
Range. Widely distributed in N and S America. Canary Islands, Australia.

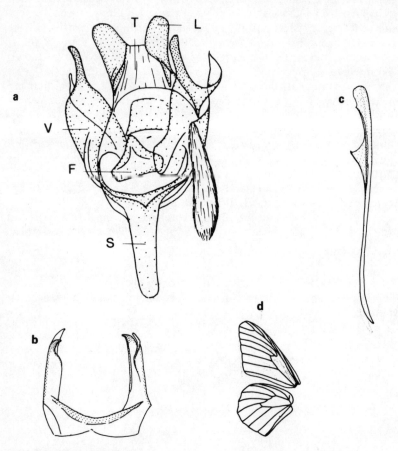

401. *Danaus plexippus,* Canary Islands: **a,** genitalia: **b,** 8th abdominal sclerite which supports the genitalia: **c,** penis: **d,** wing venation.

DANAUS CHRYSIPPUS L. 1758   CN 30   FG p. 72; Pl. 14

Genitalia. Uncus entirely membranous; valve represented by a flat plate fused to furca and short saccus, each valve with firmly chitinised pointed process projecting below; hair pencil very large; penis massive, about twice as long as valve, with small projection on each side of apex.

Range. In tropical countries almost cosmopolitan. Recorded from Canary Isles. Absent from S America.

Note. The genus *Panlymnas* Bryk 1937, has been proposed for *D. chrysippus*, but it is not used here as the distinctive characters have not been defined. The name remains valid and available.

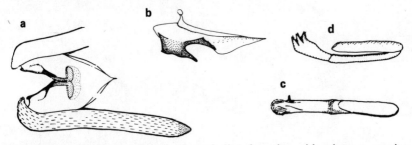

402. *Danaus chrysippus*, Egypt; **a,** genitalia; **b,** valve, side view; **c,** penis; **d,** ♀ fore-leg.

Appendix

Preparation of genitalia and of other organs for study

In order to make a satisfactory examination the genitalia must be removed from the body, cleaned and 'mounted', i.e. prepared as a permanent slide for microscopy. The procedure is to remove the abdomen, or at least the posterior segments, which are then soaked in a solution (10%) of caustic potash (KOH). This will soften the chitinous plates, dissolving fat and muscular tissues, but has little effect upon chitin if properly used. It is convenient to have the solution in test-tubes about 16mm in diameter, held upright in a simple stand, each tube to contain about 5ml of solution, i.e. about 2cm deep of caustic potash. After soaking for some hours, the time necessary will vary with the size of the specimen, the abdomen will become quite soft. The time required for this process can be shortened if the tube is warmed. After suitable soaking the specimen is placed upon a glass slide and covered with a few drops of distilled water or filtered rain water, when the contents of the abdomen and the genitalia can be teased out with a dental seeker and mounted needles. Generally this is quite easy, but a small hand lens or better a pair of jeweller's magnifying glasses will be useful if the parts are small. Alternatively, a small clip with lenses of about +2 can be had to fix on to ordinary glasses. A dissecting microscope is sometimes used, but in my experience these are mostly too high and I prefer a small low box to support the slide as described below. I find there is some *mystique* about these preparations. It is thought sometimes that a binocular microscope is essential but I very rarely use one. If such a microscope is to be used, the lenses should not be of the Huygenian type, giving an inverted image. It is important to make sure that all soft tissues and fragments of sclerite are removed and this will require a certain amount of kneading and squeezing with the seeker or needles. It is surprising how strong the chitin is, and even very delicate genitalia will stand up to quite firm treatment. If some muscle fragments are tenacious it may be necessary to return the genitalia to the potash to be boiled up for a few moments. Sometimes this will dislodge adherent fragments. Finely pointed forceps are often useful at this stage to extract the penis or to remove pieces of tissue or hair. If, during these proceedings, the penis is dislodged unintentionally, the organ is to be carefully preserved. During cleaning and preparation of the parts the glass microscope slide should be supported on a small box about 2½cm deep and 5cm wide. A piece of white paper fitted in the bottom of the box gives a good background and reflects light. In this way the hands are resting firmly upon a table and manipulations are under good control while movement is completely free. An Anglepoise lamp which will focus directly upon the genitalia is most valuable. When the whole abdomen is to be mounted, the body segments are opened by cutting along the dorsal or ventral aspect with fine scissors. Androconial scale patches are present upon the abdomen in various species, especially common in Satyridae.

After cleaning, the specimen must be dehydrated by soaking for several hours in alcohol, since most mounting media do not mix well with water. Rectified spirit may be used for this purpose but this is expensive and ordinary methylated spirit (but not 'surgical' spirit) is perfectly satisfactory. Thorough dehydration is important, and unless this is done carefully the chitin will not become transparent. A simple method is to have the spirit in two or three small corked tubes labelled 1, 2, 3, and the specimen is left in each tube for an hour or so in the proper order. Once dehydrated, the specimen can be left in spirit for an indefinite period, when it can be examined superficially and a decision is made on the best aspect to show. In order to see clearly the details of all parts, the specimen must be mounted as a microscope slide. Everyone has his own ideas about the best method of doing this, and I will describe my own procedure. A supply of glass slides and cover-slips will be needed, and a mounting medium. Euparal has largely taken the place of the old-fashioned Canada balsam, since the refractive index is said to be more suitable and Euparal does not discolour with age. A drop or two of Euparal is placed upon a glass slide, using a narrow glass rod or an old knitting needle, the dehydrated specimen is lifted on a needle point or with forceps, and arranged in the drop to display important characters, when the whole can be sealed with a cover-slip. Parts of genitalia, e.g. a valve or penis, may give more information if detached and mounted separately. This may involve simple dissection which can be done in the Euparal drop before sealing or in spirit immediately before mounting. Since some distortion is inevitable when the parts are pressed flat, a specimen mounted in a shallow cell will sometimes give important information. A cell can be made with small plastic or metal rings which are obtainable of the same diameter as the cover-slips. A single preparation is rarely sufficient to show all parts of the genitalia. A side view of the whole organ with penis *in situ* and a dorsal or A.-P. view will be necessary, and sometimes additional preparations of certain parts, e.g. in Lycaenidae. It is helpful if the parts are mounted to give comparable views of each species.

Very small genitalia and minute organs are easily lost and need special treatment. They should be washed on the slides in two or three different lots of water and mounted without dehydration in Berlese's fluid mountant. This fluid is slightly hygroscopic, so the cover-glass should be ringed with Euparal a few weeks after mounting, to give an air-tight seal. In many ways the old-fashioned Canada balsam is a splendid mountant, but preparation is more elaborate, since spirit must be removed by soaking the specimen in xylol for some hours. This makes the chitin brittle but beautifully transparent, giving brilliant definition especially good for large, robust genitalia. Unfortunately the balsam will become yellow after a few years, and today Euparal, which remains colourless, is preferred.

Preparation and mounting of legs, palpi etc.

If the parts are fairly large, boiling in water for a few moments will drive out air-bubbles, when the specimen can be mounted after dehydration in alcohol. Small legs and palpi are so easily lost or damaged that I find it best to mount them 'dry' in Euparal, or sometimes in Canada balsam. The last can be warmed over the lamp to drive out air from the segments. Legs and palpi are often very hairy. To remove hair the parts should be soaked in Eau de Javelle (chlorinated potassium hydrate) which will bleach the scales and will make the hair easy to detach by light brushing. This solution is sensitive to sunlight and must be kept shaded in a dark bottle. If legs and palpi are left too long in the solution, the chitin will be softened and their structure will collapse. Eau de Javelle is also most useful for cleaning scales from wings in order to examine venation. The wing is floated on the surface of a little reagent in a watch-glass, first on one side and then on the other side, for about 15 minutes each, until the scale colours are bleached. It is then placed on a slide with a little water, when the scales can be brushed away, using great care to avoid damage to the wing-membrane. The cleaned wing should be carefully washed and then mounted dry between two slides held together with adhesive tape.

Practical hints

Caustic potash is a very strong reagent; it will burn and stain fingers and make marks on furniture. I keep all test-tubes, dissecting needles, spirit lamp, slides etc. on an unpolished tray which is easily moved on to my desk when required and removed when it is not wanted. The tray may get stained but my furniture does not.

I prefer to treat specimens by leaving them for several hours (over night) in cold reagent. If they are large or very hard, I often boil up the specimen in the reagent for a few moments, which drives out air bubbles and allows the caustic potash to soak in. The flame of the lamp must be directed to the upper layers of potash solution. If the bulb of the test-tube is put into the flame, the lowest layers of liquid boil first and the whole contents of the tube will suddenly blow away, with permanent damage to any furniture or carpets within range. If it is important to make an examination rapidly, the test-tube plugged with cotton-wool, numbered and containing the abdomen may be partially immersed in a beaker half filled with water which is brought to the boil and left to simmer for about 20 minutes. Heated in this way the KOH solution will soften the parts very quickly. To express the genitalia from the softened abdomen as it lies in water on the slide, the proximal end of the abdomen can be held firmly by something blunt (e.g. a wooden match) while the genitalia are expelled by gently kneading and pushing. I find the dental seeker invaluable for this and for many other purposes.

Reference. Bourgogne 1963.

Essential apparatus and materials

Test-tubes 16mm in diameter (with corks) and test-tube stand.

Small corked tubes about 10mm in diameter × 7cm long, for dehydrating specimens in alcohol; name and number of specimen to be pinned to the cork.

Microscope slides (standard size 3in × 1in), round coverslips and rings (if obtainable) about 16mm diameter are convenient for most specimens.

Caustic potash (KOH) 10% solution. Distilled water, filtered rain water or melted 'defrosting' ice from refrigerator. Tap water is not suitable.

Small spirit lamp or small gas flame.

Glass pipette (5cc) and glass rod. I use the rod to transfer a few drops of water to the slide when a specimen is to be cleaned.

Two or three needles mounted on handles. Dental seeker or crochet-hook, not too short, for hooking specimens out of the KOH tube.

Forceps with really sharp needle-points.

Jeweller's spectacles or clip-on lenses to give slight magnification; useful during preparation of small specimens.

Microscope. A simple microscope giving magnification up to × 50 or little more is generally adequate. Magnification to × 300 or more will be needed for study of androconial scales. Expensive binocular microscopes are not essential.

Slides should be named and numbered as they are made, and recorded in a book. The same number on a small paper label must be pinned to the specimen from which it is taken. Boxes of trays for storing finished slides are available in wood or in strong cardboard. The slides must be stored flat; if stored vertically the object may move about in the mountant.

Glossary

The nomenclature of the anatomical parts of genitalia, legs etc. fully explained on pages 19–29, are not included in the Glossary.

Acuminate   slender and pointed like a needle.
Adaptation   in living creatures, modification of structure, function etc. to suit a particular environment.
Allele   an alternative expression of a gene.
Allopatric   of distribution, occurring in mutually exclusive different geographical areas.
Anal   associated with the anus or inner margin of the hw; anal angle, anal vein etc.
Anastomosed   of wing veins, those united for part of their length.
Androconia   scales of special form occurring only in males.
Binominal nomenclature   the system in which the scientific name of an animal is composed of two words, generic and specific names.
Biotope   environment, including soil, altitude, humidity, fauna and flora etc.
Boreal   associated with the arctic regions.
Caudal   associated with the tail.
Cell   of wings, part of the membrane enclosed completely by veins, used especially for the discoidal cell.
Cephalic   associated with the head.
Chitin   a hard organic substance forming the integuments of insects.
Chromosomes   small particles of protein within the nuclei of living cells, containing the genes that transmit hereditary characters.
Cline   a character gradient; see p. 12.
Code   the rules for zoological nomenclature adopted by the International Congress of Zoology in 1964. The Code is published by the International Trust for Zoological Nomenclature and is obtainable from the Secretary, 41 Queen's Gate, London SW7.
Congeneric   a term applied to species of the same genus.
Conspecific   a term applied to individuals belonging to the same species.
Cremaster   a set of minute hooks at the caudal extremity of a pupa, by which the insect is attached to a silken pad spun before pupating.
Dimorphism   occurrence of two distinct morphological types in a species, often seasonal or sexual.
Discoidal   associated with the central area of the wing, especially around the transverse discoidal veins.
Distal   away from the centre of the body.
Dominant   in genetics, of a gene, able to express a character to the exclusion of other characters.
Ecology   the study of the relationship between organisms and their environment.
Environment   the total physical and chemical conditions surrounding an organism.

Facies   in taxonomy, the general habitus or aspect of a species.

Falcate   hooked, of the fw the apex extending beyond the outer margin.

Family   a term used for a (large) group of animals or plants all with certain similar characters and considered closely related on this account.

Fauna   the animals of a region collectively.

Frons   the front of the head, especially the part between the eyes.

Fusiform   spindle-shaped, centrally wide and tapering at each end.

Gene   a particle of living matter carrying hereditary material, present within the chromosomes of body cells.

Gene flow   exchange of genetic material between populations.

Genetics   experimental study of the laws of heredity.

Genitalia   male genitalia are referred to unless qualified.

Genotype   the class within which an individual falls on the basis of its genetic (hereditary) constitution. See also phenotype.

Genus   a taxonomic category; see p. 9.

Hibernation   survival through winter in a dormant state.

Holarctic Region   the extra-tropical areas of the northern hemisphere.

Homologous   of organs, having the same derivation.

Homonym   identical name applied to different things, see p. 13.

Hyaline   resembling glass.

I.C.Z.N.   abbreviation for International Commission for Zoological Nomenclature. The Commission publishes the Code, last revised in 1964, which includes the rules for nomenclature adopted by Zoologists throughout the world.

Imago (pl. imagines)   the final phase in a butterfly's life, the perfect insect.

Karyotype   the number and disposition of the chromosomes within the cell nucleus.

Jullien Organ   modified scales along the caudal margin of the last abdominal tergite in some Satyrid species; see p. 221.

Larva   the second (growth) stage of a butterfly's life.

Lamella   a small plate.

Macular   of a wing-marking – composed of spots.

Mediterranean Subregion   an important zoogeographical area with characteristic flora and fauna, extending from the Mediterranean coastal regions across W Asia to Iran and the western frontiers of India.

Mendelian Heredity   the theory of particulate heredity first enunciated by Gregor Mendel (1822–84).

Morphological   concerned with structure and markings.

Morula   in Melitaeini, a small spiculate structure present in the ostium-folds (probably = cornutus).

Mutation   in genetics, a discontinuous change in a genetic factor.

N Africa   Morocco, Algeria and Tunisia referred to together.

Nearctic Region   the extra-tropical areas of America.

Obsolescent   becoming obsolete.

Ocellus   1. of an insect the simple true eye.
         2. of wings, a round spot resembling an eye, often including a white central pupil.

Onisciform   like a wood-louse (Oniscus).

Osmaterium   a fleshy, glandular forked organ situated behind the head in Papilionid larvae.

Palearctic Region   Europe and the extra-tropical areas of Asia and NW Africa.

Phenotype   the total characteristics of an individual or population.

Phylogeny   the origin and evolution of an organism or group of organisms.

Pilose   covered with fine hair.

Polymorphism   occurrence together in the same habitat of two or more forms of a species in such proportions that the rarest of them cannot be maintained by recurrent mutation.

Postdiscal   of a wing, the area beyond the discal area and before the marginal area.

Produced   extended.

Proximal   near or towards the centre of the body.

Pubescent   covered with short fine hair.

Race   subspecies, sometimes used for poorly defined subspecies.

Ramus   a branch esp. a slender branch (anatomy).

Region   Europe, west of the USSR frontier and Bosphorus; N Africa, Canary Islands, Madeira and Azores.

Recessive   in genetics, the opposite of dominant q.v.

Rugose   wrinkled.

Sagittate   shaped like an arrow-head.

Sclerite   the chitinised exoskeleton of an insect's body segment.

Serrate   with teeth like a saw.

Seta   a very fine bristle.

Sex-brand   androconial scales collected into a conspicuous patch.

Sibling species   Pairs or groups of closely related species morphologically nearly identical.

Space   the area between two wing-veins.

Spatulate   shaped like a spade.

Species   a 'kind' of something; see p. 10.

Sphragis   the horny structure secreted during copulation around the ostium bursae in females of the genus *Parnassius*.

Symbiosis   two or more species living together and dependent upon one another.

Sympatric   a term applied to two or more species which occupy identical or broadly overlapping areas.

Synonym   different names applied to the same thing are synonyms.

Systematics   application of the principles involved in the classification of animals or plants.

Taxon   a unit of classification, i.e. a genus or species.

Taxonomy   the branch of science that deals with classification.

Trabecula   a small bar or rod.

Type   in zoology, the base for the name of a taxonomic unit, e.g. type specimen of a species, type species of a genus.

Valid name   the name of a taxon available under the rules of the I.C.Z.N.

Vein   of insect wings, minute rigid tubes which support the wing-membrane.

Venation   the pattern of veins in an insect's wing.

Vicariant   taking the place of something.

Bibliography

Agenjo R.   1956   Consideraciones sobre el estudio de las formulas cromo-
somicas en los Lepidopteros . . . de grupo *Plebejus* (*Lysandra
coridon* Poda). Graellsia **14**: 73–87.

ibid. 1963(A)   Morfologia y distribución geográphica de los *Satyrus actaea*
(Esp. 1780) y *bryce* (Hb. 1790–93) en España. Eos **39**:
313–36.

ibid. 1963(B)   Estudio de la 'Moradilla del Fresno' *Laeosopis roboris* (Esp.),
Bol. del Servicio de Plagas Forestales **6**: 129–39).

ibid. 1963(C)   Distribución geographica y morphologia del *Pyrgus alveus*
Hb. en España. Eos **39**: 7–22.

ibid. 1967   Morphologia y distribución geográphica en España de la
'Niña del Astrágalo' – *Plebejus pylaon*. Eos **43**: 21–5.

Amarsden C. A. and Wright P. L. 1971.   A note on the distribution of the
Rhopalocera on the island of Sao Jorge – the Azores. Ent.
Rec. **83**: 179–86.

Aurivillius C. 1925   Seitz **13**: 546 (Heteropterinae).

Bang-Haase O.   1926–30.   *Novitates   Macrolepidopterologicae*.   Dresden-
Blasewitz. 5 parts.

Bates H. W.   1861   Papilionidae of the Amazon Valley. Journ. Ent. **1**: 220.

Bethune Baker G. T.   1914   On the correlation of Pattern and Structure in
Rhopalocera . . . Ent. Rec. **26**; 177–84.

ibid. 1917(1918)   A revision of the genus *Tarucus* Trans. ent. Soc. Lond.
269–96.

Berger L. A.   1948   A *Colias* new to Britain. Entomologist **81**: 129.

Berger L. A. & Fontaine M.   1947   Lambillionea **47**: 91–8. 1948, **48**: 12 et
seq. (figures).

Bernardi G.   1945   Revision de la classification des espèces paléarctiques du
genre *Euchloe* Hb. Misc. Ent. **42**: 65–105.

ibid. 1947(A)   La nomenclature de quelques formes Européennes de
l'*Euchloe ausonia* Hb = *belia* auct. Misc. Ent. **44**: 1–24.

ibid. 1947(B)   Notes sur l'article de L. Berger – '*Maculinea rebeli* Hirschke,
bonne espèce. Bull Soc. ent. Mulhouse p. 61–7.

ibid. 1951   La détermination des *Maculinea* françaises. Rev. fr.
Lépidop. **13**: 16–18.

ibid. 1960   La répartition insulaire de deux espèces jumelles d'*Aricia*
R.C.Bull. Soc. ent. Fr. **65**: 49–52.

ibid. 1964   Endémisme et catégories taxonomiques modernes. C.R.
Soc. Biogéog. Fr. **360**: 115–29.

ibid. 1971   Note sur la variation geographique d'*Allancastria cerisyi*
(Godart). Lambillionea **70**: 55.

Beuret H.   1953   *Die Lycaeniden der Schweiz*: Lycaeninae
1957   *Die Lycaeniden der Schweiz*: Plebejinae
1961   *Die Lycaeniden der Schweiz*: Plebejini (2).

ibid. 1958   Zur systematischen Stellung einiger wenig bekannter
Glaucopsychidi. Mitt ent. Ges. Basel **8**: 61–100.

ibid. 1959   Versuch einer taxonomisch Deutung der schweizerischen *agestis*-formen. Mitt. ent. Ges. Basel **9**: 84.

ibid. 1960   Versuch einer taxonomischen Deutung der schweizerischen *agestis*-formen. Mitt. ent. Ges. Basel **10**: 1–96.

Bigger T. R. L.   1960   Chromosome numbers of Lepidoptera. Pt. 1, Ent. Gaz. **11**: 149–52. Pt. 2, idem 1961, **12**: 85–9.

Boisduval J. B. A.   1833–34   Icones historique des Lépidoptères. Roret, Paris.

ibid. 1836   Species Général des Lépidoptères. Roret, Paris.

ibid. 1840   Genera et Index Methodicus. Roret, Paris.

Bollow Chr.   1929   In Seitz, **1**: Supplement p. 20. *Parnassius.*

Borner C.   1938   Verh. VII Internat. Ent. Congress, Berlin **2**: 1372.

Bowden S. R.   1954–55   Hybrids within the European *Pieris napi* group. Proc. S. Lond. Ent. Nat. Hist. Soc. pp. 135–59.

ibid. 1963   Polymorphism in *Pieris*: forms *subtalba* and *sulphurea* (Lep. Pieridae). Ent. **96**: 77–82.

ibid. 1966a   *Pieris napi* in Corsica (Lep. Pieridae). Ent. **99**: 56–68.

Bourgogne J.   1953   *Melitaea athalia athalia* et *M. athalia helvetica* Rühl (*pseudathalia* Reverdin) en France. Etude biogéographique. Ann. Soc. ent. Fr. **122**: 131–76.

ibid. 1951   In Grassé, *Traité de Zoologie* tome **10** – Ordre des Lépidoptères: p. 364.

ibid. 1963   La préparation des armures génitales des Lépidoptères. Alexanor **3**: 61–

Bryk F.   1915   *Parnassius apollo* und sein Formenkreis. Nicolaische Verlags-Buchhandlung. Berlin.

ibid. 1937   Lep. Cat. **78**: 56 (*Panlymnas* gen. n.).

ibid. 1930–39   Parnassiana vol. 1–6. Verlag Gustav Feller, Neubrandenburg.

ibid. 1962   Parnassiidae. Lep. Cat. Pars 27.

Burmeister   1878   Descr. Phys. Rep. Arg. **5**: Lep. 1.

Butler A. G.   1869   Cat. of Diurnal Lep. Fabricius (Theclinae).

le Cerf   1913   Contribution à la faune .lépidopterologique de la Perse. Ann. d'Histoire Nat. **2**. Entomologie p. 3–22.

ibid. 1914   Etude Comparée . . . Satyrus Algériens in Oberthur, Lép. Comp. **10**: 289–344 (*Satyrus abdelkader*).

Catherine G.   1920.   In Oberthur, Et. Lép. Comp. *XVII*: 48–52. Notes sur *Anthocharis.*

Chapman T. A.   1910(B)   On *Zizeeria* (Chapman), *Zizera* (Moore), a group of Lycaenid Butterflies. Trans. ent. Soc. Lond., p. 480.

ibid. 1910(A)   On the generic characters of the ancillary appendages of the Plebeid section of the Lycaenids. Ent. Rec. **22**: 101–3.

ibid. 1912   An unrecognised European *Lycaena* identified as *Agriades thersites* Cantener. Trans. ent. Soc. Lond., pp. 662–76.

ibid. 1916   On the pairing of the Plebeid blue butterflies. Trans. ent. Soc Lond. pp. 156–80 (many figures).

ibid. 1919   Notes on *Lycaena alcon* F. reared in 1918–19 (early stages). Trans. ent. Soc. Lond. pp. 443–65.

Clench H. K.   see Ehrlich & Ehrlich 1961.

Comstock J. H. & Needham J. G.   1918.   The wings of Insects. American Naturalist **32**: 253–7.

Courvoisier 1916 Verh. nat. Ges. Basel 27. *Everes.*

Corbet S. 1948 Observations on species of Rhopalocera common to Madagascar and the Oriental Region. Trans. R. ent. Soc. Lond. **99**: 595.

Cribb P. W. et alia 1973. Genitalia of Lepidoptera, pp. 1–16. Pub. The Amateur Entomologist's Society. Available from L. Christie, 137 Gleneldon Road, Streatham, London, S.W.16.

Crosson du Cormier A. et Guérin P., 1947. A propos de la division spécifique du genre *Boloria* Moore; *B. aquilonaris* Stichel en France. Rev. fr. Lépid. **11**: 177–95.

Crosson du Cormier A., Guérin P. et H. de Toulgouet 1953 Nouvelle note sur *Boloria aquilonaris* Stichel. Rev. fr. Lépid. **14**: 21–3.

Cuvier G. C. L. G. 1798 *Tableau Elémentaire.* Paris.

ibid. 1799–1805 *Leçons d'Anatomie Comparée.* Paris.

Darwin C. 1859 *The Origin of Species.* London.

Descimon H. et de Lesse H. 1953 Découverte d'un nouvel *Erebia* dans les Hautes Pyrénées. Rev. fr. Lépid. **14**: 119–22.

Duponchel P. A. J. 1832 *Histoire Naturelle des Lépidoptères.* Supplément **1**. Paris.

ibid. 1844 *Catalogue Méthodique des Lépidoptères d'Europe.* Paris.

Ehrlich P. R. & Ehrlich A. H. 1961. The Butterflies. Dubuque, Iowa.

Eisner C. 1954–66 Kritisches Revision der Gattung *Parnassius.* Parnassiana Nova **33–40**. Zool. Meded. Leiden.

Eliot J. N. 1969 An analysis of Eurasian and Australian Neptini. Bull. Br. Mus. nat. Hist. (Ent.). Supplement 15.

Eller K. 1936 Die Rassen von *Papilio machaon* L. Verlag des Bayerıschen Akademie der Wissenschaften, München.

Elwes H. J. & Edwards 1898 Revision of the Oriental Hesperiidae. Trans. Zool. Soc. Lond. **14**: 160. (*Pyrgus malvoides*).

Esper E. J. C. 1781 De Varietatibus. Essay. (ref. Rothschild & Jordan 1906).

Evans W. H. 1949 *A Catalogue of the Hesperiidae from Europe, Asia and Australia.* British Museum, London.

Federly H. Chromosomenzahlen finnländischer Lepidopteren. 1. Rhopalocera. Heriditas, **24**: 397–464.

Ford E. B. 1944 The Classification of the Papilionidae. Trans. R. ent. Soc. London. **94**: 201–23.

ibid. 1945 *Butterflies.* Collins, London.

ibid. 1964 Local Races arising in isolation. Ecological Genetics pp. 290–1. Methuen & Co. N.Y.

Forster W. 1936 Beitrag zur Systematik der Tribus Lycaenini (*argus* Gruppe) Mitt. münch. ent. Ges. **26**: 41–150.

ibid. 1938 Das System der Paläarktischen Polyommatini (Lep. Lyc.). Mitt. münch. ent. Ges. **28**: 97–118.

ibid. 1956–60 Bausteine zur Kentniss der Gattung *Agrodiaetus* Scudder. (Lep. Lycaenidae). Z. wien. ent. Ges. **41**: 42–127.

ibid. 1961 Idem Part 2. Z. wien. ent. Ges. **45**: 8–142. **46**: 8–116.

Frohawk 1924 *Natural History of British Butterflies.*

Fruhstorfer H. 1923 In Seitz, Macrolep. d. Erde **9**: 891–2 (Tarucini).

BIBLIOGRAPHY

Godman F. D. & Salvin O.   1889   Biol. Cent. Amer. 1(2): 113 & 173 (Pierini & Dismorphina).

Gosse P. H.   1881   On the clasping organs . . . Trans. Linn. Soc. Lond. (2): Zool. **2**: 265–345.

Grassé P-P.   See Bourgogne 1951.

Grote A. R.   1895   Systema Lepidopterorum. Mitt. Roemer Mus. Hildersheim **1**: 24. Riodinidae.

ibid. 1897   Mitt. Roemer Mus. Hildersheim **8**: 20. (Araschniinae, Maniolinae).

ibid. 1900   Mitt. Roemer Mus. Hildersheim **11**: 2. (Zerynthiinae).

Guénée A.   1865   In Vinson, Voyage Madagascar, Annexe. (Charaxinae).

Guillaumin M.   1962   Etude des formes intermédiares entre *Pyrgus malvae* et *P. malvoides*. Bull. Soc. ent. Fr. **67**: 168–73.

ibid. 1964   Les espèces françaises du Genre *Pyrgus* Hübner. Alexanor **3**: 293–305.

Hemming A. F.   1929   Revision of the *baton*-group of the genus *Turanana* Bethune Baker. Ent. **62**: 27 et seq.

ibid. 1931   Revision of the genus *Iolana* B. Baker. Trans. ent. Soc. Lond. **79**: 323–33 (*Apelles*).

ibid. 1934   Revisional notes on certain species of Rhopalocera. Stylops **3**: 193.

ibid. 1943   On the occurrence in Europe and the distribution of *Hipparchia syriaca* . . . Ent. **76**: 68–72.

ibid. 1967   *Generic Names of the Butterflies*. Bull. Br. Mus. nat. Hist. (Ent). Suppl. 9. London.

Herrich-Schäffer   G. A. W.   1843–44.   Systematische Bearbeitung . . . Regensburg.

Heydenreich G. H.   1851   *Lepidopterorum Europaeorum Catalogus*. Leipzig.

Higgins L. G.   1932   Some observations on *Melitaea athalia*. Ent. **65**: 217.

ibid. 1941   An illustrated Catalogue . . . Trans. R. ent. Soc. Lond. **91**: 175–365.

ibid. 1944   An illustrated Catalogue . . . Errata. Proc. R. ent. Soc. Lond. **13**: 44–5.

ibid. 1950   A descriptive catalogue of the Palearctic *Euphydryas* (Lep. Melitaeinae). Trans. R. ent. Soc. Lond. **101**: 435–99.

ibid. 1955   A descriptive catalogue of the genus *Mellicta* Billberg. Trans. R. ent. soc. Lond. **106**: 1–131.

ibid. 1956   Bemerkungen zu *Melitaea* . . . Z. wien. ent. Ges. **41**: 10–15.

ibid. 1967   *Hipparchia* (*Pseudotergumia*) *wyssii* Christ, with description of a new subspecies. Ent. **100**: 169–71.

ibid. 1969   Observations sur les *Melanargia* dans le Midi de la France. Alexanor **6**: 85–90.

Hoegh-Guldberg   1961   *Aricia agestis* Schiff. and *A. allous* Hb. (Lep. Rhopalocera) in northern Europe. Opuscula Ent. **26**: 161–76.

ibid. 1966   Northern European *A. allous*. Nat. Jutlandica No. 13.

ibid. 1968   Evolutionary trends in the genus *Aricia*. Nat. Jutlandica No. 14.

Hoegh-Guldberg O. & Jarvis F. V. L.   1969   Central and North European *Ariciae* (Lep.). Nat. Jutlandica No. 15.

Hogben L.   1940   In Huxley, *The New Systematics*. Oxford. p. 271.

Hübner J.   1818–23   *Verzeichniss bekannter Schmetterlinge*. Augsburg.

Huxley J.   1942   *Evolution*. G. Allen & Unwin. London.

Illiger K.   1807   Magazin f. Insektenkunde Vol. 6.

Imms A. D.   1964   *General Text-book of Entomology* Ed. 9.

Jarvis F. V. L.   1962   The genetic relationship between *Aricia agestis* (Schiff.) and its ssp. *artaxerxes*, Proc. S. Lond. ent. nat. hist. Soc. pp. 106–22.

ibid. 1966   The genus *Aricia* (Lep. Rhopalocera) in Britain. Proc. S. Lond. ent. nat. hist. Soc. pp. 37–122.

Jordan K.   1903   The variation in the genital armature of certain Papilios. Nov. Zool. **3**: 458 et seq.

Jullien J.   1909   Un problème résolu. *Satyrus hermione, syriaca, alcyone*. Bull. Soc. Lép. Genève **1**: 361.

Kaaber Sv. & Hoegh-Guldberg O.   1961   *Aricia allous* Hb. ssp. *vandalica*. Flora og Fauna **67**: 122–8.

Karsch   1893   Berl. ent. Z. **38**: 169 (in Key) Grypocera, replacement name for Netrocera Haase preocc. (Ent. Nachr. 1892; **18**: 177.)

Kauffmann   1955   *Spialia sertoria* Hoffmannsegg en Corse. Rev. Fr. Lépidop. **15**: 38–40.

Klots A. B.   1930   Brooklyn ent. Soc. **25**: 80–95 (Anthocharinae).

ibid.   1931–32   Ent. Americana **12**: 139 et seq. (Pieridae).

Kluk K.   1788 (Ed. 1).   1802 (Ed. 3).   *Zweirat domowych i dzikich* . . . Vol. 4 Warsaw.

König F.   1965   *Erebia melas runcensis* ssp. nova. (Lep. Satyridae) aus den Westtranssylvanischen Karpathen. Ent. **98**: 161–6.

Latreille P. A.   1804   *Histoire Naturelle des Crustacés* . . . Vol. **9**. Paris.

ibid. 1809   *Genera Crustaceorum et Insectorum* **4**. Paris.

ibid. 1810   *Considérations Générales* . . . Paris.

de Lattin G.   1949   *Hipparchia semele* L. Gruppe. Ent. Z. **59**: 113–18; 124–6; 131–2.

ibid. 1950   Türkische Lepidopteren. Rev. Fac. Sc. Univ. Istanbul **15**: Ser. B: fasc. 4. 301–31.

Leach W. E.   1815   Zool. Miscellany in Edinburgh Magazine.

de Lesse H.   1947.   Contribution à l'étude du Genre *Erebia*. Rev. fr. Lép. **11**: 97–118. *E. e. fauveaui* nova; *E. m. lioranus* nova.

ibid. 1949(A)   Contribution à l'étude du Genre *Coenonympha*. Lambillionea **49**: 68–80.

ibid. 1951(A)   Contribution à l'étude du genre *Erebia*. Vie et Milieu **2**: 95–123. (*E. tyndarus* et *E. cassioides*).

ibid. 1951(B)   Dicisions génériques et subgénériques des anciens genres *Satyrus* et *Eumenis*. Rev. fr. Lép. **13**: 39–41.

ibid. 1951(C)   Revision de l'ancien genus *Satyrus* (S.l.) (with bibliography). Ann. Soc. ent. Fr. **121**: 77–101.

ibid. 1951(D)   Contribution à l'étude du genre *Erebia*. Vie et Milieu **2**: 268–77. (*E. pandrose* et *E. sthennyo*).

ibid. 1951(E)   Sur . . . *Hipparchia wyssii* Christ. Bull. Soc. ent. Fr. **121**: 50–3.

ibid. 1952(A)   Contribution à l'étude du genre *Erebia*. Rev. fr. Lép. **13**: 217–19. (*E. pandrose* et *E. sthennyo*).

ibid. 1952(B)   Revision des *Neohipparchia* (Satyridae) de l'Afrique du Nord. Bull. Soc. Sci. Nat. Maroc **43**: 91–105.

ibid. 1952(C)   Sur la validité spécifique de *Pararge xiphia* F. et *P. xiphioides* Stgr. Bull. Soc. ent. Fr. **122**: 152–5.

ibid. 1952(D)   Revision des genres *Pararge* et *Maniola*. Ann. Soc. ent. Fr. **121**: 61–76.

ibid. 1953(D)   Formules chromosomiques nouvelles du genre *Erebia*. C. R. Acad. Sc. **237**: 758–9.

ibid. 1953(C)   Formules chromosomiques de *Boloria aquilonaris* Stichel, *pales* D. & S., *napaea* Hoffmannsegg etc. Rev. fr. Lép. **14**: 24–6.

ibid. 1954   Formules chromosomique nouvelles chez les Lycaenidae. C. R. Acad. Sc. **238**: 514–16.

ibid. 1955(B)   Distribution holarctique d'un groupe d'espèces du Genre *Erebia* . . . C. R. Soc. Biogéogr. **276**: 12–18.

ibid. 1959(A)   Caractères et repartition en France d'*Erebia aethiopellus* et *E. mnestra*. Alexanor **1**: 72–81.

ibid. 1959(B)   Séparation spécifique d'un *Lysandra* d'Afrique du Nord à la suite de la decouverte de sa formule chromosomique. Alexanor **1**: 61–4.

ibid. 1960(A)   Spéciation et variation chromosomique chez les Lépidoptères Rhopalocères. Ann. Sci. Nat. Zool. **1** 1 223.

ibid. 1960(B)   Les nombres de chromosomes dans la classification du groupe d'*Agrodiaetus ripartii* Freyer. Rev. fr. d'Entomol. **27**: 240–64.

ibid. 1961(A)   Signification supraspecifique des formules chromosomiques chez les Lépidoptères. Bull Soc. ent. Fr. **66**: 71–83.

ibid. 1961(B)   Cohabitation en Espagne d'*Agrodiaetus ripartii* Freyer et *A. fabressei* Oberthur. Rev. fr. d'Ent. **28**: 50–3.

ibid. 1966   Variation chromosomique chez *Agrodiaetus dolus* Hübner. Ann. Soc. ent. Fr. **2**(1): 209–14.

ibid. 1969   Les nombres chromosomiques dans le groupe de *Lysandra coridon* (Lep. Lycaenidae). Ann. Soc. ent. Fr. (N.S.) **5**(2): 469–522.

ibid. 1970(A)   Les nombres de chromosomes à l'appui d'une systématique du groupe de *L. coridon* (Lycaenidae). Alexanor **6**: 203–24.

ibid. 1970(B)   Les nombres de chromosomes dans le groupe de *Lysandra argester* et leur incidence sur sa taxonomie. Bull Soc. ent. Fr. **75**: 64–8.

Lindsey A. W., Bell E. L. & Williams R. C. junr.   1931   The Hesperioidea of N America. Denison University Bull. Journ. Sci. Lab. No. 26.

Linnaeus C.   1735   *Systema Naturae* Ed. 1. Lund.
ibid. 1758   *Systema Naturae* Ed. 10. Lund.

Lorković Z.   1938   Artberichtigung von *Everes argiades* Pall., *E. alcetas* Hffmgg., und *E. decolorata* Stgr. Mitt. münch ent. Ges. **28**: 215–46.

ibid. 1950   Neue ostasiatische Arten und Rassen der Gattung *Leptidea* nebst Nomenclaturberichtigungen. Bioloski Glasnik **2**(B): 57–76.

ibid. 1952   Beiträge zum Studium der Semispecies. Specifität von *Erebia stirius* Godart und *E. styx* Frr. (Satyridae). Zeitschr. Lepidopt. **2**: 159–76.

ibid. 1955   Die Populations-analyse zweier neuen sternochoren *Erebia*-Rassen aus Kroatia. Bioloski Glasnik **8**: 53–76.

ibid. 1957   Die Speciesstufen in der *Erebia tyndarus* Gruppe. Bioloski Glasnik **10**: 61–110.

ibid. 1961   Abstufungen der Reproductiven Isolationsmechanismen in der *Erebia* . . . Verh. Int. Kongress für Ent. Wien 1960: 134–42.

ibid. 1962   The genetics and reproductive isolating mechanism of the *Pieris napi bryoniae* group. J. Lep. Soc. **16**: 5–19 & 105–27.

ibid. 1965   Ueber die neuerliche Verwirrung um die 2 Generation von *Euchloe orientalis* Bremer. NachrBl. bayer Ent. **14**: 1–15.

ibid. 1968   Karyologischer Beitrag zur Frage der Verhalthisse Sudeuropaischen Taxone von *Pieris napi* (L). Lep. Pieridae. Bioloski Glasnik **21**: 95–136.

ibid. 1968(B)   Systematische-genitische und oekologische Besonderheiten von *Pieris ergane* Hb. Mitt. schweiz. ent. Ges. **41**: 233–44.

ibid. 1970   Karyologischer Beitrag zur Frage der Fortpflanzungs verhaltnisse Sudeuropäischer Taxone von *Pieris napi* (L). Bioloski Glasnik **21**: 96–136.

Lorković Z. & de Lesse H.   1954(A)   Experiences de croisements dans le genre *Erebia*. Bull. Soc. ent. Fr. **79**: 31–9.

ibid. 1954(B)   Nouvelles decouvertes concernante le degré de parenté d'*Erebia tyndarus* et *E. cassioides* Hohenw. Lambillionea **54**: 58–86. (*E. nivalis*).

ibid. 1965   Note supplémentaire sur le groupe d'*Erebia tyndarus*. Lambillionea: **55**: 55–8.

Lorković Z. & Herman C.   1961   The solution of a long-outstanding problem in the genetics of dimorphism in *Colias*. J. Lep. Soc. **15**: 43–55.

ibid. 1958   Genetics of morphism in *Colias crocea* Fourcroy. Bioloski Glasnik **11**: 55–9.

Lorković Z. & Sijarić R.   1967   Der Grad der morphologischen und oekologischen Differenzierung zwischen *Aricia agestis* Schiff. und *A. allous* (Hubn.) in der Umgebung von Sarajevo. Posebni Otisak Glasnika, Zemaljskog Musela N.S. sr. 6.

Maeki K. & Remington C. L.   1960   Studies of the chromosomes of North American Rhopalocera. J. Lep. Soc. **13**: 193–203. idem. 1960. **14**: 37–56.

Malicky H.   1969   Uebersicht über präimaginal Stadien, Bionomie und Oekologie der mitteleuropäischen Lycaeniden (Lepidoptera). Ent. Ges. Basel **19**: 25–91.

Mayr E., Linsley E. G. and Usinger R. L.   1953   *Methods and principles of Systematic Zoology*. McGraw-Hill Book Co.

Mayr E. 1970 *Principles of Systematic Zoology.* McGraw-Hill Book Co.

McDunnough J. 1911 On the nomenclature of the male genitalia in Lepidoptera. Can. Ent. **43**: 181-9.

Merian M. S. 1705 *Metamorphosis Insectorum Surinamensium.* Amsterdam.

Le Moult 1945 Nouvelles remarques sur *Lycaena (Heodes) dispar* Haworth. Misc. Ent. **42**: 41-60.

Munroe E. 1961 The classification of the Papilionidae (Lepidoptera). Can. Ent. Suppl. 17.

Müller L. & Kautz H. 1939 *Pieris bryoniae* O. und *Pieris napi* L. Oesterreischischen Ent.-Ver. Wien.

Nguen Thi Hong 1970 Note sur deux espèces jumelle d'*Apatura* Fabr. Lambillionea **68**: 76-80.

Niculescu E. V. 1963 Fauna Republicii Populare Romine. **11**: (6) Pieridae.

Nordström F. 1955 *De Fennoskandiska Dagfjärilarnas Utbredning.* Lund.

Oberthur C. 1891 Lépidoptères du genre *Parnassius.* Et. d'Ent. **14**: 1-18.
  ibid. 1913 A propos des Races géographiques occidentales de *Parnassius apollo.* Lep. Comp. **8**: 9-82.
  ibid. 1914 See Le Cerf.

Ochsenheimer O. 1806 Die Schmetterlinge Sachsens, Leipzig.
  ibid. 1808 Die Schmett. von Europ. **1**(2): 210. (*Pap. proto*).

dos Passos C. F. & Grey L. P. 1945 A genitalic survey of Argynninae (Lepidoptera Nymphalidae). Am. Mus. Novit. No. 1296, pp. 1-29.

Petersen B. 1955 Geogr. variation of *Pieris (napi) bryoniae.* Zool. Bidr. Upps. **30**: 366-97.
  ibid. Breakdown of differentiation between *Pieris napi* and *Pieris bryoniae* and its causes. Zool. bidr. Upps. **35**: 205-62.

Picard J. 1946 Notes sur *Pyrgus cacaliae* Rbr. Rev. fr. Lép. **10**: 300-2.
  ibid. 1948(1950) Etude sur les Hesperiidae du Maroc. Bull. Soc. Sci. Nat. du Maroc **28**: 121 et seq.

Pierce F. N. 1909 and later. Studies of genitalia of Lepidoptera 1941. *Genitalia of the British Rhopalocera* . . . Oundle.

Ragusa 1919 Nat. Sicil. **23**: 172. Lepidoptera Siciliana (*Reverdinus*).

Reissinger 1960 Die unterscheidung von *Colias hyale* L. und *C. australis* Verity (Lep. Pieridae). Ent. Z. **70**: 117.

Remington C. L. see Maeki & Remington.

Reuter E. 1897 Über die Palpen der Rhopaloceren. Acta Soc. Sci. Fenn. **22**: 1-578.

Reverdin J. L. 1911 *Hesperia malvae* L., *H. fritillum* Rambur, *H. melotis* Duponchel. Bull. Soc. Lép. Genève **2**: 59-77.
  ibid. 1913 Notes sur les genres *Hesperia* et *Carcharodus.* Bull. Soc. Lép. Genève **2**: 212-37.

Reverdin J. L. & Chapman T. A. 1917. Note sur *Lycaena argus* L. In Oberthur 1917, Lep. Comp. **14**: 1-74.

Riley N. D. 1925 Species usually referred to the genus *Cigaritis* (Lep. Lycaenidae). Nov. Zool. **32**: 70.

Rocci 1930 *Melitaea melathalia.* Boll. Soc. ent. It. **62**: 184.

Rothschild W. 1895 Monographic revision of the Papilios of the Eastern Hemisphere. Nov. Zool. **2**: 167-463.

Rothschild W.   1914   Notes on Mr Charles Oberthur's Faune des Lép. de la Barbarie. Nov. Zool. **21**: 301–5. (*Euchloe crameri*).

Rothschild W.   1917   Supplemental notes on Mr Charles Oberthur's Faune des Lépidoptères de la Barbarie. Nov. Zool. **24**: 81–4; 271. *Euchloe ausonia* and regional forms.

Rothschild W. & Jordan K.   1906   A revision of the American Papilios. Nov. Zool. **13**: 413–753.

Rösel A. J.   1740–46   Der Monatlich-herausgegebenen Insectenbelustigung. Nürnberg.

Schima   1909.   Verh. zool.-bot. Ges. Wien: 376. idem. 1910: 268–303.

Schrank F. P.   1801   *Fauna Boica*. Nürnberg.

Seba A.   1734–65   *Lucopletissimi rerum* . . . Amsterdam.

Shirozu T. & Yamamato H.   1956   A generic revision and the phylogeny of the tribe Theclini (Lepidoptera Lycaenidae). Sieboldia **1**: 329–421.

Seitz. A.   1907   et seq. Macrolepidoptera of the World. Vol. **1**. idem. 1932, Supplement.

Sloane H.   1707   *Voyage to the Islands of Madeira* . . . London.

Staudinger O. & Rebel   1901   *Catalog der Lepidopteren des Palaearctischen Faunengebietes*. Berlin.

Stempffer H.   1927   Description d'une forme nouvelle de *Cupido minimus* Fuessli. Bull. Soc. ent. Fr. p. 244. (*C. carswelli*).

   ibid. 1937   Contribution à l'étude des Plebeiinae palaéarctiques. Bull. Soc. ent. Fr. p. 211–19; 297–300.

   ibid. 1964   Determination facile des espèces du group de *Lycaeides idas*. Alexanor **3**: 339–44.

   ibid. 1967   *The genera of the African Lycaenidae*. Bull. Brit. Mus. nat. Hist. (Ent.) Suppl. No. 10. London.

Stichel H.   1907(A)   Gen. Ins. Subfamily Parnassiinae **58**: 1–18.

   ibid. 1907(B)   Gen. Insect. Subfamily Zerynthiinae **59**: 1–27.

Swainson W.   1827   Phil. Mag. (N.S.) **1**(2): 187. Coliadinae; Polyommatinae.

   ibid. 1840   Nat. Hist. of Insects in Lardener's Cabinet Cyclopedia.

Swinhoe C.   1912   Lepidoptera Indica **9**: 156. (Aphnaeinae).

Talbot G.   1939   *Fauna of British India* **1**. (Papilionidae).

de Toulgouet H.   1952   Note sur les premiers états de *Boloria pales* Schiff. et *napaea* Hb. Rev. fr. Lép. **13**: 162–5.

Toxopaeus   1927   Tijdschr. Ent. **70**: 286 *nota*.

Turati E.   1909   Revisione della forme di *Epinephele lycaon* Rott. Nat. Sicil. **21**: 56–73.

Tutt J. W.   1896   *British Butterflies*. London.

   ibid. 1905–6   *British Lepidoptera* vol. 8. Lycaeninae.
      1907–8   idem   vol. 9. Thecla etc.
      1908–9   idem   vol. 10. Polyommatini.
      1910–14   idem   vol. 11. Polyommatini.

Tuxen S. L.   1970   *Taxonomist's Glossary of genitalia of insects*. Copenhagen.

Urbahn E.   1952   Die Unterschiede der Jugenstände . . . *Melitaea athalia* Rott., *britomartis* Assmann, und *parthenie* Borkh. = *aurelia* Nickerl, in Deutschland. Z. wien. ent. Ges. **37**: 105–21.

Urquhart F. A.   1960   *The Monarch Butterfly*. Toronto.

Varin G. 1953 Les races d'*Arethusana arethusa* Schiffermüller. Rev. fr. Lépid. **14**: 77–84.

Verity R. 1905–11 *Rhopalocera Palearctica*. Firenze.

ibid. 1940–53 *Le Farfalle Diurne d'Italia*. Vol. 1–5. Firenze.

Wallengren H. D. J. 1853. *Lepidoptera Scandinaviae*. Rhopalocera.

Warren B. C. S. 1926 Monograph of the tribe Hesperiidi. Trans. ent. Soc. Lond. **74**: 1–170.

ibid. 1936 Monograph of the genus *Erebia*. British Museum (N.H.).

ibid. 1942 Genus *Pandoriana* gen. nova. Entomologist **75**: 245.

ibid. 1944 Review of the classification of the Argynnidi. Trans. R. ent. Soc. Lond. **94**: 1–101.

ibid. 1949 Three hitherto unrecognised species of *Erebia*. Entomologist **82**: 103.

ibid. 1953 Three unrecognised species of *Pyrgus* (Lep. Hesperiidae). Entomologist **86**: 103.

ibid. 1952 *Pyrgus reverdini* Oberthur, a European species. Entomologist **85**: 38–41.

ibid. 1961 The androconial scales and their bearing on the question of speciation in the genus *Pieris* (Lepidoptera). Ent. Tidskr. **82**: 121–48.

ibid. 1963 The androconial scales of the genus *Pieris* (2). The nearctic species of the *napi* group. Ent. Tidsk. **84**: 1–4.

ibid. 1965 Notes on various Pierid species. Ent. Rec. **77**: 121.

Wheeler G. 1903 Butterflies of Switzerland p. 121. (Oeneini; Melanargiinae).

Wilmot A. J. 1942 The nature of the genotype. Entomologist **75**: 113–16.

Wyatt C. 1952 Einige neue Tagfalterformen aus Marokko. Z. wien. Ent. Ges. p. 174–6 (*P. manni haroldi*).

Zander E. 1903 Beiträge z. Morphologie d. männlichen Geschlechtsanhange der Lepidoptera. Z. wiss. Zool. **74**: 557–615.

Zerny H. 1935 Die Lepidopterenfauna des Grossen Atlas in Marokko. Mem. Soc. Sci. Nat. de Maroc. No. 62: p. 34 et seq.

Checklist of Species

Family **HESPERIIDAE** Latreille 1809

Pyrgus Hübner

Pyrgus malvae L.
  m. malvae L.
  m. malvoides Elwes & Edwards
  m. melotis Duponchel

Pyrgus alveus Hübner
  a. alveus Hübner
  a. centralitaliae Verity
  a. alticolus Rebel
  a. numidus Oberthur

Pyrgus armoricanus Oberthur
  a. armoricanus Oberthur
  a. maroccanus Picard

Pyrgus foulquieri Oberthur

Pyrgus serratulae Rambur
  s. serratulae Rambur
  s. major Staudinger

Pyrgus carlinae Rambur

Pyrgus cirsii Rambur

Pyrgus onopordi Rambur

Pyrgus cinarae Rambur

Pyrgus fritillarius Poda

Pyrgus sidae Esper

Pyrgus andromedae Wallengren

Pyrgus cacaliae Rambur

Pyrgus centaureae Rambur

Spialia Swinhoe

Spialia sertorius
  s. sertorius Hoffmannsegg
  s. orbifer Hübner
  s. therapne Rambur
  s. ali Oberthur

Spialia phlomidis Herrich-Schäffer

Spialia doris Walker

Syrichtus

Syrichtus proto Esper

Syrichtus mohammed Oberthur

Syrichtus tessellum Hübner

Syrichtus cribrellum Eversmann

Syrichtus leuzeae Oberthur

Carcharodus

Carcharodus alceae Esper

Carcharodus lavatherae Esper

Carcharodus boeticus
  b. boeticus Rambur
  b. stauderi Rambur

Carcharodus flocciferus
  f. flocciferus Zeller
  f. orientalis Reverdin

Erynnis Schrank

Erynnis tages L.

Erynnis marloyi Boisduval

Heteropterus Duméril

Heteropterus morpheus Pallas

Carterocephalus Lederer

Caterocephalus palaemon Pallas

Carterocephalus silvicola Meigen

Thymelicus Hübner

Thymelicus acteon Rottemburg

Thymelicus hamza Oberthur

Thymelicus lineolus Ochsenheimer

Thymelicus flavus Brünnich

303

Hesperia F.

Hesperia comma L.

Gegenes Hübner

Gegenes pumilio Hoffmannsegg
Gegenes nostrodamus F.

Ochlodes Scudder

Ochlodes venatus Bremer

Borbo Evans

Borbo borbonica Boisduval

Family **PAPILIONIDAE** Latreille 1809

Papilio L.

Papilio machaon L.
Papilio hospiton Géné
Papilio alexanor Esper

Iphiclides Hübner

Iphiclides podalirius
  p. podalirius L.
  p. feisthamelii Duponchel

Zerynthia Ochsenheimer

Zerynthia polyxena D. & S.
  p. polyxena D. & S.

p. cassandra Geyer
Zerynthia rumina L.

Allancastria Bryk

Allancastria cerisyi Godart

Archon

Archon apollinus Herbst

Parnassius Latreille

Parnassius apollo L.
Parnassius phoebus F.
Parnassius mnemosyne L.

Family **PIERIDAE** Duponchel 1832

Aporia Hübner

Aporia crataegi L.

Pieris Schrank

Pieris brassicae
  b. brassicae L.
  b. cheiranthi Hübner

Artogeia Verity

Artogeia napi L.
  n. napi L.
  n. meridionalis Heyne
  n. bryoniae Ochsenheimer
  n. segonzaci Le Cerf
Artogeia ergane Geyer
Artogeia rapae L.
Artogeia mannii Mayer
Artogeia krueperi Staudinger

Pontia F.

Pontia daplidice L.
Pontia chloridice Hübner
Pontia callidice Hübner

Colotis Hübner

Colotis evagore Klug

Catopsilia Hübner

Catopsilia florella F.

Euchloe Hübner

Euchloe ausonia
  a. ausonia Hübner
  a. insularis Staudinger
Euchloe crameri Butler
Euchloe tagis
  t. tagis Hübner

t. bellezina Boisduval

Euchloe falloui Allard

Euchloe belemia
  b. belemia Esper
  b. hesperidum Rothschild

Euchloe pechi Staudinger

Elphinstonia Klots

Elphinstonia charlonia Donzel

Anthocharis Boisduval

Anthocharis cardamines L.

Anthocharis belia L.

Anthocharis damone Boisduval

Anthocharis gruneri Herrich-Schäffer

Zegris Boisduval

Zegris eupheme Esper

Colias F.

Colias hyale L.

Colias australis Verity

Colias hecla Lefèbvre

Colias nastes Boisduval

Colias phicomone Esper

Colias erate Esper

Colias palaeno
  p. palaeno L.
  p. europome Esper
  p. europomene Ochsenheimer

Colias chrysotheme Esper

Colias libanotica Lederer
  l. heldreichi Staudinger

Colias myrmidone Esper

Colias balcanica Rebel

Colias crocea Geoffroy

Gonepteryx

Gonepteryx rhamni L.

Gonepteryx cleopatra
  c. cleopatra L.
  c. cleobule Hübner

Gonepteryx farinosa Zeller

Leptidea Billberg

Leptidea sinapis L.

Leptidea duponcheli Staudinger

Leptidea morsei Fenton

Family **LYCAENIDAE** Leach 1815

Lycaena F.

Lycaena phlaeas L.

Lycaena helle D. & S.

Lycaena dispar Haworth

Heodes Dalman

Heodes virgaureae L.

Heodes tityrus Poda

Heodes ottomanus Lefèbvre

Heodes alciphron Rottemburg

Thersamonia Verity

Thersamonia thersamon Esper

Thersamonia phoebus Blachier

Thersamonia thetis Klug

Palaeochrysophanus Verity

Palaeochrysophanus hippothoe
  h. hippothoe L.
  h. leonhardi Fruhstorfer
  h. eurydame Hoffmannsegg

Cigaritis Donzel

Cigaritis zohra Donzel

Cigaritis allardi Oberthur

Cigaritis siphax Lucas

Cigaritis myrmecophila Dumont

Thecla F.

Thecla betulae L.

Quercusia Verity

Quercusia quercus

q. quercus L.
q. iberica Staudinger

Laeosopis Rambur

Laeosopis roboris Esper

Nordmannia Tutt

Nordmannia ilicis Esper

Nordmannia esculi
  e. esculi Hübner
  e. mauretanica Staudinger

Nordmannia acaciae F.

Strymonidia Tutt

Strymonidia spini D. & S.

Strymonidia w-album Knoch

Strymonidia pruni L.

Callophrys Billberg

Callophrys rubi L.

Callophrys avis Chapman

Tomares Rambur

Tomares ballus F.

Tomares nogellii Herrich-Schäffer

Tomares mauretanicus Lucas

Tarucus Moore

Tarucus theophrastus F.

Tarucus balkanicus Freyer

Tarucus rosaceus Austaut

Syntarucus Butler

Syntarucus pirithous L.

Cyclyrius Butler

Cyclyrius webbianus Brullé

Lampides Hübner

Lampides boeticus L.

Azanus Moore

Azanus jesous Guérin

Azanus ubaldus Stoll

Cupido Schrank

Cupido minimus Fuessli

Cupido osiris Meigen

Cupido lorquinii Herrich-Schäffer

Cupido carswelli Stempffer

Everes Hübner

Everes argiades Pallas

Everes alcetas Hoffmannsegg

Everes decoloratus Staudinger

Zizeeria Chapman

Zizeeria knysna
  k. knysna Trimen
  k. karsandra Moore

Celastrina Tutt

Celastrina argiolus L.

Pseudophilotes Beuret

Pseudophilotes baton
  b. baton Bergsträsser
  b. panoptes Hübner
  b. schiffermuelleri Hemming

Pseudophilotes abencerragus Pierret

Scolitantides Hübner

Scolitantides orion Pallas

Scolitantides bavius
  b. bavius Eversmann
  b. fatma Oberthur

Glaucopsyche Scudder

Glaucopsyche alexis Poda

Glaucopsyche melanops Boisduval

Maculinea van Ecke

Maculinea alcon D. & S.

Maculinea arion L.

Maculinea teleius Bergsträsser

Maculinea nausithous Bergsträsser

Iolana B. Baker

Iolana iolas Ochsenheimer

Turanana B. Baker

Turanana panagaea Herrich-Schäffer

Freyeria Courvoisier
Freyeria trochylus Freyer

Plebejus Kluk

Plebejus argus L.

Plebejus pylaon
  p. sephirus Frivaldsky
  p. trappi Verity
  p. hespericus Rambur

Plebejus martini Allard

Plebejus vogellii Oberthur

Lycaeides Hübner

Lycaeides idas
  i. idas L.
  i. bellieri Oberthur
  i. magnagraeca Verity
  i. lapponica Gerhard

Lycaeides argyrognomon Bergsträsser

Aricia Reichenbach

Aricia agestis
  a. agestis D. & S.
  a. cramera Eschscholtz

Aricia artaxerxes
  a. artaxerxes F.
  a. allous Hübner
  a. montensis Verity

Aricia morronensis Ribbe

Aricia anteros Freyer

Pseudaricia Beuret

Pseudaricia nicias Meigen

Eumedonia Forster

Eumedonia eumedon Esper

Kretania Beuret

Kretania psylorita Freyer
Kretania euripylus Freyer

Vacciniina Tutt

Vacciniina optilete Knoch

Albulina Tutt

Albulina orbitulus de Prunner

Agriades Hübner

Agriades glandon
  g. glandon de Prunner
  g. zullichi Hemming
  g. aquilo Boisduval

Agriades pyrenaicus
  p. pyrenaicus Boisduval
  p. asturiensis Oberthur
  p. dardanus Freyer

Cyaniris Dalman

Cyaniris semiargus Rottemburg
Cyaniris (antiochena Lederer)
  a. helena Staudinger

Agrodiaetus Hübner

Agrodiaetus damon D. & S.

Agrodiaetus dolus
  d. dolus Hübner
  d. virgilius Oberthur

Agrodiaetus ainsae Forster

Agrodiaetus pseudovirgilius de Lesse

Agrodiaetus ripartii

Agrodiaetus admetus Esper

Agrodiaetus fabressei Oberthur

Agrodiaetus amanda Schneider

Agrodiaetus thersites Cantener

Agrodiaetus escheri Hübner

Agrodiaetus coelestina Eversmann

Plebicula Higgins

Plebicula dorylas D. & S.

Plebicula golgus Hübner

Plebicula nivescens Keferstein
Plebicula atlantica Elwes

Lysandra Hemming

Lysandra coridon
  c. coridon Poda
  c. caelestissima Verity

Lysandra hispana Herrich-Schäffer

Lysandra albicans Herrich-Schäffer

Lysandra bellargus·Rottemburg

Lysandra punctifera Oberthur

Meleageria Sagarra

Meleageria daphnis D. & S.

Polyommatus Kluk

Polyommatus icarus Rottemburg

Polyommatus eroides Frivaldsky

Polyommatus eros Ochsenheimer

Family **RIODINIDAE** Grote 1895

Hamearis Hübner

Hamearis lucina L.

Family **LIBYTHEIDAE** Boisduval 1840

Libythea F.

Libythea celtis Laicharting

Family **NYMPHALIDAE** Swainson 1827

Araschnia Hübner

Araschnia levana L.

Nymphalis Kluk

Nymphalis polychloros L.

Nymphalis xanthomelas D. & S.

Nymphalis vau-album D. & S.

Nymphalus antiopa L.

Inachis Hübner

Inachis io L.

Vanessa F.

Vanessa atalanta L.

Vanessa indica Herbst

Vanessa cardui L.

Vanessa virginiensis Drury

Aglais Dalman

Aglais urticae
  u. urticae L.
  u. ichnusa Hübner

Polygonia Hübner

Polygonia c-album L.

Polygonia egea Cramer

Argynnis F.

Argynnis paphia
  p. paphia L.
  p. immaculata Bellier
  p. dives Oberthur

Pandoriana Warren

Pandoriana pandora D. & S.

Argyronome Hübner

Argyronome laodice Pallas

Mesoacidalia Reuss

Mesoacidalia aglaja L.

Fabriciana Reuss

Fabriciana n. niobe L.
  n. auresiana Fruhstorfer

Fabriciana elisa Godart

Fabriciana adippe
  a. adippe D. & S.
  a. chlorodippe Herrich-Schäffer

Issoria Hübner

Issoria lathonia L.

Brenthis Hübner

Brenthis hecate D. & S.

Brenthis daphne D. & S.

Brenthis ino Rottemburg

Boloria Moore

Boloria pales
  p. pales D. & S.
  p. pyrenesmiscens Verity
  p. palustris Fruhstorfer

Boloria napaea Hoffmannsegg

Boloria aquilonaris Stichel

Boloria graeca
  g. graeca Staudinger
  g. balcanica Rebel

Proclossiana Reuss

Proclossiana eunomia
  e. eunomia Esper
  e. ossianus Herbst

Clossiana Reuss

Clossiana selene D. & S.

Clossiana freija Thunberg

Clossiana dia L.

Clossiana polaris Boisduval

Clossiana thore
  t. thore Hübner
  t. borealis Staudinger

Clossiana frigga Thunberg

Clossiana improba Butler

Clossiana titania Esper

Clossiana euphrosyne L.

Clossiana chariclea Schneider

Melitaea F.

Melitaea didyma Esper

Melitaea deserticola Oberthur

Melitaea trivia
  t. trivia D. & S.
  t. ignasiti Sagarra

Melitaea arduinna
  (*a. arduinna* Esper)
  a. rhodopensis Freyer

Melitaea phoebe D. & S.

Melitaea aetherie Hübner

Melitaea cinxia L.

Melitaea diamina
  d. diamina Lang
  d. vernetensis Rondou

Mellicta athalia
  a. athalia Rottemburg
  a. celadussa Fruhstorfer
  a. norvegica Aurivillius

Mellicta deione
  d. deione Geyer
  d. berisalii Rühl
  d. nitida Oberthur

Mellicta parthenoides Keferstein

Mellicta britomartis Assmann

Mellicta aurelia Nickerl

Mellicta varia Meyer-Dur

Mellicta asteria Freyer

Euphydryas Scudder

Euphydryas intermedia Ménétriés

Euphydryas maturna L.

Euphydryas cynthia D. & S.

Euphydryas iduna Dalman

Euphydryas aurinia
  a. aurinia Rottemburg
  a. debilis Oberthur

Euphydryas desfontainii Godart

Charaxes Guénée

Charaxes jasius L.

Apatura F.

Apatura metis Freyer

Apatura ilia D. & S.

Apatura iris L.

Limenitis F.

Limenitis populi L.

Limenitis reducta Staudinger

Limenitis camilla L.

Neptis F.

Neptis sappho Pallas

Neptis rivularis Scopoli

Family **SATYRIDAE** Boisduval 1833

Satyrus Latreille

Satyrus actaea Esper

Satyrus ferula
  f. ferula F.
  f. atlanteus Verity

Minois Hübner

Minois dryas Scopoli

Brintesia Fruhstorfer

Brintesia circe D. & S.

Arethusana de Lesse

Arethusana arethusa D. & S.

Berberia de Lesse

Berberia abdelkader Pierret

Hipparchia F.

Hipparchia fagi Scopoli

Hipparchia alcyone
  a. alcyone D. & S.
  a. genava Fruhstorfer
  a. vandalusica Oberthur
  a. caroli Rothschild
  a. syriaca Staudinger

Hipparchia ellena Oberthur

Hipparchia neomiris Godart

Hipparchia semele
  s. semele L.
  s. cadmus Fruhstorfer
  s. cretica Rebel

Hipparchia aristaeus
  a. aristaeus Bonelli
  a. algirica Oberthur
  a. siciliana Oberthur
  a. maderensis B. Baker
  a. azorica Strecker

Neohipparchia de Lesse

Neohipparchia statilinus Hufnagel
Neohipparchia fatua Freyer
Neohipparchia hansii

h. hansii Austaut
h. powelli Oberthur

Pseudotergumia Agenjo

Pseudotergumia fidia L.

Pseudotergumia wyssii
  w. wyssii Christ
  w. bacchus Higgins

Chazara Moore

Chazara briseis L.

Chazara prieuri Pierret

Pseudochazara de Lesse

Pseudochazara atlantis Austaut

Pseudochazara hippolyte
  (*h. hippolyte* Esper)
  h. williamsi Romei

Pseudochazara mamurra
  (*m. mamurra* Herrich-Schäffer)
  m. graeca Staudinger

Pseudochazara anthelea
  (*a. anthelea* Hübner)
  a. amalthea Frivaldsky

Pseudochazara geyeri
  (*g. geyeri* Herrich-Schäffer)
  g. occidentalis Rebel & Zerny

Erebia Dalman

Erebia ligea L.

Erebia euryale
  e. euryale Esper
  e. ocellaris Staudinger
  e. adyte Hübner

Erebia eriphyle Freyer

Erebia manto
  m. manto D. & S.
  m. constans Eiffinger
  m. pyrrhula Freyer

Erebia claudina Borkhausen

Erebia flavofasciata Heyne

Erebia epiphron
  e. epiphron Knoch

e. mnemon Haworth
e. aetheria Esper
e. orientalis Elwes

Erebia serotina Descimon & de Lesse

Erebia christi Rätzer

Erebia pharte Hübner

Erebia melampus Fuessli

Erebia sudetica Staudinger

Erebia aethiops Esper

Erebia triaria de Prunner

Erebia medusa
  m. medusa D. & S.
  m. hippomedusa Ochsenheimer

Erebia polaris Staudinger

Erebia disa Thunberg

Erebia embla Thunberg

Erebia alberganus de Prunner

Erebia pluto
  p. pluto de Prunner
  p. alecto Hübner
  p. nicholli Oberthur
  p. oreas Warren

Erebia gorge
  g. gorge Hübner
  g. ramondi Oberthur
  g. triopes Speyer
  g. erynis Esper
  g. carboncina Verity

Erebia aethiopella
  a. aethiopella Hoffmannsegg
  a. rhodopensis Nicholl
  a. sharsta Higgins

Erebia gorgone Boisduval

Erebia mnestra Hübner

Erebia epistygne Hübner

Erebia tyndarus Esper

Erebia cassioides Hohenwarth

Erebia hispania
  h. hispania Butler
  h. rondoui Oberthur

Erebia nivalis Lorković & de Lesse

Erebia calcaria Lorković

Erebia ottomana
  o. ottomana Herrich-Schäffer
  o. balcanica Rebel

Erebia pronoe
  p. pronoe Esper
  p. vergy Ochsenheimer

Erebia scipio Boisduval

Erebia malas Herbst

Erebia lefebvrei
  l. lefebvrei Boisduval
  l. astur Oberthur

Erebia stiria Godart

Erebia styx
  s. styx Freyer
  s. triglites Fruhstorfer
  s. trentae Lorković

Erebia montana de Prunner

Erebia zapateri Oberthur

Erebia neoridas Boisduval

Erebia oeme
  o. oeme Hübner
  o. lugens Staudinger
  o. spodia Staudinger

Erebia meolans
  m. meolans de Prunner
  m. valesiaca Elwes
  m. bejarensis Chapman

Erebia palarica Chapman

Erebia pandrose
  p. pandrose Borkhausen
  p. sthennyo Graslin

Erebia phegea Borkhausen

Oeneis Hübner

Oeneis glacialis Moll

Oeneis norna Thunberg

Oeneis bore Schneider

Oeneis jutta Hübner

Melanargia Meigen

Melanargia galathea
  g. galathea L.
  g. lachesis Hübner
  g. lucasi Rambur

Melanargia russiae
  (*r. russiae* Esper)
  r. cleanthe Boisduval
  r. japygia Cyrillo

Melanargia larissa Geyer
Melanargia occitanica
  o. occitanica Esper
  o. pelagia Oberthur
  o. pherusa Boisduval
Melanargia arge Sulzer
Melanargia ines Hoffmannsegg

Maniola Schrank

Maniola jurtina
  j. jurtina L.
  j. hispulla Esper
  j. telmessia Zeller
Maniola nurag Ghiliani

Hyponephele Muschamp

Hyponephele lycaon Kühn
Hyponephele lupina
  l. lupina Costa
  l. rhamnusia Freyer
  l. mauretanica Oberthur
Hyponephele maroccana Blachier

Aphantopus Wallengren

Aphantopus hyperantus L.

Pyronia Hübner

Pyronia tithonus L.
Pyronia bathseba F.
Pyronia janiroides Herrich-Schäffer
Pyronia cecilia Vallantin

Coenonympha Hübner

Coenonympha oedippus F.
Coenonympha pamphilus
  p. pamphilus L.
  p. lyllus Esper
  p. thyrsis Freyer
  p. sicula Zeller
Coenonympha tullia

  t. tullia Müller
  t. demophile Freyer
  t. rhodopensis Elwes
Coenonympha arcanioides Pierret
Coenonympha dorus
  d. dorus Esper
  d. bieli Staudinger
  d. fettigii Oberthur
Coenonympha austauti Oberthur
Coenonympha corinna Hübner
Coenonympha elbana Staudinger
Coenonympha hero L.
Coenonympha darwiniana Staudinger
Coenonympha leander Esper
Coenonympha vaucheri Blachier
Coenonympha gardetta de Prunner
Coenonympha arcania L.
Coenonympha glycerion
  g. glycerion Borkhausen
  g. iphioides Staudinger

Pararge Hübner

Pararge aegeria
  a. aegeria L.
  a. tircis Butler
  a. xiphioides Staudinger
  a. xiphia F.

Lasiommata Westwood

Lasiommata megera
  m. megera L.
  m. paramegaera Hübner
Lasiommata maera L.
Lasiommata petropolitana F.

Lopinga Moore

Lopinga achine Scopoli

Kirinia Moore

Kirinia roxelana Cramer

Family **DANAIDAE** Bates 1861

Danaus Kluk

Danaus plexippus L.   *Danaus chrysippus* L.

Index

including synonyms and homonyms in current use

For technical terms not included here see Glossary p. 29

317

318